Adeline and Julia

Adeline, Julia, and Thomas Lee Wilkinson, Jr., ca. 1885

Adeline and Julia

GROWING UP IN MICHIGAN AND ON THE KANSAS FRONTIER

Diaries from 19th-Century America

edited by

Janet L. Coryell

and

Robert C. Myers

Michigan State University Press
East Lansing

∞The paper used in this publication meets the minimum requirements of ANSI/NISO Z39.48–1992 (R 1997) (Permanence of Paper).

Printed and bound in the United States of America.

Michigan State University Press
East Lansing, Michigan 48823–5202

05 04 03 02 01 00 1 2 3 4 5 6

Library of Congress Cataloging–in–Publication Data

Graham, Adeline, 1864–1934.
Adeline and Julia : growing up in Michigan and on the Kansas frontier : diaries from 19th-century America / edited by Janet L. Coryell and Robert C. Myers.
     p.   cm.
Annotated diaries of two young sisters, Adeline and Julia Graham, written during their adolescent years growing up in Berrien Springs, Michigan in the 1880s. Also includes Julia's diary from the year she spent homesteading with three other young women on the Kansas frontier.
ISBN 0–87013–513–9
1. Graham, Adeline, 1864–1934—Diaries. 2. Graham, Julia, 1862–1900—Diaries. 3. Sisters—Michigan—Berrien Springs—Diaries. 4. Young women—Michigan—Berrien Springs—Diaries. 5. Berrien Springs (Mich.)—Biography. 6. Berrien Springs (Mich.)—Social life and customs. 7. Frontier and pioneer life—Michigan—Berrien Springs. 8. Frontier and pioneer life—Kansas—Greeley County. 9. Young women—Kansas—Greeley County—Diaries. 10. Greeley County (Kan.)—Social life and customs—19th century. I. Graham, Julia, 1862–1900. II. Coryell, Janet L., 1955–   III. Myers, Robert C. IV. Title

F574.B47 G73 2000
977.4'11—dc21

99–050969

Book design by Michael J. Brooks
Cover design by Heidi Dailey

Visit Michigan State University Press on the World Wide Web at:
     www.msu.edu/unit/msupress

Contents

Preface

Janet L. Coryell and Robert C. Myers

On a cold winter day, Adeline Graham ditched school, pulled taffy, giggled with her friend, teased the boys who followed her home, and sat down at night to write it all down in her diary. A few years later, her sister Julia wearily shoveled the last of the snow that had drifted into the interior of her sod "hotel" and sat down to write to her sister all about the blizzard that had buried her and her friends inside for days.

Americans of the late twentieth century seldom record their thoughts or write letters on paper anymore, preferring to rely instead on the speed and convenience of telecommunications. But vast numbers of nineteenth-century Americans kept journals and diaries, and many more used the mail as their only method of communication, despite new-fangled inventions such as the telegraph (in 1847) or the telephone (in 1876). Today, their thoughts and deeds, their lives and loves, their dreams and disappointments, preserved in ink and pencil on paper, become part of an open book to students of the past.

Two such recorders of lives lived were diarists Adeline and Julia Graham, sisters who lived in the second half of the nineteenth century. Residents for a time of Berrien Springs, Michigan, their experiences were common to many women of the period—education, marriage, children. And, like many women, they occasionally had grand adventures, the grandest perhaps being Julia's homesteading attempt in Greeley County, Kansas, near the Colorado border. Their adventures and everyday lives were recorded in lined blank books, sold widely in the nineteenth century for this very purpose. To remember and reflect on adventures and daily life were important parts of learning how to grow up.

We edited this collection of Adeline and Julia Graham's diaries in order to illuminate the past through the presentation of original documents. We have kept the spelling, grammar and punctuation that the "Graham Girls" used in their original documents, although minor

vii

changes have been added in brackets for clarity's sake when needed. We defined some of the words unfamiliar to modern Americans in the notes to provide additional explanation and context, and we included the names of their relatives or people who showed up frequently in their writings. For more information, two appendices are attached for those interested in further details: Appendix 1 includes information about the people Addie knew and mentioned; Appendix 2 lists the books she enjoyed or studied. Those items are highlighted in the text with an asterisk (*) to indicate more information is available at the back of the book.

The editors wish to acknowledge the aid and support they received from the following persons: Mary "Polly" Preston Parrett, Cynthia Burkholder Grootendorst and the late Sally Berk Roe, who donated Adeline's diaries to the Berrien County Historical Association; Julia Caldwell Mitchell, who owns Julia Graham's Kansas diary and made it available for publication; Kay Mantegna, who owns Mary Garrow Graham's letters and made them available to help with the annotation of these diaries; Jan H. House, former director of the Berrien County Historical Association, who helped with initial research on the Graham family; Virgil W. Dean, Ph.D., editor at the Kansas State Historical Society; Diether Haenicke, president of Western Michigan University, whose timely donation of grant funds allowed the purchase of a computer to make the editing process much easier and faster; Bonnie Coryell Hatch and Homer Hatch for information regarding Kansas traditions and terminology; Rachel Lynn Ayers and Bethany Leigh Ayers for a careful reading of the manuscript; and most especially Candace Seymour Myers, whose support is always a timely affair, and James Smither, for taking on extraordinary amounts of childcare so Momma could work on this.

For those wishing to learn more about the times in which Addie Graham lived, her journal is used as a resource for part of the permanent exhibit, "Growing Up in Michigan" at the Michigan Historical Museum in Lansing, Michigan.

Introduction

Susan Armitage

Y ou are about to meet two engaging young nineteenth-century women and share important experiences with them. Adeline and Julia Graham, daughters of a prosperous Michigan farm family, kept diaries during key moments in their young lives. Addie, the younger sibling, consciously kept a very personal and literary record of her adolescence (ages 15–19) during the years 1880–84. The next year, older sister Julia penned a less personal but equally interesting account of her great "adventure" homesteading in western Kansas. Taken together, these two diaries tell us many things about the opportunities and challenges facing white, middle-class women in the latter part of the nineteenth century.

Adeline Graham's diary affords us a fascinating glimpse into the difficulties young girls of the middle class experienced as they confronted nineteenth-century notions of appropriate gender roles. Addie, (or Adam, as her family and best friends called her) was a "tomboy." In part the term described a joy in physical activity such as the riding and ice skating that Addie and many other young girls so enjoyed but that they were expected to give up as they became "young ladies." Young girls on farms and ranches like Addie who enjoyed the freedom and physicality of horseback riding may have most regretted the changes of adolescence. Agnes Morley Cleaveland, growing up on a New Mexico ranch during the same time period, saw a sharp divide between the free horseback-riding life of her childhood and her expected female adult role: ranching was, she said, "no life for a lady."[1] In Addie's account, the moment of truth occurs when her new sidesaddle arrives, without the leaping horn that would have allowed her to continue to jump fences. Bicycles, which

---

[1] Agnes Morley Cleaveland, *No Life for a Lady* (Boston: Houghton Mifflin Company, 1941; reprinted Lincoln: University of Nebraska Press, 1977).

1

were to allow the next generation of women some opportunity for physical activity, were not widely available until the 1890s, by which time Addie was irrevocably mature.

"Tomboy" had another, less openly acknowledged meaning: it denoted a young girl who resisted expected notions of heterosexuality. Perhaps the best-known western tomboy was Willa Cather, who was growing up in Red Cloud, Nebraska, at about the same time Addie was in Berrien Springs, Michigan. Cather frequently dressed in boys' clothes and was known as Will to her friends. Like Addie, she aspired to be a doctor. As is now widely acknowledged by literary scholars, Cather maintained a lesbian preference throughout her life. Addie Graham married in her mid-twenties, but her diary makes clear that in adolescence she had great difficulty figuring out how to deal with the opposite sex. At times, she wanted to be "one of the boys" while at others, especially in her temperance efforts with Jule Brown, she tried on the role of womanly reformer and at other times allowed herself to be mildly courted. Working out a satisfactory attitude toward young men is a major theme of Addie's diary. After her early rebellious outburst ("wish I *was* [a boy] . . . but since I can't be a boy the next best thing is to act as much like one as possible."[vol. 1 p. 35]), she makes a slow but steady accommodation to contemporary norms of heterosexual behavior.

In this accommodation, Addie was greatly aided by the novels of Louisa May Alcott, and especially by *Little Women*, published in 1868–69. Alcott's heroine Jo aspired to be an independent woman and was deeply suspicious of what literary scholars have termed "the romance plot." In creating the character of Jo, Alcott gave voice to the hesitations and worries that many young women on the verge of adulthood felt, and by voicing them made them acceptable. Addie clearly modeled herself on Jo, and felt authorized by this fictional creation to express her own very similar ambivalent thoughts about men and marriage.

Addie followed Alcott's model in another sense as well: the diary is a literary creation to which Addie (an aspiring writer as well as a wishful doctor) devoted considerable time and effort. One reason why it is such delightful reading is that it is so consciously self-revelatory and descriptive. Addie wrote it with readers, and the Alcott novels, clearly in mind. This writerly urge makes the diary no less honest, but it is true that Addie's selfconsciousness makes it more accessible and understandable than many other nineteenth-century diaries.

One way to appreciate Addie's talent as a writer is to compare her diary with that of her sister Julia. Julia did indeed have a great adventure when she decided (for reasons her diary does not explain) to homestead in western Kansas with three other women in 1885–86. The fact that she was a woman homesteader is not quite so startling as later histories of the American West might lead one to believe. Studies of Colorado and North Dakota indicate that before 1900, unmarried females accounted for 5 to 10 percent of homesteaders; after 1900, the percentage rose as high as 18 percent.[2] Thus we can say that although Julia Graham was not the only single woman to choose to homestead, she certainly was among the first women to do so. However, although she was unmarried, she was certainly not alone: "the Greeley Girls" as the four women homesteaders called themselves, seem rarely to have spent a day without male company. Indeed, this must be one of the most sociable accounts of homesteading ever written! All the more pity, then, that Julia Graham, unlike her younger sister, did not use her diary for introspection or even for detailed description. How nice it would be, for example, to have a full picture of "the Palace Hotel," the dugout boardinghouse that Julia and her friends established in mid-December 1885, or a fuller sense of the severe blizzard that struck in early January 1886. Julia provides a few details about this famous storm, but soon gives up the literary effort, saying, "I cannot describe how dreadful it all is."

Julia Graham endured some very bad weather and some primitive living conditions, but she had steady companionship and another advantage many other homesteaders lacked: money. Julia and her friends could afford to hire labor to dig a well, to construct a dugout, to supply them with coal and water, and to plow their fields. Many other homesteaders were less affluent, and the lack of cash frequently condemned them to failure. Several poignant memoirs, among them Alice Day Pratt's account of her solitary life in Oregon, *A Homesteader's Portfolio*, and Sanora Babb's evocative memoir of her family's fruitless efforts in eastern Colorado, *An Owl on Every Post*, compound the sense of loss with a nearly overwhelming love of the land.[3] Julia Graham did not fail. She achieved what she set out to do: she demonstrated her ability to live on the land long enough to

[2]Katherine Harris, *Long Vistas: Women and Families on Colorado Homesteads* (Boulder: University Press of Colorado, 1993), 61; H. Elaine Lindgren, *Land in Her Own Name: Women Homesteaders in North Dakota* (Norman: University of Oklahoma Press, 1996), 51.

[3]Alice Day Pratt, *A Homesteader's Portfolio* (New York: Macmillan, 1922; reprinted Corvallis, Oreg.: Oregon State University Press, 1993); Sanora Babb, *An Owl on Every Post* (New York: McCall Publishing Company, 1970; reprinted Albuquerque: University of New Mexico Press, 1994).

claim it as her own. We can have little doubt that she recalled her home-steading adventure fondly for the rest of her life.

Challenges and opportunities faced Adeline and Julia Graham and they made choices between them. Growing up; striking out on one's own: these were issues for the Graham sisters just as they are, in different form, for young women today. Seen from that perspective, the diaries of the Graham girls are a small but interesting part of the larger and continuing history of women in America.

Addie's Diary

Growing Up in Michigan: The Diary of Adeline Graham

Adeline Eliza Graham was born at her family's farm just outside Berrien Springs, Michigan, on August 26, 1864, the youngest child of George and Mary Graham. Her parents named her for her mother's sister, Adeline Eliza Murdock.

Adeline's father, George, the eldest of seven children, was born in Stoystown, Pennsylvania, January 31, 1826. He came to Berrien County, Michigan, in 1843 and was joined three years later by his widowed mother, two brothers (John, who settled in Buchanan and James, who settled in Berrien Springs), and two sisters. George married Mary Bacon Garrow on December 19, 1849, and the couple lived on the west edge of Berrien Springs until 1879, when they moved to a new house on Ferry Street in town. Tax rolls show that by 1880 George Graham was by far the wealthiest man in the township. He was not particularly active in politics, but supported the Republican party all his life. His wife, Mary, born in Auburn, New York, in 1830, came to Berrien County with her family in 1848. She gave birth to six children: John (1851–65); William Holmes (1853–1930), who appears in Addie's diary as "Will"; Mary L. (1855–56); George (1857–61); Harry Kimmel (1860–1942); Julia (1862–1900), whom Adeline called "Jude"; and Adeline (1864–1934), known as both "Addie" and "Adam."

Besides her immediate family, Addie enjoyed having an extended family in Berrien Springs and Niles, Michigan: Her maternal aunt and uncle Adeline and George Murdock and their children, George and Henrietta ("Et" in Addie's diary); paternal uncles and aunts, including John and Frances (Aunt "Frank") and widowed Aunt Harriet Graham and Nelson and Julia Graham Higby and their son Graham; first cousin Robert Dougherty ("Cousin Bob"); and both grandmothers. Her cousin Georgianna Holmes ("Daisy") visited from Cincinnati for an extended time; Addie's one surviving grandfather, John Garrow, lived in Liberty, Mississippi.

Addie's diaries of her daily life begin while she was still in high school in Berrien Springs and reflect many of the pastimes common to children of the time. Despite the Grahams' wealth, Addie's life as a teenager was probably not much different from that of most schoolgirls of the age, except in her education. Unlike most of her contemporaries, after graduating high school in 1882, Addie went to the Michigan Female Seminary in Kalamazoo, from which she graduated in 1884. After her years at the Seminary, Addie's diaries come to an abrupt end. She did attend Olivet College in 1885 for a short while and, although she planned to attend medical school to become a physician, she never did so. On April 1, 1886, two years later, she arrived in Greeley County, Kansas, to visit her sister Julia, who was homesteading there. She remained until July 12, helping her sister prove up her claim. Seven years later, Addie shows up in the public records again, as she married Thomas Lee Wilkinson, Jr., the oft-mentioned "Lee" in her diaries from high school, at her parents' home in Berrien Springs. Lee by then was a partner in the abstract and title firm of Dix and Wilkinson. Addie and Lee had four daughters: Phyllis (born 1894); Frances (born 1898); Doris (1900–1901); and Mary Elizabeth (born 1903).

Addie and Lee lived in Berrien Springs until 1900, when they moved to St. Joseph. The county seat of Berrien County had moved to that city in 1894, and Lee Wilkinson chose to move his business and home to that city as well. In St. Joseph, Addie became a prominent lady in society, holding memberships in the Daughters of the American Revolution, the auxiliary of the Michigan Children's Home, the Needlework Guild of America, and the Log Cabin Club. Despite her status in St. Joseph, a few traces of Addie's tomboy nature seem to have lingered: in corresponding with her, friends and family still called her by her old nickname, "Adam."

❧

Volume 1

May 10, 1880–June 6, 1881

Evening. Mon. May 10th '80

I just spilt my ink to commence with. Well I've made up my mind to keep a journal at last. I've been making up my mind for about two years now; so to night I went down town and got this little book and commenced in dead earnest.

I just got back from Niles this evening and feel rather blue after bidding my dear cousin Martha a good bye.[1] I will miss her so much after being with her all winter. I took her up to Niles Saturday with the carriage and Charlie and Pa took Daisy, Aunt Ella, and Ma up in the two seated buggy.[2] Ma and Pa came back the same night but the rest of us stayed. Mr. Bates monopolized Martha almost all the time and I didn't see her half as much as I wanted to. I think it was horrid when he is going to have her all the time most in Cincinnati. I think it horrid to be engaged anyway and never intend to get into that fix my self. I like Mr. B. well enough and we are good friends but what does he want to carry Martha away with him for?

Martha wants me to come East this summer with Aunt E. and Daisy and meet her at the sea side but I don't think there is any hopes of it. I've been crying most all afternoon but I didn't cry near as much as I should have if I hadn't divided it up and did some yesterday.

It rained most all day yesterday and all last night and this morning so it was quite a suitable time to cry when the sky was crying to. I read the "Ancient Mariner" by [Samuel Taylor] Coleridge yesterday and there

---

[1]"Cousin Martha" Holmes was the daughter of William and Ellen Holmes, Addie's paternal aunt and uncle.

[2]"Charlie" was the horse Adeline rode. He died at the advanced·age of twenty-five, a rarity so unusual the local paper, the *Berrien Springs Era*, printed his obituary. "Daisy" was Adeline's first cousin, Georgiana Holmes, daughter of her paternal aunt, "Aunt Ella," and uncle William Holmes.

is a quotation I want to write down here. It is one that is heard quite often so I want to remember

"Water, Water <u>everywhere</u> nor yet <u>one</u> <u>drop</u> to drink."[3]

Martha told me of a splendid way to do when ever I am reading and come across any thing that pleases me to write it down and remember it. And I intend to do it. She read me parts of her journal and she had lots of quotations, and I will copy some of them in here . . . .[4]

I must stop for to night and go to bed. I guess it must be after ten.

Tuesday 4 P.M. May 11th '80

Jude and Daisy have gone riding.[5] I am blue clear through and lonesome without M. So I thought I would come up and write in my little journal and see if scribbling a little wouldn't cheer me up. It usually does.

Et was here this after noon.[6] We went riding out to the cemetery (cheerful?) and I took Grandma Graham riding. On the whole I think I ought to have the "blues" but then it is [a] lovely day, just warm enough to be pleasant; trees are green and thick, and perhaps I oughtn't after all.

Aunt Ella got back from Niles to day. I'm going to write down some more of the quotations I got out of Martha's journal . . . .[7]

Here is a parody on the "Sorrows of Werter" which I think real good.
"Sorrows of Werter"
"Werter had a love for
Charlotte
Such as words could never
utter.
Would you know how first
he met her?
She was cutting bread and
butter.

---

[3]Properly, "Water, water, everywhere, nor any drop to drink," from Samuel Taylor Coleridge, *The Ancient Mariner*, Part 1.

[4]Adeline's quotes were passages from German philosopher Arthur Schopenhauer, English poet Alexander Pope, Greek philosopher Anaxagoras, and English playwright William Shakespeare, all evidence of her education in classical literature.

[5]"Jude" was Adeline's sister Julia, two years Addie's senior.

[6]"Et" was Adeline's cousin, Henrietta M. Murdoch, born the day before Addie.

[7]Here Adeline quotes from Scottish essayist and historian Thomas Carlyle.

"Charlotte was a married
lady
And a moral man was
Werter
And for all the wealth of India
Would do nothing for
to hurt her.
"So he sighed, and pined,
and ogled;
And his passion boiled and
bubbled,
Till he blew his silly
brains out;
And no more was by it
troubled.
"Charlotte having seen his
body,
Borne before her on a shutter
Like a well conducted
Person
Went on cutting bread and
butter."
Wm. M. Thackery[8]

. . . .

I guess I've got over my blueness slightly and will stop now. Martha promised to write to me as soon as she arrived at Cincinnati and I will look for a letter about Thursday.

6 o'clock

Jude and Daisy have got back. I've been looking up about the "seven wonders of the world," "the seven sleepers," and "the seven wise men of Greece," and will write down what I have learned, as it may be useful sometime . . . .[9]

---

[8]German playwright Johann Wolfgang von Goethe wrote the original "Sorrows of Young Werther" of which this is the condensed version.

[9]The seven Wise Men of Greece most likely referred to philosophers Socrates, Aristotle, Plato and four others; the Seven Wonders of the World were the Hanging Gardens of Babylon, the Tower of Pharos in Alexandria, the Mausoleum in Pergamun, the Sphinx, the Pyramids, the Colossus of Rhodes, and the Parthenon.

The seven sleepers, according to an old legend they were seven Christian young men of Ephesus who were persecuted because of their religion. They fled to a large cavern. Their persecutors followed and closed up the cavern so they could not escape. Tradition says that they were put to sleep and slept two centuries and so escaped being starved to death, I suppose.

May 13th 1880

Just got back from taking a walk. Went down to Et's and she went with me down to Cousin Ellen Kepharts after Martha's bird but did not get it as Cousin Ellen wishes to keep it longer.[10]

Yesterday Daisy and I went horse back riding. She is very cowardly about horses so we didn't ride fast, but after we came back I had a jolly ride up to the farm and down to the woods. Charlie went beautifully and we tore along. The woods were so lovely and green and thick.

I wrote a long letter to Harry yesterday and Jude got one from him this morning. He said he thought Will would be home the first of June. I hope he will, for it is very lonesome to be without brothers.[11]

I did not get the expected letter from Martha today, but Aunt Ella got a postal yesterday.[12] She had got as far as Kalamazoo when she wrote and must have got into Cincinnati last night, so I guess I looked a day too soon for my letter. Daisy wrote to her this morning and I put in half a sheet.

I read old Macaulay yesterday after noon and found a splendid seet up in a little cherry tree, and the leaves are so thick no one can see me.[13] I ought to read some more to day. Guess I will this evening. I haven't quite caught up to Martha yet and want to tonight. Ma has called and I must go down and practice.

[10]Ellen Kephart was the wife of town pharmacist Henry Kephart.

[11]"Harry" and "Will" were Adeline's and Julia's brothers. Harry Kimmel Graham was farming in southeastern Kansas; William Holmes Graham was at the University of Notre Dame.

[12]A "postal" is a postcard. Aunt Ella moved to Cincinnati after her marriage to W. N. Holmes.

[13]"Old Macaulay" refers to English historian Thomas Macaulay. Addie here exhibits the influence of one of the nineteenth century's best-sellers, Louisa May Alcott's *Little Women*, as she imitates Jo March, the novel's leading character who also read books while perched in trees. See also Appendix 1.

May 14th

Been cooking maple sugar; its prime.[14] We had a serenade on the dishpan last night and yelled negro Melodies. Bony joined in the chorus.[15] Guess the neighbors were edified. Went over to Ralph's and teetered with him. Went around to play croquet, but one of Kit's* beaus came and I "glode" out. This morning Ralph and I went up to the farm and got some pieplant.[16] Didn't read hardly any in Macaulay yesterday and haven't read any yet to day.

I just tore out to the barn and back. Heard the pups yelping and thought they must be half killed. Two were shut up in their box and the other got lonesome, so he amused himself by serenading the other two. That was all.

I will write down some quotations from the "Merchant of Venice." I think Portia is just splendid . . . .[17]

I'm going to roost now.

I had just got roosted comfortably in the cherry tree and read about one paragraph of old Mac. when along came Et and wanted me to go down town with her. I went, and when I got back Daisy and I went horse back riding.

We started to go up to the farm and I was trying to open the gate with out getting off when suddenly the saddle turned. I had to lean over so far, and I would have fallen if the fence hadn't been there and kind of held me up. Got off and examined the saddle and found that the girth strap had broken.[18] Went back and changed saddles and started forth again. Daisy says it was providential about my trying to open the gate and

[14]"Prime" meant first-rate. May was very late for making maple syrup from sap, usually done in March and April. Unless 1880 had been very cold, most likely Addie was cooking maple syrup down to make maple candy.

[15]"Bony" was Will Graham's hound dog.

[16]"Teetered" means teeter-totter; "croquet" is a lawn game played with wooden mallets and balls; "glode" serves Adeline as the past tense of glide; and "pieplant" is garden rhubarb. A "beau" is a boyfriend or, at the very least, an interested young man.

[17]"Portia" from Shakespeare's play, The Merchant of Venice, is the leading lady and a forceful, intelligent and well-read woman.

[18]The girth strap runs from the saddle sides and buckles underneath the horse's belly.

breaking the girth, for it might have broken when I was riding fast and I would have got a tumble.

Had a very nice ride, and when we got back Jude and Daisy went; Ralph got on behind me and we rode up and down the lane. He made Peg kick up almost every step.[19] It was lots of fun and very exciting, for you would be away up in the air one minute and expecting to light on the horse's ears the next, so it was a continual surprise to find yourself sitting in the saddle.

Aunt Ella got a letter from Martha to day. She said in it that she would write to me soon.

Tuesday 18th May

Got a nice long letter from Martha yesterday. Saturday Mrs. Reiter died. And Mate didn't get here till two o'clock Sunday morning.[20] I haven't seen Mate for a year.

Puss Hall came to see me Saturday after noon. Sunday I went to Sunday school. Mrs. Reiber* explains the lessons so splendid we can't help understanding them. I wrote a long letter to Martha Sunday evening and Ma got one from Harry yesterday.

It is very warm to day. Aunt Julia is here. She came down in the stage yesterday and last night I took her and Grandma down to Mr. Dix's, and while I waited for them Roscoe, Win, Frank Murdock, and Eddie Aymar* all piled in and we rode all over town.

Mosquitoes are very bad this year. I've practised an hour this morning.

Wed. May 19th

Had quite a big thunder storm this morning, and it is pouring down now. Looks like an all day drizzle.

Mrs. Kephart brought back our bird last night. Daisy went down to Platt's last eve.

Aunt Ella is reading one of Miss Mulock's . . . novels "The Head of the Family"* aloud evenings for Grandma's benefit. I think it is kind of a

[19]"Peg" is the horse.

[20]Anna M. Reiter died on May 15, 1880, of consumption, or tuberculosis. She was the wife of the Reverend D. H. Reiter. "Mate" was her eldest daughter Mary, then 15, and a good friend of Addie's.

love-sick book, but there are many good things in it which rather make up for that; I have written to Martha to have her tell me about it. Daisy says Miss Mulock never writes trash anyway. I think parts of this is trashy. Here is a quotation from it which is splendid: "When two paths of duty bewilder thee, and thou knowest not which it is right to follow, choose the one which to thyself is the fullest one therein."

I've just got back from taking Aunt Julia down town, and have just had a nice long talk with my dear old friend Mate Reiter. It is the first time I have seen her for a year. She goes back to Fulton tomorrow, says she had much rather stay here. She hasn't changed a bit. I guess Et, Jude, and I will go down to her Grandmother's and see her this evening and then our glorious old P. C. will be together once more.[21] Mate is coming back "Young Settler's Day," which will be next August and will stay two or three weeks.[22]

Today is the "Odd Fellows Picnic," but I guess there will not be much of a crowd as it is so wet.[23] It has stopped raining but must be very wet down in the grove. Jude and Daisy have ridden down town to see the crowd. I don't think they'll see much, for when I was down town there were fewer people than ever.

It's night and I'm going to bed soon. Spent a very pleasant evening at Mate's: George, Et, Jude, and I. And Miss Eply and Ella Platt* called in while we were there to say good bye.

This after noon didn't do much but ride around. I took Aunt Ella and Ma riding. Aunt E. was so afraid of the band that her ride was short. We were riding along quietly when suddenly she grew almost frantic, grabbed my arm, and begged me to turn around quick, the band was coming and Charlie would be frightened. I told her that Charlie was used

---

[21]The term "P. C." may refer to Alcott's *Little Women* again. The March girls' secret literary society, the Pickwick Club, is referred to by Alcott in the chapter title as the "P.C."

[22]"Young Settlers' Day" was the annual meeting of the Young People's Picnic Association of Berrien County. The Association, formed in 1877, held a picnic meeting in what is today Grove Park ("down in the grove"), a wooded area of about seven acres on the south edge of Berrien Springs. By 1878, attendance was estimated at 6,000 people.

[23]The Independent Order of Odd Fellows was a secret, fraternal benevolent association of British origin, formed for mutual aid and socializing.

to it, but she was so afraid that Charlie would be afraid that she begged me to drive fast, something she never did before, I guess. I pulled Charlie out of the road to pass a team. He started and went up the hill so fast it raised me up on my feet to hold him. Aunt E. didn't seem to mind that at all, she was so afraid he would see the band.

Fleas bite and I must go to bed.

Sun. May 23rd '80

I went to Sunday school. The lesson was glorious. Subject—"The Marriage Fruit—" and Mrs. Reiber is a jewel of a teacher.

It [is] pretty hot to day and I think we will have a thunder storm before long.

Got our hats and other things from Cincinnati yesterday. I like them very much.

Mr. Marquissee,* our Sunday school superintendant, reminds me of "Mr. Pecksniff" in "Martin Chuzzlewit."[24]

Mon. May 24th 80

It's very warm to day. Didn't have the storm expected last night.

Bob Dougherty came up in the after noon and stayed to tea. In the evening, Daisy, Jude, Bob, Ma, Aunt Ella, and Grandma Garrow went to church.[25] Grandma Graham and I kept home. I read "The Head of the Family" aloud to her till Pa came home, then finished the book to myself.

We commenced cleaning house to day though we will not clean very extensively as we moved in so late in the fall. I took all the tacks out of the dining room carpet this morning and Ma and I washed the wood work this after noon.[26]

[24]"Mr. Pecksniff" from Charles Dickens' novel, Martin Chuzzlewit, was a tall, thin, long-necked most moral man—a comic figure, so this is not a compliment on Addie's part.

[25]"Bob Dougherty" was Addie's cousin Bob, son of her aunt, Julia A. Kimmel Dougherty. "Grandma Garrow" was Addie's maternal grandmother, Mary Seymour Garrow.

[26]To make it easier to keep the house clean during summers when there was more foot traffic and to keep the house cooler, nineteenth-century housewives pulled up area carpets, beat the dust out of them and rolled and stored them until fall, when they replaced them, tacking them down to the floor. Addie's parents' new house was celebrated by a housewarming party reported in the local newspaper on November 19, 1879. A good time was had by all.

I was scrubbing away at the folding doors when Daisy called me. I was getting interested in my work and said something cross under my breath at being interrupted, but when she told me there was a letter from "Sister," it more than made up for the interruption.[27] She answered all my questions about "Miss Mulock." She says "Miss Mulock is very much admired and ranks high among the novelists of the day." I asked her how to tell a "trashy" novel. She says "If the characters are natural, the thoughts pure and ennobling, and the tone of the book good and healthy, you may always know that it is not trash, even if there is a good-deal of lovemaking in it."[28] She has not got "Macaulay" yet, and I'm about eighty pages ahead.

Cousin Bob has promised to come up and ride horse-back with me some day. I was so glad to get a letter from "Sister" that when I got to my work again I jumped upon the stand to wash the top of the door, caught my dress on the inkstand, pulled it down, and spilt the ink all over the floor, and then got meekly down on my knees and wiped it up.[29] Luckily, there was no carpet down or there would have been a pretty mess. Ma's dreadfully good about such things and didn't scold.

Sun May 30th

As I am up here scribbling and got stuck, I thought I would write in my journal for a change. I wrote a letter to Martha Thursday and Daisy got one from her yesterday. She says she is getting aged and grey associating with old folks so much.

Friday had a school picnic down to the grove. It was a lovely day and we had a better time than I expected to. There was a splendid big swing down there. We girls—Allie,* Fanny,* Et, May,* and I—ate our dinner on a seperate table from the little children and Q. M. came and ate with us. My cake was splendid.

It is rainy and disagreeable to day. Friday, Neppa [the cat] got into my room and ate my dear little canary. At least I suppose he ate it, for the cage was tipped over and the bird gone when I went into the room,

[27]"Sister" probably refers to Cousin Martha Holmes. Addie's fondness for her cousin made her think of Martha as another sister.

[28]"Lovemaking" in the nineteenth century usually referred to intimate conversation, not physical passion.

[29]An inkstand was a stand with fittings for ink and pens.

though Neppa was no where to be seen. We hoped that the bird had escaped through the window and set the cage out on the roof in hopes that it would come back, but he hasn't yet.

Here is something good:

"We may glean knowledge by reading, but the chaff must be separated from the wheat by thinking. Knowledge is proud that he has learned so much—wisdom is humble that she knows no more."

Tues. June 1st 1880

This has been such a nice day, and I have enjoyed it so much. I don't know why I should have enjoyed today any more than other days but I have.

Pa and the hired man went to Niles today, and as I am generally "The Man of the Family" when they are both gone he left the horses and things in my care, and I always like that more than most anything. So I watered the horses first thing. Then Daisy gave me a music lesson. Then Et came up for a few minutes and I lent her "Martin Chuzzlewit" as she wanted something to read as she most always does, and I like to have her read Dickens.

Then Daisy and I played about two hours, reading new duets and such things. Then we all turned out and picked strawberries. They were <u>immense</u>. It was fun to pick them, for it didn't take many to make a quart.

Ralph went down in the country to pick berries this morning and got back this noon. I <u>thought</u> he wouldn't stay long—he hasn't much "stick-to-it-iveness." I got a handful of big strawberries and went out to the barn and divied with him and we traded knives, marbles, and most everything under the sun. Then we fed and watered the horses and I bathed Peg's eyes and teased the Tudor children.

After dinner we (Jude, Daisy and I) hitched up and went to look at the sheep as Pa directed me to. Got there and couldn't find the sheep anywhere. So we all got out and hunted through the woods. I believe I enjoyed this more than anything, but the others didn't. Daisy was so afraid she'd see a snake that she couldn't enjoy herself a bit and would get on top of stumps and beg us to go back. Jude was afraid too, but didn't act like Daisy. I'm afraid of snakes when I see them, but I didn't see the use of being afraid when I don't see them.

Well, we hunted and hunted but couldn't find no sheep. There was fresh tracks everywhere but no animals, so we went back and I made up my mind to go home and get Ralph and come back horseback. So we drove towards home. When we got to the gate there were all the sheep.[30] I was rather disappointed, for I wanted to hunt them some more and had been kind of looking forward to a horseback ride. So we came home.

I picked another quart of strawberries and took them over to Mrs. Ewalt,* then I read awhile. Cut some clover for Peg. Pa brought an immense snapping turtle home. Went riding in the evening.

I nearly forgot the best thing of all. My little bird is not lost after all but is down to Aunt Hattie's.[31] If the cat did tip the cage over, the bird must have got out of the window. He went down to Aunt Hattie's and flew on her bird cage and she caught it and I am so glad.

Sun. June 13th

Been a jolly day, a trifle warm but pretty good considering the storm this morning. About six o'clock this A.M. we had a pretty hard blow and rain storm. It blew Mrs. Hall's* big Balm of Gilead down, which also mashed her cherry tree, but did not hurt the house or fence, which is a wonder.[32]

Considerable has happened since I wrote last. Firstly, Will got home from Kansas, for which, Oh be Joyful! Daisy goes away to morrow for which we might as well be joyful for also as we have our hand in. Old Settler's Day has also been and gone.[33] Gertie Stevens* spent a couple of days with us about that time.

Friday the 4th, Daisy, Jude, Laura Platt,* and I took an eight mile horseback ride over to Tom Mar's at Berrien Center and back. It's only

[30]Sheep are herding creatures; where the leader goes, the flock follows. If the lead sheep takes it into his head to travel far from home, sheepherders, sheepdogs, or, in this case, farm girls, must chase after them and head them for home.

[31]"Aunt Hattie" was Harriet Graham, widow of Addie's late uncle, James. The miraculous reappearance of Addie's canary might also have resulted from her father's trip to Niles that same day. Niles was a much larger town than Berrien Springs, and George Graham might well have procured an identical canary to comfort (and deceive) a grieving daughter.

[32]The Balm of Gilead was probably a balsam poplar tree.

[33]As is true today, towns regularly celebrated anniversaries of when towns were founded. Michigan became a state in 1837; many celebrations of this Old Settlers' Day variety were held literally by the original settlers of a town some thirty to sixty years afterward. The Pioneer Association of Berrien County, formed in 1875, was made up of members who had emigrated to Berrien County no later than 1850. Like the Young People's Picnic Association, they too held their annual meeting in Grove Park. These meetings attracted thousands and were major events in county social life.

seven miles over and back, but we explored new roads and made out about another mile.

Friday June 11th after noon Daisy went to Niles with Bob Dougherty, and in the evening we all went to the Methodist social at Aunt Hattie's. It was a lawn social and was lit with Chinese lanterns. Had a poky old time. Mate Dunn,* Jude, and I poked around to gether till the mosquitoes chewed us pretty awful. We had to keep on the "Rampage" all the time or they wouldn't have left a piece big enough for a remembrance.[34]

Just as we were ready to go home, Jen Boon* and Howard Miller* wanted to dance, so I got up on the stairs and whistled a waltz. The refreshments were Ice cream and strawberries, Lemonade and candy. Ma made the ice cream so of course it was good.

I've got a little pet orphan lamb, but its fleece isn't "white as snow," but on the contrary rather inky, but I'll give him a bath when he gets a little fatter, which I think will improve his looks. Oh yes, and Jude's got two little young golden woodpeckers.[35] They came out of Mrs. Hall's tree when it fell. There was seven of them. One was killed by the fall, Jude took two to raise, and Hall's are going to try to raise the other four.

Spent my after noon in the cherry tree reading "Idylls of the Kings"* and eating strawberries. I have finished the second volume of "Macaulay." I guess I'll give him a rest now for awhile, though Martha is ever so far ahead of me.

Daisy, Jude, and I went riding this evening. It wasn't very agreeable, for Daisy had on her 'injured innocent' air, and Jude and I teased her and snubbed her all the way. I don't know what makes her act so injured unless its because Jude and I are not sorry that she is going tomorrow. I felt so joyful about it that I gave "vent" to my feelings by striking attitudes behind her back while she was driving and poor Jude snorted, while Daisy looked daggers and more injured than ever. My opinion of her is that she is a regular spoiled grown up babe and when she can't have her own way and do just as she wants to, she pouts and sulks, sheds copious tears & makes everybody cross.

I've just finished reading "Little Women"* for the second time. Et asked Mrs. Kephart if I could take it like a goody girl.[36] I think "Jo" is

---

[34]Insecticides were invented in the 1850s; insect repellent maybe what Addie is referring to here, or it could simply be the "slap and brush" method of repellant common among Michiganders.

[35]Probably the yellow-shafted version of the northern flicker.

[36]"Goody girl" possibly meaning a sensible girl.

just to jolly for any use and intend to be like her. I think I am naturally something like her, for everybody says I'm a "perfect Jo March." Martha told me I was several times, and I say three cheers for Jolly Jo!

Thur. Niles July 7th '80

Uncle Nelson, Aunt Julia, and Graham have gone to Sister Lakes, and Grandma Graham and I are keeping bachelors Hall.[37] It isn't an enviable job, I can tell you. Well, I'll go back to the beginning and tell how I got here.

Last Sunday after noon, about four o'clock, I was up in my cherry tree reading "Bonnie Lesley" when Jude came out and said "hurry up if you want to go to Niles." I didn't believe her at first and thought she only wanted to get me down, so of course I stayed up. But I soon found she was in dead earnest about it; and Pa was running out the buggy.

So in about fifteen minutes we were on our way. Pa had suddenly made up his mind he wanted some more wire for the machine, so he sent us up and we were to come down next morning early.

When we got here, Uncle N., Aunt J., and Graham were getting ready to start, and they wanted one of us to stay with Grandma.[38] Jude offered to if she could, but we both had to go home first. On the way, Jude got to thinking it over and wished she hadn't offered to. So I said I would. I thought it would be kind of fun and I would have plenty of time to read and scribble. But one can't read all the time, and as for scribbling, I don't feel a bit like it. I've only been here a little over two days but it seems at least two weeks. I came up Tuesday in the stage.[39]

Grandma is a fussy old lady and is in a fidget all the time for fear I'll break something. So most every time I touch anything, she utters a little scream and flies at me till I feel like throwing it at her head.

Oh, we have "such drowsy" 'most make me go to sleep to think of them. I'll give a sort of programme of yesterday.

[37]"Grandma Graham" was Addie's paternal grandmother, Mary Kimmel Graham; "keeping bachelors' Hall" means living as a bachelor would—doing all the housework without help.

[38]"Aunt J." was Addie's paternal aunt, Julia Graham Higby; "Uncle N." was her husband, Nelson F. Higby, who operated a dry goods store in Berrien Springs, moving to Niles, Michigan, in 1875. Graham was their son.

[39]"Stage" meaning stagecoach, the mass transit system of rural America in the 1880s. Berrien Springs enjoyed daily stagecoach service with Niles and St. Joseph.

Got up at eight in the morning, got through breakfast by nine, washed the two or three dishes, made the bed, read awhile, fed and watered the duckes, read Grandma to sleep or rather tried to. Then, while she was "catching a nap," I went out in the apple tree and read. Came in, commenced a letter to Martha, teased Tip, poked around till time for dinner. After dishes were washed (and that didn't take more than five minutes) I finished my letter to Martha.

An old gentleman came to see Uncle Nelson and stayed and talked to Grandma about his last sickness, and aches and pains were discussed freely. No matter how sick he had ever been, Grandma had been as sick and perhaps sicker. I think the poor man must have got discouraged.

About six I went over to Steven's after the milk. Sat in the dark till eight, then went to bed. I forgot to say I read all after noon til six, and Gertie Stevens came over a little while and sat in the dark too. Grandma can't bear lamp light or else she wants to save the oil. Gertie wanted me to come over this after noon, but it rained. Oh be joyful. I can't bear any of the Stevens, though they are my second cousins, except Wirt.* I like him better than the rest. I don't like Niles folks anyway. They look down on a fellow if he don't dress in his best harness every day.[40]

Well! I've done something desperate at last. A week ago to day I sent my little story "Jem's Day" to the children's magazine, and am waiting anxiously for the result.

Had a pretty good time on the fourth shooting firecrackers, of which a big blister on my right hand is a burning, or rather burnt, reminder.

Berrien Fri. Aug. 27th '80

Yesterday was my birthday. Sixteen years old! Didn't get a solitary thing.[41] Pa is going to send for a saddle for me, though.

Worked around all morning and in the afternoon played with May, Bert and Bunny.* I did too get a present. May and Bunny brought me over a plate of grapes and a bouquet of flowers.

Last Monday Ralph, Kit, Mate, Ottie, Jude, Et, & me went over to Little Indian Lake and stayed all afternoon.[42] Went boat riding and had a

---

[40]"In his best harness" meaning in his best clothing.

[41]Birthdays in the nineteenth century were celebrated far more quietly than in the twentieth, probably because people had more children, fewer material goods, and less emphasis on acquisition in their daily lives.

[42]Little Indian Lake lies about three miles southeast of Berrien Springs.

pretty good time. Charlie acted awful mean over there. I got on him bare back and couldn't do anything with him. He ran up in the woods and scraped me off on a tree, nearly stepped on me, and kicked at Jude. We didn't get home till way after dark, and when we went to take Etta home they were all out to the gate looking for us.

"Has Grandpa come" we all yelled together.

"Yes," Aunt Addie said, "He's up to your home."

We didn't believe it at first, but they all stuck to it, so we had too. We had been expecting him for a long time. He lives in Miss. and hadn't been to Michigan for fifteen years, so of course I didn't remember anything about him.[43]

When we got home there he was, sure enough. He is a short man, round shouldered. He has a bald head on top and grey whiskers. But his cheeks are rosy and he has bright funny brown eyes. He is seventy nine years old and is as lively as a cricket, and can read without spec's in the morning; in the afternoon, he can't.[44]

Day before yesterday, Mrs. Tudor and I went six or seven miles in the country after peaches. We stopped on the way and went to a funeral of a little boy named Ewalt.[45] We got three bushels of peaches and caught in the rain.

Cousin Lydia and Aunt Eliza Seymour are down to Aunt Addie's. A week ago Jennie, Ralph, May, Bunny, and I went out in the woods and tried to make a rustic chair.[46] We came pretty near making one, but looked more like a woodbox with the wood all on the outside.

Jude and Matie Dunn expect to go away to school this fall. They are going to St. Mary's, a Catholic school.[47] I was going too, but Pa says he

[43]John Garrow, Addie's maternal grandfather, married Mary Seymour in 1828 in Auburn, New York, where he was warden of the Auburn state penitentiary. He moved to Michigan in 1846. Due to ill health, in 1866 he moved to Liberty, Mississippi, to live with his son Nathaniel.

[44]"Spec's" meaning spectacles, or bifocals. As eyes age, their ability to focus closely for reading diminishes (a process called presbyopeia) because the lens in the eye becomes less flexible.

[45]The funeral was probably that of John K. Ewalt, eight-year-old son of George and Mary Ewalt of Oronoko Township. The onlookers may not have known the family; funerals were more open social occasions in the nineteenth century than today.

[46]A "rustic chair" was one made of wood with the bark left on, rather than of planks of finished wood.

[47]"St. Mary's" College was and is located just north of South Bend, Indiana.

can't spare both of us, and Jude is the oldest, so I'll go here again this winter. George Murdock went away Wednesday. He is going to write to me. He went to Ann Arbor.

Lee Wilk. took Jude & Et and I boat riding a week or two ago.[48] Had a glorious time. I went to camp meeting and stayed a day and a half. I didn't like it a bit. Came home in disgust and had the ague.[49]

We are thrashing today.[50] Mr. Ford is dead.* Got a letter from Martha last Monday.

My lamb is dead and the woodpeckers have fled.

The books I have been reading lately are "Queechy," "Arthur Bonnincastle," "Old town folks," "Macaulay," & "Fredrick the Great."* . . . .

Berrien Dec. 6th 1880

Last night I read over what I have written in this Journal and I find it is terribly silly. Things generally are silly after they have been written down. So I'm going to turn this Journal into a diary and every night I will set down what has happened through the day in a neet and businesslike manner.[51]

Well, this morning I got up about half past seven, helped get breakfast. Was late to school. I shall get up earlier after this. To day I took up two new studies. Physiology & Physical Geography. I also study Arithmetic, Geometry and reading. Friday I was examined in Civil Govern—I just passed and that was all, for I stood 75.

To day has been cold, snowy & blowy. We stuffed sausages to night and I wrote a letter to Jude. I must go to bed now or I won't get up at all tomorrow morning.

[48]This is the first mention of Thomas Lee Wilkinson, Jr., Addie's future husband, referred to as "Lee" in many more entries.

[49]Camp meetings were religious revivals, often lasting several days, and marked by emotional outbursts. Ague was either a sharp fever with chills, or simply a chill, marked by shivering.

[50]"Thrashing" refers to threshing the crop, presumably wheat. Threshing involves separating the grain from the chaff (or straw). The grain is ground into flour; the chaff becomes bedding for cattle.

[51]As is clear in some entries that follow, Addie regards the difference between a journal and a diary as the regularity of entry—a diary requires a daily entry.

Dec. 7th 1880.

I got up earlier this morning, I am happy to say. I also got to school in time.

Gene Howe* has got my knife and has had it for two or three weeks. I thought I would be revenged, so I thought I would put a rag doll in his desk, hoping he would pull it out after school had taken up so the scholars would all see it and tease him about it. So I took the doll to school yesterday morning and kept it in my desk most two days, waiting for a good opportunity. At recess this after noon I thought I had a good chance so I took it, all wrapped up in paper under my arm, and Et & I walked over to his desk and I sat down in it while Et talked to me as if nothing out of the way was going on. And I stuck it around into his desk and then danced a jig for joy in the aisle, flattering myself that no one had seen.

But there had, of course. I never tried to play a trick on anyone in my life but what it was spoiled some way. One of the boys saw me and tattled to Gene and he calmly took it out and threw it in the aisle. Mr. Bronson picked it up and grinned and layed it in his desk, and the scholars laughed. That was the end of the thing I layed away nights to think of.

After school I went down to Mrs. Barber's and got my mittens. The "New Church Magazine"* came to day and there is a story in it by Martha.

Dec. 12th

I've been and gone and missed six or seven days, but I won't do it any more. In looking through the "New Church Magazine" this week I saw in the back part this notice "Will the author of 'Jem's Day' please send his or her name & address." I caught my breath when I read it. For that was the first notice that had been taken of that miserable little story. I wonder now how I ever had cheek enough to send such a silly thing, for I read it through again last night and it is sickening. But I sent my address.

To day it has been thawing and I guess it is raining now, plague it all.

I went to Sunday school and got a book called "Glimpses Through."* It is very nice and comforting, though it is dreadfully solemn and the folks are all distressingly good.

I wrote a long letter to George to night, full of nonsense. Well, it is getting cold and I am getting sleepy. I intend to write every night after this.

Dec 16 1880

Here it is Thursday and I haven't written any since Sunday. So much for good resolutions.

Well, I've been out every evening this week except to night. Mon. and Tuesday I went to the Lutheran church to practice for Christmas. Wednesday, Al & I went down to Et's and spent the evening. We skated a little and practised "Jacobi."

I had an immense sty in my eye to day and tied a hand kerchief over it to go to school.[52] Ralph called me Dick Deadeye. I didn't go this after noon. Mrs. Euson* was here all day.

This evening I went to the school house after my books and went down to Aunt Addie's, and went from there with Et down to Mrs. Prestons after a bird.

I got a letter from Harry to night and an almanac. George is coming home next Saturday and Jude comes a week from to day. We are going to have two weeks vacation.

I must go to bed! Pa went to Niles to day.

Dec. 18th 1880

I don't think I'm very good at keeping a diary. It is late and I have just got my lessons and written a letter to Harry.

Yesterday George came home. I was at Al's and saw the stage come, so I trotted down town to see him and there he was, big as life. I caught onto the back of the stage and ran up to Aunt Ad's. And from there we went (Et & I) down to Al's, where Lena and she were waiting for us, then we proceeded to the picture gallery after getting the little [illeg.] out of the Methodist church.[53] For our Geometry class is going to get their picture taken in full costume as a Christmas present to Mr. Bronson.

But we were doomed to disappointment, for Carrie Mars* was there before us, and we didn't venture, for you might as well expect a sieve to hold water as to expect her not to tattle everything she knows. So we went skating instead, and I must say I was glad of it, for I hate to have my picture taken.

To day I went down and took Et & George sleigh riding. I let George drive to amuse him, and he let Charlie get to going fast and turned a

[52]A "sty" is an inflammation of an oil gland at the margin of the eyelid, resulting in a pimple or a very bloodshot eye.

[53]"Picture gallery" meaning photographer's studio.

corner and threw us all out, although I warned him. No damage was done.

I went to Sunday school to day & got a book called "Luck of Alden Farm," also the "Tangle Tales,"* but I let Fan. Bradley take them.

Gene Howe has got four jackknives belonging to me, and I had his ruler, but he took it away from me Friday and I haven't got anything. Ah me! But I will be revenged sooner or later.

Mr. Tudor is going up after Jude next Wednesday if the weather is pleasant.

Dec. 19th 1880

I went to practice to night. Et & George came up after me & George took me home. I went to school to day as usual and "flunked" in my Geography (thats a new word I learned to night—it means missed.)[54]

Et and I went up after Mr. Bronson to night.

"There was a rat run up the wall,
I saw his tail and that was all."

Mertie Matthews taught me that; she sat on my lap all evening. Rena Gaugler* taught me the following poetic inspiration:

"Up the hill and down the creek
Catch a frog to make him kick."

I must go to bed; it's as cold as ice here.

Jan. 8th 1881
morning

Its about time I was writing in my "diary." I'm afraid it will turn into a journal again.

Day after to morrow school commences again and vacation is almost over. I guess Jude will go back to morrow or Monday.

I got a good many presents Christmas. They were as follows:

a pair of chrochet slippers; a pair of girls club skates Just splendid; a book "Lucile"* by Owen Meredith; Toilet set; a neck tie; a vase; box of candy; box of prunelles; pincushion.[55]

---

[54]Actually, "flunked" has meant failed since about 1823.

[55]The slippers were crocheted, probably of yarn; the "toilet set" would be most likely a hairbrush, comb, and hair receiver (a small box with a lid in which to put hair caught in a brush or comb to use in making a hairpiece or "switch"); prunelles were a small, yellow dried plum packed without the skin.

I must go to dinner now.

❧

Evening

I took Ma down town this after noon. And while waiting for her to get her shopping done I took about two dozen boys riding. Then Jude and Al & I went down to Et's. She has got the quinsy again.[56]

Yesterday Al & I went skating. Night before last it snowed and the pond was covered with it about an inch deep and there was nobody there. We took a board and scraped off a little space, but soon got tired of it and came home pretty near froze to death. I can cut a front circle and skate pretty well, though I fall down more than I stand up and am black and blue all over.

Jude is going back to school Monday. We had a candy pull New Years night and also Christmas night.[57]

I received a letter from the Editor of the Church Magazine, saying that my story had been lost some way, but he was sure it had been accepted and would like another copy. So I sent it again. I wouldn't have if he hadn't been sure it was accepted. I expect to see it coming back soon with a note saying "It is not what I thought it was, sorry we made you so much trouble." They also asked me to send other contributions. There's sickness!

I am going to have a "Yarb" garden next spring and have written off a list of herbs and their medicinal properties, for I have serious thoughts of being a doctor.[58] I like to put folks together and make them well. I made a gorgeous New Year card and took it down to Et to day.

Pa is sick and I do the chores, take care of the horses, cow & pigs. Its jolly and I like it.

---

[56]"Quinsy" is a severe throat inflammation with swelling and fever.

[57]A "candy pull" was a party where guests made various kinds of candy, most particularly taffy, which had to be stretched or "pulled" thin until it dried so it could be eaten.

[58]"Yarb" being a dialect form of the word herb. Many forms of what were called "irregular" medicine used natural remedies developed from herbs and plants. In states with a large rural population and few medical doctors, irregular medicine developed a considerable following, especially among women, who were both patients and practitioners.

Jan. 9th

Last night Jennie Boon and Mrs. Tudor and the three children spent the evening here. We played Euchre.[59]

To day I didn't go to Sunday school. It was a cloudy day. I did the chores this morning. About half-past-four this after noon I went down to Al's to find where the Lessons were for to morrow. From there went down to Et's. She is about the same.

We all wanted to do something to distinguish ourselves and concluded to organize a secret society called the "Triangle" of which we three are corners. We are going to wear tin triangles around our necks for a badge, and when we meet every week we will all wear a white cap with a Triangle on the top and these initials inside of triangle: "M. T. S." which stands for "Member of Triangle Society." We also have a certain grip.[60] I am to make the laws and when we meet next Friday night at Et's I will read them and see if all agree upon them.

I have been studying my lesson and making up laws with Jude's help.

Tomorrow school commences again. Oh whack!

Jan. 11th

Went to school to day. Had a good lesson in geometry but a horrid one in P. Geography. I've been pegging away at it to night.[61] I was excused at recess and went down to Et's. She seemed to be a little better. Mrs. Doroughty & Mrs. Perkins* & Harry were there. After school Al came. She wouldn't be excused but she might just as well as not. Yesterday Lutie Pardee* changed seats without asking permission, changed right in school hours. Mr. Bronson hasn't said anything about it yet and I live in hopes that he won't.

We have some new scholars including Ella Graham & Charlie Smith.* Ella sits right in front of me and wears all the jewelry she can get together, I guess. She is terribly silly and affected. I <u>despise</u> such girls. I couldn't help sticking my toe up through the seet yesterday and seeing her jump. She did it quite naturally, and I flatter myself that, <u>that</u> action was not affected at least.

---

[59]"Euchre" was a popular card game in the nineteenth century, invented about 1841. Each player was dealt five cards and the player making trump had to collect three tricks to win a hand.

[60]"Grip" meaning handshake.

[61]To "peg away" at something meant to work on it persistently.

Got a letter from George to night, 11 pages of heart-rending adventures. He said he has given up lying. Yesterday I got a letter from Belle & one from Molly.

Will took Jude back to St. Mary's yesterday.

I don't believe I'll go to school tomorrow.[62] I've sprained my ancle some way and it is all swollen up and aches like Sancho.[63]

Last night I went over to spend the evening with the Tudor children. We had quite a gay time.[64]

Well, I must go to bed as it is late.

Jan. 12th

Went to school to day and was late. I didn't come home this noon but stayed intending to get my Geography lesson, but I didn't study much because Gene Howe made a racket and kept talking all the time just to bother me. He took my little knife away from me and I didn't have any peace till [I] took the poker and guarded myself, but that couldn't make him stop talking. Suffice to say I didn't have my lesson extra.

Instead of reading the regular lesson to day, Mr. Bronson had Al & I take turns reading about Elihu Burrit the Learned Blacksmith.[65]

This evening Ralph and Mrs. Martin came over to spend the evening. Pretty soon Al came up and wanted us to come down to her house as she was alone. So Ralph and I went down. Had a very pleasant time. Ralph and I are going to make a telephone.

Sat. Jan 16th 1881

It stormed nearly all day to day, but this evening it cleared up beautifully.

I went to school yesterday and had a miserable lesson in Geometry. In the afternoon I got up a tobacco pledge and passed it among the boys, but

---

[62]Michigan had no compulsory school attendance law until 1905, so children and their parents could decide when and if they went to classes.

[63]Like the expression "Oh Whack!" earlier, "aches like Sancho" is a colloquialism of the time—Addie's slang. Here she might be deriving it from Alcott's *Little Women* again—Jo March, after a trip to help a poor family, enjoyed being called an "angel-child" since she "had been considered a 'Sancho' ever since she was born."

[64]"Gay" meaning fun.

[65]"Elihu Burrett," (1810–70) "the learned blacksmith," founded the League of Universal Brotherhood (1846) and promoted the Second Universal Peace Congress held at Brussels in 1848.

could only get three to sign it.[66] Clifford Benson,* Charlie Smith and Willie Weaver.* I had counted on Jim Boon* signing it and was disappointed and rather mad. When I was going through town I met him and he yelled "Ad."

I said "What."

Says he, "Hello."

I didn't say any thing and he said "Are you mad?"

And I said "Yes I am. If I hadn't any more strength of mind than you have I'd give up."

He didn't say anything and I guess he's mad. I am sorry now that I said it, for if he couldn't keep it I didn't want him to sign, of course. I suppose I'll have to ask pardon Monday.

Last night the T. S. met at Et's. We made some changes. Et is going to be president, Al. Secretary, and I am Treasurer. We are going to read up about politics and the leading questions of the day and each must make a speech on that subject at next meeting.[67] Al staid all night with me last night. I didn't get through my work to day till four o'clock. Pa has a terrible cough yet and I still do the chores. Kit came over to night and played eight or nine games of euchre. At first Ma & I played against Kit and Pa and we beat three games. Then Will took Pa's place and they beat us all the rest.

I'm fearful sleepy and must go to bed.

Et is lots better.

I heard Pa say to day that he was going to write for Harry to come home. I hope to goodness he will. I want to see him so bad.

Jan 30th, 1881

Well, its about time I was writing in my "diary" again.

I didn't go to Sunday school to day, got up too late. Last Monday Will went to Niles and brought Aunt Ella & Daisy down. Martha was sick and couldn't come. Daisy and Aunt E. stayed till Friday, then Will took them back and Martha came down with him. She stayed till to day.

---

[66]"A tobacco pledge" would be a small card, distributed by an anti-tobacco reformer. If a person signed, that would mean he would not use tobacco. Addie is exhibiting a characteristic of many nineteenth-century women, who were thought to be more moral than men, and therefore responsible for leading men toward more moral behavior.

[67]These kinds of self-improvement groups were very common in the nineteenth century as a form of entertainment and informal education.

Yesterday Martha was making some corn muffins and asked me to get her the baking powder. I got it and she put it in. After wards Ma discovered that I had given her "Plaster of Paris" by mistake.[68] That's just my luck. I never tried to do anything yet but I spoilt it. It is needless to state that the corn muffins did not rise.

Friday night was our entertainment. In the after noon we didn't have school up stairs, and about quarter past eleven in the fore noon Et, Annie O'dell,* Mary Himes,* and myself went up to Mr. Bronson's to help get the curtains ready. I didn't do much sewing but tended baby's instead. Lu came to me first thing, which was something strange as she seldom will go to a stranger, and I felt highly flattered. They insisted upon our staying to dinner and after that we went down to the school house to help about the stage.

The entertainment went off well. I spoke "The Wonderful One hoss Shay" to the great jollification of the people, much to my discontent.[69] Had a jolly time. Took in over twenty four dollars and cleared over twenty two dollars. Pa's cough doesn't seem to get any better, and I still do the chores.

Et and I went up to see Will yesterday.

Thur. Feb. 10th 1881

It has been thawing and raining for the last two or three days, but to night; acts as if twere going to freeze up.

I wrote a composition to night on Cheating in school. We speak to morrow. Staid and practised after school.

Sunday I read "Mrs. Lirriper's Lodging & Legacy"* by Dickens. Think its splendid. Finished "Hamlet" night before last. I like the play, but not the character. He hasn't got the back-bone.[70] Have nearly finished "Fred the Great."

Got a letter from George yesterday. Am going to send him a comic valentine.[71]

---

[68]"Plaster of Paris" is white powder, like baking powder, but is mixed with water to make a quick-setting paste.

[69]Addie's public speaking was a common form of entertainment provided by children in a public setting, such as a school assembly.

[70]"Hamlet," the leading man in Shakespeare's play by the same name, spends most of the play debating whether to take action against his father's murderers.

[71]The earliest valentines in the nineteenth century were postcards and so rude and abusive that one year the Chicago Post Office refused to deliver them because they were deemed vulgar.

Yesterday we stayed after school a little while to practice. Gene Howe came prowling around and when I wanted to go home he took my books and wouldn't give them to me. I at last got his hat and said I'd give it to him if he'd give up my books. Wouldn't do it, said he didn't want hat. I put hat in my pocket and said I was going home. He said he didn't care, so I went. It was raining and I guess he went home bare headed. Found my books in Mr. Bronson's desk this morning.

With the money made by our entertainment, Mr. Bronson bought Encyclopedias for school and had the book-case fixed up. Have some money left.

Pa is lots better. Will got a letter from Harry to night. He says we won't hear of him being in bad company again. It makes me feel good— hope we won't. Jude were home last week and staid three or four days. They will not be home again till June.

Mon. Feb. 14th 1881

Didn't get any Valentines. Went to school to day as usual. Has been a very pleasant day.

Mr. Bronson sent Jim Boon & Elmer Gorham* home to day for acting bad. Saw Jim after school; says he's going back to morrow. He says he wasn't as bad as Teacher thought. Hope he wasn't, I will miss him if he doesn't come back.

When I was coming home from school to night saw Nal Colvin* & Charlie Shearer* with their skates. They told me to come on and go skating. Told them I didn't know there was any [ice]. Said they were going up to see. So I ran in the house and got my skates and went. Ma wasn't at home. Didn't find any good skating. Snow was about an inch deep on the pond. Got disgusted. Left the boys to clean it off and came home. I would have stayed and helped, but it was so late when I came home. Ma asked me who went skating. I [told] her Charlie, Nal, & I. She looked sort of amused about something—guess twas because I went off with two boys. So, I don't care, I like boys better than girls.

Friday night I went to a surprise party on Ella Graham. We met at Hattie Smith's.* It was an oyster supper. Walter Kephart was there and said he had got a letter from George.

"He is the queerest boy I ever saw," said he, "You remind me of him, not like any body else."

"Yes," said Al, "They are both odd."

I think I will take that as a compliment. I sort of like to be odd.

Walter and I sat and told each other marvelous stories for about half an hour. I guess each trying to tell a bigger.[72] We didn't have supper till twelve o'clock. I think that was heathenish. I didn't get home till two in the morning. It rained like sixty, too.

Saturday Et and I went down to see how much the river had raised, and while down there saw some little boys sliding down the big hill, although it has been forbidden by the marshal, for it is not only very dangerous for the children, but makes the hill so icy it is almost impossible for teams to drive up.[73] Nevertheless, Et & I longed to slide down, for the boys went awful fast and there was plenty of danger. If the sled isn't steared just right it will run into the side of the bridge and knock your brains out, or you will fall into the river.

After while Jim Platt* came down with a great long sled. He slid down several times and steared splendidly. He invited one of us to go down with him. We were only too glad of the chance, but Et said she wouldn't go first, and I said I would. So I got on in front and he sat behind. The hill is long, and as we neared the bottom the sled was going so fast that things at the side of the road were just one blur. We ran into another sled with two boys on, but didn't hurt anyone. If it hadn't been for them we would have gone clear across the bridge. Et went next and the sled never stopped till it had gone clear across the bridge and to where the water crosses the road in the other side.

Yesterday I went to Lutheran Sunday school, although it stormed awfully. In the evening I wrote a long letter to George & Jude and fixed four Valentines to send to Nellie Hall* & the Tudor children. I must stop, for my oil is low.[74]

Wed. Feb. 16th 1881

Went to school today as usual. I got my [grade] card yesterday. General average 8 4/5, which is 2/5 better than last month. Et, Al, and I went skating last night after school. There is quite a large pond in Snider's field. Had a good enough time, not extra.

---

[72]A "bigger" meaning a tall tale.

[73]The "big hill" Addie refers to led up a steep riverbank from the bridge across the St. Joseph River to Ferry Street, the main business route in Berrien Springs. It was heavily traveled and the children's sled runners would indeed have packed the snow into ice and created quite a hazard.

[74]"Oil" here referring to lamp oil.

Jim Boon came back yesterday & Gene Howe was sent out to breathe the fresh air today. I expect to go next.[75] Staid after school and practiced songs. Have been studying a little this evening, but not much.

Got a letter from Mollie. Wrote in Walter Martin's* autograph album. Mary Himes says I'm queer because I always have three or four children around me. I can't help it. I like 'em and they like me.

Et is getting so she is troubled by pressing attentions. Tom Dispennet* pesters her most awfully, although she snubs and makes fun of him unmercifully. And Rome Knight* wanted her to go to Ella Graham's party with him. Thank goodness I'll never be bothered that way! The boys all treat me as if I was one of them, and we converse about jack-knives, revolvers, and other congenial topics with animation, and I like that way best; wish I <u>was</u> one of them, but since I can't be a boy the next best thing is to act as much like one as possible.

Thur. Feb. 16th

Went to school. Was imperfect. Cut up fearfully this morning.[76] After school, Mary Himes and I went skating. Et couldn't & Al wouldn't go. Mary took her sled and we had a first rate time. She seems to be a very sensible girl, and to crown all she doesn't wear bangs: that fact sort of drew me towards her from the first. She is very tall, about half an inch taller than I am, and is only fourteen years old. She found out to day that I was sixteen and would hardly believe it. I feel as if she was the oldest, sometimes.

May & Bert Tudor spent the evening with me. We played Euchre, and I saw them nearly home.

I have been practicing reading out of my old reading book to night.

There is a social at Nichols' to morrow night. Guess I'll go. Mary is going.

The second division comes to morrow. I look forward to it with pleasure, for someone else will have to suffer as I did last Friday.

The End

---

[75]In other words, Gene was suspended from school for a few days for poor behavior and Addie expects the same fate for a similar reason.

[76]"Cut up" meaning misbehaved.

Sun. 19 Feb.

Went to Sunday school to day. Friday, the second division came off. It wasn't near as good as ours. Many failures.

After school, Al had the first division stay to choose a captain, as she has resigned. Mary Himes & I were nominated. We voted by ballot. I got sixteen votes and Mary got four, so I am captain. I am going to pick out pieces for most of my division. And I won't have a bit of instrumental music, for that organ is about as musical as a cross-cut saw. I am going to speak a piece, "The Lightning rod dispenser,"* by Will Carleton.

Yesterday I took Ma calling down to the Shaker farm, Aunt Hattie's and Minnie's.*[77] In the evening I went down to Al's. Et was there. We made plans for our division. Mrs. Ewalt is down stairs.

Yesterday I was walking down town, and had got to the brick store, where there was quite a crowd around, as there always is Saturday, when Eddie Aymar yelled "Has your sister gone back yet?"[78]

I said "Yes."

"Well," says he, "You've got her thing on anyway." He meant my cloak, which Jude wore most of the time when home. I had to laugh; though it was impudent of him, he said it as innocently as if it was a common occurrence. When I went through town yesterday, all the boys yelled "Hello, Captain."

Good gracious, I've got to get my lessons.

Tue. Feb. 22nd

Well, Will's gone and done it at last. Was married this after noon and started for Chicago as soon as the ceremony was over, and I didn't see him.[79] I wasn't invited to the wedding and am firy mad. The poor fellow was so scared he came pretty near not inviting Ma. We weren't sure he would do it this after noon or not, so I went to school as usual and missed the fun.

[77]The Shaker farm refers to a farm on the north edge of Berrien Springs, bought by the Shakers, a religious sect, in 1858, and used for commercial seed production until they sold the property in 1872. Although no Shakers actually lived there, the work was done by hired hands, it was and is still known as the "Shaker Farm."

[78]"The brick store" refers to Berrien Springs' one and only brick commercial building; it still stands at the corner of Cass and Ferry streets.

[79]Brother Will married Laura Platt, daughter of James M. and Aurelia Platt. Like birthdays, nineteenth-century weddings were often much more casual affairs than those of the late twentieth century.

This is rather an eventful day. Harry's and Washington's birthday. Will's wedding day. Al had a tooth pulled. I was perfect and Et got scolded twice.

I went to a social at Nichol's; a dry affair.[80] Paid twenty-five-cents for a cup of coffee (which I didn't drink), 1 piece of cake, 1 biscuit, 1 cookie, and a pickle.

It was a very pleasant day to day until about four o'clock, when it cloudeded up, snowed, and now it is most awful cold and windy.

Last night I had my division meet up here.

Got a long letter from George to night.

Pa got me some beautiful chromos and a paper that comes monthly.[81]

I went up to Mr. Bronson's to night and played with the babies for about half an hour.

Carrie Mars asked me if her frizzes looked horrid. I was thinking about something else and said yes. Made her mad, although I immediately begged pardon and told her they were immense.[82]

Feb. 28th Mon.

It is terribly stormy to night. Yesterday it was warm and rained steadily all day; at night it got colder, turned to snow, the wind blew so it fairly shook the house, and this evening the snow was drifted so I had to climb the fence when I went to school, and jumped in a snow drift nearly up to my waist. But to night I couldn't even do that, for the snow would have been up to my neck.

I went to Sunday school yesterday through the rain. Mary Himes was the only other one in my class. Mrs. Reiber didn't come, so we went into Mrs. Howe's* class. She has a class of boys: Jim Boon, Herm[an] Gaugler,* & Tom Dispennet were there. Mrs. Howe asked me what leprosy was like. She meant in a spiritual sense, but I didn't know it, so I said "small-

---

[80]"A dry affair" may be a reference to lack of punch rather than liquor, which is its usual meaning, or it may simply mean it was dull.

[81]"Chromos" are chromolithographs, or color prints. These were printed by using stones with different parts of a single picture drawn on each stone with a different colored ink. When printed in succession on a single piece of paper, the combined sections created a complete picture of scenes or people.

[82]"Frizzes" is a reference to tightly curled hair; "immense" would be slang for nice.

pox," thinking I was very smart.[83] I should have said it was like sin. Got laughed at.

Thursday noon Jim asked me if I couldn't go out to a Lutheran social at Rockies, five miles in the country.[84] His mother and father were going, also Al, Fan., Et., Frank Kephart, & Herman Gaugler, & Clara Elliot,* all in a big bob, and lots of fun.[85] After much urging from Et and myself, I got permission to go. We had a glorious time, and the only thing that spoiled the serenity of the evening for me was that in playing Snap-and-Catch-'em (a heathenish kind of game), I had to kiss Reiber's Wonderful-What-is-it.[86] It makes me sick to think of it, for I detest him above all others and can't imagine what induced him to snap me.

I got better acquainted with Frank Kephart than ever before, and really begin to like him. I always thought he was bashful, green, and stupid, and everything else, but he isn't—he is full of fun and seems to have an extensive imagination.

We didn't start back till nearly one o'clock. Before we left, the country young people got awful mad at us. Though for a long time we couldn't imagine what about. But we found out afterwards. Mrs. Boon came upstairs where we all were and cautioned us not to make so much noise; Jim said, just for fun, that it wasn't us, it was the country folks. I heard him, but didn't know there was any others but our party around. And I don't think he did either, but there was and they were furious.

Coming home, Jim & Fan were fearfully spoony, pulled the robe over their heads, and monopolized each other.[87] Clara, Et, Frank, and I did all the talking. I guess Herm. & Al. dozed, for they didn't say much. We grew quite poetic, or rather Frank did. Here is a sample:
"The boy stood in the door
The mule was in the stable;

---

[83]"Leprosy" was a disease marked by the formation of nodules, ulcerations and deformities, and by a loss of sensation. It receives prominent mention in the Bible; "smallpox" was a viral disease that caused lesions and pockmarks. It has since been eradicated from Earth with vaccines.

[84]"Rockies" was probably owned by George C. Rockey—a large farm in Royalton Township, north of Berrien Springs.

[85]A "bob," short for bobsleigh, two short sleds coupled together side-by-side.

[86]These terms refer to games, most likely similar to spin-the-bottle or other kissing games enjoyed (or suffered through) by teenagers in other times.

[87]"Spoony" meant kissing, caressing, or conversing amorously.

The boy thought he was stronger
And the mule thought he was able.
"He lifted up his hoof
Kicked the boy upon the jaw;
The boy was so scared he didn't know
Whether it was his hind foot or his paw."

The metre is perfectly astonishing. I stayed all night at Et's and we didn't get to sleep till nearly four o'clock, and got awake again at seven. I wasn't a bit sleepy Saturday morning.

Ma went up to the farm to prepare for Will, and left me to get dinner. I managed to fall down cellar during her absence and skin my arm. In the after noon she went up again and Et came up. I tried to teach her to play Euchre, but we were both so sleepy we didn't do much but sit and blink at each other. Afterwards, Al came up and taught me the chords to "Golden Slippers."

Well, I must stop.

June 6th 1881

Four more days and school is out! I don't know as I am very glad. I've had pretty jolly times this winter. We have examination in Physical Geography tomorrow after noon, and I ought to be studying this minute.

Jude will be home in nearly three weeks.

Grandma Graham is dead. Sorry I wrote what I did July 27th.[88] She was ~~most~~ always good to me, and I ought to have remembered she was old and could not stand my racketing.

She and Aunt Julia and Graham were driving down to come to Old Settler's day. The horse scared at the top of Mar's hill and ran away. Aunt Julia fell out on the hill and was terribly bruised.

Graham was thrown over on to the thil[l]s between the horse and dash-board and was not hurt.[89] But Grandma knelt in the bottom of the buggy and held to the dash-board with both hands, and stayed in until the buggy ran over a little log, when she was thrown up in the air and

---

[88] A reference to Addie's entry of July 7, 1880.

[89] "Thills" being the long wooden shafts between which the horse is hitched to a vehicle. The dash-board was a wooden screen at the front of the buggy that protected occupants from mud, snow or water kicked up by the horse's hooves. The three were on their way to the annual meeting of the Berrien County Pioneer Association when their horse ran away.

came down on her head and was almost instantly killed. It is well that she was not compelled to suffer long. But I cannot help thinking how she must have suffered after Aunt Julia and Graham were thrown out, not knowing but that they were both killed, and expecting as she knelt on the floor of the buggy that every moment would be her last.

But her face in death was calm and peaceful, and showed none of the agony she must have suffered. I can hardly realize yet that she is gone.

Volume 2

December 21, 1881–May 28, 1882

We have such comical and funny times I am going to keep an account of them as well as I can, although they will sound silly written down. Jude advised me to and I always take her advice; when she advises me to do something I intend to do.

Cousin Bob got up a dancing school this winter. He likes to dance. I don't unless I can have the whole floor to myself. It's lots of fun to go though, and I wouldn't miss it for a good deal. George generally takes Jude and I and Et has to go with Cousin Bob and stand his conversation which has about as much substance to it as moonshine. I asked him one night if he didn't like the poem "Miles Standish."[1]

"Yes," said he, "It's by Whittiah, is it not? Very fine poem."

He is great on literature. At Aunt Addie's one night they were speaking about "Thaddeus of Warsaw."*

"Yes, I read that," he said. "Thaddeus was the fellah who tied his horse to a twig in the snow and there came a big thaw and in the morning his horse was in the top of a tree."

George wrote for West and Keisler to come and spend the holiday with him, but West's mother is dead and they will not come.

---

[1] *The Courtship of Miles Standish* (1858) was by Henry Wadsworth Longfellow. Cousin Bob erred in both pronunciation and identification.

Our dancing club meets Saturday nights. One week from tomorrow night we are going to have a masquerade.

Dec. 26th Monday

Christmas is over and now I may get some chance to write in this book. It seems so funny to have Christmas without a bit of snow. It was warm and pleasant yesterday.

I got a good many presents, three books, "Andersen's Fairy Tales," from Et, "Tom Brown's school days" from Jude, and "Among the Poets" from Pa.* Besides I got a pair of kid mittens, two handkerchiefs, an old paper knife that was my grandfathers.[2] Aunt Jude gave me a pretty Christmas card, from Graham a gold collar button, and a bottle of perfumery from Cousin Bob.

Mrs. M.Mc.C.D.W.,* Et and George took dinner with us. I asked George "What is the difference between a Hairdresser and a Sculptor." The answer is "One curls up and dies and the other makes faces and busts." Jude tried to repeat it and innocently told Et "one curls up and busts and the other makes faces and dies," to the great edification of her hearers.

When it began to get dark we all started down to Aunt Addie's to spend the evening, taking M.Mc.C.D.W. home on the way. Just as we started M. Mc. said "Who will take me home."

"I will," said George.

"It is nice for young men to escort old ladies around," said she. "They can practise on them and mistakes are not noticed."

Then George, just to take off Lee Wilkinson, said "I've got six girls and I'm the nicest young man in town."

M. Mc. thought he was in earnest, never having heard Lee joke before, gave quite a lecture on conceit and poor [George] was so mortified he didn't have the heart to explain himself. They two went first and through town we three went single file behind with our handkerchiefs to our eyes.

Well, to continue we reached Aunt Addy's at last and Jude and Et were determined to go to church. George and I didn't want to go and tried to persuade them to stay at home, but to no purpose and they went. They had not been gone long e'er we longed to pay them back for leaving us and I knew of nothing that would cause Jude more agony than to go to church just as I was, without one plea so we went, I in my old hood

---

[2]"Kid mittens" would be made of goatskin.

and no gloves.[3] And to add to the harmony, we were late. And took a seat near the front. When we sat after the hymn, what should I do but sit down on George's hat and mash it flat. To our great horror instead of the the usual preacher who is poor enough, Rev. John Boon arose in the pulpit. But it came to an end at last and we all went back to Aunt Addie's and ate popcorn.

Jude got a watch for a Christmas present and keeps every one well posted on the time of day, as she looks at it about every five minutes. Coming home we were all hilarious and conversation ran on something like this.

Jude: "I think you will make a very good cupid at masquerade."

George: "Cupid? Yes, just so, Cupid, Ah yes (giggles—)."

Jude: "Isn't that a splendid sky?"

George: "Sky? ah yes, splendid sky. Cupid flying through a splendid sky, yes, yes."

Ad: "There is a light in Mrs. Ewalt's house."

George: "Mrs. Ewalt's house? Oh yes, Cupid flying through a splendid sky over Mrs. Ewalt's house, just so."

And a whole rigmarole more interspersed with giggles. Jude and I went down there this afternoon to look over old fashioned dresses and choose something for masking. I am going to be a Quakeress, wear a plain green silk of old fashioned make, a square of white around my neck and crossed in front, and a white cap.[4] We all dressed up and pranced around in them. Mine won't come together. George is getting up a remarkable costume, I guess, and won't tell us anything about it, for which I am glad as 'twill be more fun. I wish Et didn't know what I am to be.

Et and I want to play some trick on George that night though we don't know what it will be yet. He and Jude are always trying to get up some joke on us, and think they are awfully cute if they happen to succeed. On hallowe'en a lot of us girls were invited down to Ella Graham's to spend the evening. About ten o'clock we started home serenading people on the way. We had just finished singing at Vinton's and were walking along when we saw a man staggering along on the other side of the street.[5] Of course, we ran, who wouldn't, although there were eight of us

---

[3]"Just as I was, without one plea" is a spoof on the old hymn, "Just as I am, without one plea. . . ." by Charlotte Elliott, and L. M. Woodworth (1834).

[4]A "Quakeress" was a woman Quaker, a member of a religious sect known for its simplicity of dress. They did not wear green.

[5]"Vinton's" refers to the blacksmith's shop of Harlow Vinton.

and only one of him. Well, we took Annie O'dell home and had just finished piling the drug store steps full of wood and were walking down toward Gaugler's when we saw that man stagger against a tree and fall clear across the walk not far in front of us.[6]

It is needless to say that we crossed the road in a way that would have done credit to a circus performer for neatness and dispatch. That man stumbled after us. When we reached the walk we all broke into a dead run and of course I lost my hat. So, Carrie Mars and I plucked up courage to go back after it, although that awful man stood just where it was. When we got to the corner he advanced and holding out his coat remarked, "Ad, I wish you'd take this coat home to Jude, I borrowed it for the occasion"—

It is needless to say that I pounded him. He had been up to our house all evening planning some way to scare us. I will tell of more of their cuteness next time Jude's watch says half past nine.

Jan. 2nd Monday

It has been snowing for the last few days and is now. Yesterday we were invited down to Aunt Addie's to dinner, had a very pleasant time.

I must tell about the masquerade. I was a "Spanish Lady" instead of a Quakeress as I intended to be. Jude and Et were both little "Bo Peeps" and looked very well, wearing old fashioned high hooped overskirt and quilted skirts.[7]

I must must set the table now.

We had [a] very good time and hardly anyone knew me. It would have been a success but for one thing and that made it a failure. Two or three of the young men had been drinking and though only enough to make them very jolly, it was enough to spoil the evening, for I don't see why boys can never attend anything of that kind without making fools of themselves. Jim Platt was one of those who were a little off. I did not know it and when he came and engaged me for the next quadrille I accepted.[8] But before the quadrille came, George told me and promised

---

[6]Daniel George Washington Gaugler was the town undertaker and furniture dealer. "Gaugler's" probably refers to his business rather than his residence since Addie and her friends were downtown.

[7]"Bo Peep" is a reference to Mother Goose's Little Bo Peep, who lost her sheep and didn't know where to find them. Hoops made skirts stand out from the body.

[8]A "quadrille" was a popular nineteenth-century square dance of five figures for four couples, chiefly in 6/8 or 2/4 time.

to dance it with me himself. But Jim had forgotten his engagement by that time and to my delight took another partner.

George was disguised as a clown and had the cutest suit of any boy there. Knee breeches of many coulered calico, a pointed collar with tiny bells all over him. I got an inkling that he was to wear bells and knew him at once. He soon found me out and let me know it by asking his favorite connundrum—"why is the first u in the word cucumber like the isthmus of Suez?"[9]

Jude had a blue ribbon on her crook. George declared that Jule Brown asked her for it—"Miss Julia, may I have this ribbon," and that Jude said "Yep." George thought Miss Epley was Fanny Kesler* and asked her to waltz with him. They waltzed and he thought they were getting along splendidly but she begged to be excused and took her seat. Says he don't know why.

Et came up this afternoon, had lots of fun. Went to town and wished Mr. Sheldon "Happy New Year," and he gave Et and I a stick of candy. Took Mr. Tudor's cutter and had a sleigh-ride.[10] Mr. Morton jumped in behind. Jule Brown snow balled us. Went into Walter's after Arnica, wished Happy New Year.[11] He gave us each his card. Met Cousin Bob, he invited us to attend the minstrels with him tonight, am going. It is Negro minstry.[12]

Went down to Aunt Addie's. George came up with us and borrowed "History of Rome." He and Jude fight like everything. He tells everyone about "Yep" and makes her awful mad. I would tell about "Valerian" if I was her. At the first dance we had, George intended to take Mate Reiter home and took it all as a matter of course and said "ain't you pretty near ready to go?" She said "no, I ain't" short as pie crust. He felt awfully cut up about it. Went home and Aunt Addie had to give him Valerian to quiet his nerves.[13] They are friendly now but George has never offered to take her home since. Jule and George want to come up tomorrow night and play whist.[14] Guess they will.

[9]Because it lies between two "Cs" (seas).

[10]A "cutter" is a light, small one-horse sleigh.

[11]"Walter's" referred to Walter Kephart's pharmacy in Berrien Springs. Arnica is a tincture derived from the species *Arnica montana*, used to treat bruises and sore muscles.

[12]Minstrel shows in the late nineteenth century were performed by African Americans, as was the case here, or by whites who had blackened their faces. The shows included songs, dances, comic routines, and sentimental skits that were based on and included traditional African American folk songs and humor.

[13]"Valerian" is a drug made from garden heliotrope that works as a sedative.

[14]"Whist" is a card game similar to bridge.

Tuesday
Jan 3rd 1882 A.M.

We did an awfully mean thing last night. Et came up and said the church was crowded, so not waiting for Cousin Bob we trotted off. Got a good seat and watched for him. He had got Walter and gone up to our house. No one was at home so they came to the church. Saw us. Cousin Bob came and sat with us. He wasn't mad. I would have been if I was him.

Query: Why is Cousin Bob like charity. Because he suffereth long and is kind.

Tonight he wants to get a lot of young people and go down and call on Mary Hime's aunt. I had rather go to the minstrels again. It was splendid. There is good skating, the boys say. I am going this P.M. Makes me wild to see the boys going and me not.

Jan 8th Sun.

Cousin Bob is here. He and Jude are singing duets.

I did go to the Minstrels Tuesday night. They were not so good as the first night. I also went skating that afternoon with Mate Himes.

Wednesday, Fanny Bradley, Mate, Et and I went again. We skate down by the Indian fields where the river over flow. It is quite a large pond with not much water under it. Coming home we met Jule Brown and all went up to Aunt Addie's to see about calling on Mate's aunt, Miss McClellan, in the evening. George was sick and we didn't find out anything more than we knew before. So I told Jule to come up about half past seven and Cousin Bob would stop with Et for us. They did. We spent a very pleasant evening playing Euchre, casino, etc.[15]

Jule is a trump, I think.[16] He is so jolly and seems to see the ridiculous side of everything. He makes fun of every body in a good natured way and gets off the dryest jokes without a smile. He seems to be a natural gentleman yet is blunt and boyish enough to suit even me.

Thursday afternoon I went skating again and got in. Ottie Statler and I were jumping. He jumped over a log and I after him. He didn't get in but of course I did, but water is shallow and I only got one foot wet. When I got home Aunt Ella and Aunt Julia were here.

---

[15]"Casino" is a card game where each player wins cards by matching or combining cards in the hand with those exposed on the table.

[16]"Trump" is slang for a fine fellow.

Went skating again Friday afternoon, Jude went with me. Had just lots of fun. Jule Brown was there, he was awfully good to me. Skated with me most all the time. He says I skate better than any of the girls. Jude never skated but once before and I was pulling her around. He looked at us a minute and then said in his blunt way—"Adam, I believe you would have had lots of fun if your sister hadn't come."[17] Another time Jude was skating along and thought she was doing remarkably well, looked up and he was laughing with all his might. She asked him what he was laughing at and he said, "Oh, I'm laughing at you."

Herm Gaugler gave me an apple and Lee Wilkinson said he was going to take it away from me. We had a race and he got it. He was eating it and gabbing as usual when I hit his hand and knocked it out. He said "Adam, that was nothing but cussedness." Then I went for him. I told him that no gentleman would talk that way. It did make me mad and I skated off by myself to cool off. I am getting so I despise that little bunch of egotism. I quarrel almost everytime I come near him. His conversation consists largely of I's. Sade Reiber* skated with him afterwards and run him into a stump. As I have a revengeful spirit, I rejoiced.

As we went home we stopped and slid down hill ever so long. That night it thawed and so yesterday there was no skating. Et came up in the afternoon and we went around making calls New Year calls although rather late in the day.

Heard there was to be a dance last night but made up our minds not to go because of the bad conduct of several at the masquerade. As we were coming home Jule Brown and Cousin Bob met us. Cousin Bob said the boys were all ashamed of themselves and had sworn it should never happen again; and as Walter was getting it up he thought we had better go. He said he would stop for Ettie and Jule would come for us, as George swore he would not go. So we agreed to go.

When Jule came for us we got to speaking about Huntley. I said, "I have no patience with anyone who will make such a fool of himself."

"I know," he said, "but I look at it this way, when a fellow does get to going down hill that isn't the way to bring him up again," and I think he spoke from experience. I liked him all the better for saying that. As we were going he said "Whose poems do you like best?"

"I don't know, Longfellow, I guess. Do you like poetry," I asked, for I was surprised and didn't suppose he was one of the poetic kind. He said

---

[17]"Adam" is Addie's nickname. She was a confirmed tomboy and preferred to be called Adam or Addie, never Adeline.

he liked poetry better than prose unless it was about war. He said he had four volumes of the Last Rebellion that he had read through three or four times. Tennyson is his favorite poet and he thinks "Lady of the Lake" is splendid. These facts take him up another notch in my estimation. We had a real good time at the dance though Et didn't go. I'm glad I did.

The M. P. C. has dissolved and is going to reorganize. Cousin Bob says we will have about eight couples and meet at private houses which I think will be much nicer. Today was rainy and disagreeable. I went to Sunday school, only eight there. Had a doleful time.

School tomorrow, makes me sick. <u>Ugh</u>.

Jan. 10th Tuesday

Second day of school. The physiology class is reciting and I can write about ten minutes.[18]

School passed off very well yesterday. After school Jude and I went skating. The ice is just like glass. Stayed till it got quite dark. Just before I started home I fell and caught my whole weight on my left hand and sprained my wrist pretty badly. I ought to be satisfied now I have sprained both ankles and both wrists. Jule says all I've got to do is to dislocate a bone in my neck and I will be fixed. He walked to town with me and rejoiced my heart by telling me he had turned over a new leaf New Year.

Jule and George and Et came after us to go skating after dark but we couldn't go, so Et spent the evening with us, and Jule and George went. When they came back we played cards awhile and then they went home.

Must go to philosophy.

Tis night now and I ought to be studying my lessons but I ain't going to. Aunt Julia and Ellie have gone back to Niles, went on the train this evening. This afternoon it commenced to snow and is snowing yet. I guess snow is about three inches deep. Of course, skating is spoiled.

Et and I feel as if we ought to do something and do it quick. We are trying to think of some way to keep our school boys out of bad company. Herm Gaugler, they say, spends half his time and money in Aymar's bowling alley.[19] He has reached the age when he thinks it manly to smoke,

---

[18]"Reciting" meant the class was saying the lesson out loud. Rote memorization was a favorite teaching method in the nineteenth century.

[19]Bowling has been around since the sixteenth century. Bowling alleys suffered from a somewhat unsavory reputation in the nineteenth century, and some towns banned them.

gamble, and so forth. Something must be done. Scolding has no effect, he really seems to enjoy having us scold and coax him and is as stubborn as a mule.

Sunday
Jan. 15th 1882

Last Wednesday morn I rec'd a letter from Et while I was eating my breakfast saying she had the quinsy again. Its just too bad how she suffers with that. She has had it once before this winter.

Thursday noon when I went down to see Et, George told me he had seen Mate Himes and she told him to have Jule Brown, Jude and I come down that night and her father would teach us to play cribbage.[20] George came after us and said Jule Brown had made an engagement to go to a dance at Pipestone and of all things in the company of John Whaley.[21] I am so afraid that if he goes much in the company of such fellows his leaf will not stay turned and he will get to going wrong again. I will do my best to help him keep it down. It seems as if I could sympathise with boys in their failings more than other girls for I am more like a boy than a girl in my tastes, and I really think I have a little influence there, and will use it to the best advantage. I do want to help the boys keep straight so bad.

Well to continue, we spent a very pleasant evening at Mr. Himes. And he insisted upon our staying until almost eleven o'clock. Cribbage is a noble game. I like it better than any game with cards that I ever played. Coming home, George told us a frightful ghost story. It ended in this way,

"Where is that beautiful hair of yours?"
"Gone to dust!"
"Where are those bright blue eyes of yours?"
"Gone to dust."
"Where are those pearly teeth of yours?"
"Gone to dust."
"Where is that beautiful hand of yours?"
"You've got it."

And as [he] said these last words he jumped at Jude and she screamed.

---

[20]"Cribbage" is a card game in which two players try to form various counting combinations of cards. Score is kept with a cribbage board.

[21]Pipestone was a township northeast of Berrien Springs.

It was a very impressive scene. The above dialogue represented a conversation between a man and the ghost of his wife.

Friday afternoon Mr. Bronson read my composition aloud and had the class help correct it. None of them knew it was mine so I didn't care. The subject was one I know but little about, "Early Rising."

A thought just struck me that makes me howl. I have got to write a composition on "Carpets" for tomorrow afternoon and how I am to get it done by that time is more than I know.

After school Friday, Mate Reiter and I went skating up to Boons pond. It was rather rough, didn't stay long. When got home, Jude and I went down to Aymar's after bread. As we were about to go in we heard an awful racket as if some one was having a fight, and when I went in, there was Jim Boon. I don't know what the matter was but I saw a billiard table in the distance.[22] He looked rather sheepish and I didn't speak to him. Saturday afternoon I went skating for a little while. Jim was there and didn't have much to say for himself. When I skated with Herm he told me that he (Herm) hadn't been into Aymar's since New Year. I hope he hasn't.

I went down to Et's after I got through skating. George got to teasing us about some thing and I told him Mate Reiter said he had written to her all about the masquerade and that it was a very long letter though there was not much in it, and that most every sentence began with an I. Of course it was all a fib except that she told me that he wrote to her all about the masquerade. I supposed he knew I was just fooling. He came after us in the evening to go to the dance and coughed pathetically all the time he waited.

As we were going along he said: "I want to ask you a serious question, did Mary Reiter honestly make fun of my letter?"

"Oh you big goose," I said, "don't you know I was only fooling?"

"Now I want to know honestly if she said I wrote a good deal and didn't say much. I have an awful hacking cough, it is the kind that wears people away. Why if I thought she made fun of that letter I'd never speak to her again."

I assured him that I had been fibbing and he recovered from his hacking cough on short notice.

Had a real pleasant time at the club. Didn't get home until after eleven. We told George we were going out to the pantry, as soon as we went in and he said he would come around to the window and we had to open it and give him some pie. When we got to the pantry there he was

[22]A billiard table would be comparable to a pool table today. Like bowling, billiards had a shady reputation.

at the window. We opened it and had a gay time poking pie, cheese, and cookies through the crack to him.[23] It was very romantic and reminded me of feeding the elephant at the circus. But this morning Ma discovered a man's tracks leading around the house. She examined it and found that they went to the pantry window and then stopped. She thought it very mysterious and told Pa and he went out and examined them very closely. I pretty near died laughing. Pa looked like Robinson Crusoe and the footprint on the sand while he was tracking the man around.[24] We told Ma about it and told her not to tell but of course she did.

It has thawed all day to day. This P.M. went down to see Et. She was much better. It was too good to keep so we told her and Aunt Addie about George's consumption.[25] He made us solemnly promise never to tell anyone else.

Coming home we met Cousin Bob. He had been up to our house about an hour. He is a splendid fellow, just as kind-hearted as he can be, if he is rather odd. I like him but I can't talk to him to save my life.

Jude and I just disposed of two eggs. We cooked them on our stove and ate them with a paint blender. They were hard ones, too. Guess I shall dreem to night.

Jan 16th 1882. Mon.

Went to school to day. It has been bitter cold all day. I didn't come home to dinner but stayed and tried to write that composition on carpets. Didn't get it done and have just finished it to night.

When I was up here studying my lessons this evening, Herm Gaugler stopped in for me to go skating. I never went after dark before. Had a very pleasant time but didn't skate more than half an hour. Mr. Essick* taught me to cut a circle and skate backward a little. He says he is going to make a skater of me. Hope he will.

When I got home, I found Mary Himes and her aunt here. They spent the evening. Aunt seems to be quite jolly. Mary told me something that makes me melancholy. She saw Jule Brown coming out of a saloon. What

[23]A nineteenth-century pantry would be like a small closet next to the kitchen. There housewives would store staples such as flour and sugar, and would also keep baked goods they had prepared on baking day, usually one day a week, for use the rest of the week.

[24]In *Robinson Crusoe,* by Daniel Defoe, an English castaway discovers he is not on a deserted island when he sees a man's footprints in the sand.

[25]"Consumption" was tuberculosis; in this case, fake.

shall I do with that boy? I have a lecture ready for a convenient opportunity and if he doesn't behave shall cut his acquaintance.[26]

Jude's eyes are troubling her. Must go to bed now.

Thurs. Jan 19 1882

Tuesday after school I went skating with Jim Boon. In the evening, George, Mary Himes and Aunt came up and we played cribbage. Wednesday as I was coming from school, Jule Brown came out of Kephart's with his skates on his arm and asked me if I wasn't going skating. Of course I said I was, for I saw a chance to deliver a lecture in the distance and find out if he had kept his leaf down. George was here amusing Jude, for her eyes were no better, and she gets very lonesome sitting around doing nothing.

Well, I got my skates and we trotted off up to the pond. Had a splendid time but suffered with my ankles all night and all day today to pay for it. I didn't hardly know how to commence my lecture for I hate to have the boys think I am always scolding but at last I made a start.

"I want to ask you a question," I said in a desperate way as we were coming home.

"What is it," said he, cool as an icicle.

"I want to know if you keep your leaf down."

"What do you mean?"

"Why, the new leaf you turned over New Years."

"What part of it do you mean."

"Why, all of it. I don't know what you had on your leaf."

"Well, part of it was not to play billiards any more and the other—"

He paused there and sort of changed the subject. When he got through talking about something else, I said

"Well, what was the rest of it?"

"Well, the other part was not to go into saloons any more. Two or three others turned over a leaf when I did and some of them had to resolve not to drink any more, but I didn't have to do that because I never drink. And I kept down all I turned over this far. But I have been into a saloon three times since New Years but honestly it [was] necessary every

[26]To "cut" someone was to ostracize them socially. Addie, if she wanted to "cut" Jule, would ignore him when she saw him, pretend not to see him, refuse to converse with him, and cross the street to avoid coming near him. In a small town, being "cut" by a family member with the status Addie held might have serious repercussions to one's social life.

time. I had to see a fellow who was in there and I only went in and right out again. Have you been hearing something about me?"

"Yes, I heard you had been into a saloon."

"It was necessary, honestly."

"You should have hung around the corner till he came out," said I.

"Well, but it was one of those old loafers and I would have had to hang around the corner all day," he said laughing. "Its getting so now that if I am not invited out to spend the evening I have to go straight home if I want to be good."

"Why don't you read," I inquired.

"Read? I've read everything we've got. I've read the History of Rome, Greece, Italy, two or three histories of the United States and the War of the Rebellion. We take four or five newspapers and I read them all through."

"Do you like history?"

"Yes, first rate."

Well, we went on talking about books. He said he wished he could get hold of Shakespere's complete works, says he likes that kind of reading. I offered to lend him mine. He has good literary taste. He asked if he might take me to the dance Saturday and I said yes. He took my skates down to get sharpened for me. I do wish he wouldn't go into saloons even to see a man, for those who see him come out don't know what he went in for. I will tell him so when I get a chance. He really is trying to do better and I will help him all I can.

Went to school today.

Jude's eyes do not get any better. George came up this afternoon while I was at school and took the liberty, read the letters I wrote him when he was at Ann Arbor aloud to her. Et came up after school. I didn't go skating but am saving up my ancles. They ache like everything tonight. Wrote a composition on "Coal" today. I don't think Jule was in town today. At least I didn't see him. Wish he'd stay at home more. Will tell him so if he don't look out.

Mon. Jan 23 1882.

Haven't been skating since Thursday Wednes[?]. But it doesn't seem to improve my ankles much to rest them although they are some better, I must admit. Why must I be tormented with ancles and wrists when I love to skate, row and drive so much? And there's Cora Nichols who doesn't care a cent about such things and doesn't use her joints enough to find out when they are sprained, hasn't a sprain to her name, I believe. I think she would really enjoy a sprained ancle for then she would have a good excuse to sit still.

It thawed all day Saturday and Jude's eyes were much better, so we went with Mate Dunn to call on Mate Himes. Jude didn't dare go to the dance in the evening as lamp light is bad for her eyes. I went and didn't have a very good time. In the first quadrille that I danced I was so awkward as to slip and come down on my knees and felt so ashamed I didn't enjoy myself all evening and almost wept in my anguish. George didn't take anyone. Hugh Mars* wanted him to go after Carrie but he not being a bit gallant said the walking was too bad. He danced the first quadrille with her and I made his hair stand on end by telling him that he was always expected to see the lady home that he danced first with. I told him it would be perfectly awful if he didn't, and he writhed in his anguish and vowed he would leave before the dance was out. Finally, as I do not like to see a fellow creature suffering, I took back all that I said and made him happy once more.

Coming home, Jule said he had just as soon talk to a statue as to Ella Graham or Cora Nichols. Said he has to do all the talking and answer himself, too, tells them something he thinks rather interesting or funny and they look at him and say in their slow way, "Why,—what was that you said?", tells it all over and they say "W-h-y."

Saw the sweetest little negro baby at Reeds.[27] A little boy about two years old. Chubby and the brightest eyes. He's a perfect little cherub. I think they are lots prettier and sweeter than white babys.

Sunday I stayed at home all day. It was awfully cold. I read "Aunt Serena"* to Jude. It is a splendid story. I think Miss Howard writes in such a fresh crisp style, but I believe I liked her "One Summer"* better than this. George came up about three and stayed till dark. We have planned to have a candy-pull some night this week. Went to school today—very cold.

Jude's eyes are much worse. At noon I told George to come up in the afternoon and "lighten up de gloom." He came like the good boy that he is and when I came home at night he and Cousin Bob were here. Cousin [Bob] soon left and George, Jude and I played Euchre. We call Jude "Job" and George "Jeremale" after the "Faltyplace boys" in "[illeg.] girls." Kitt Ewalt came over and we played four handed Euchre; played two games, Jude & Kit against Geor. & I. Each beat once.

---

[27]"Reeds" refers to the Reed House, a small hotel/boarding house in Berrien Springs, run by Otis Reed.

Oh, my skates are just splendidly sharp and I expect to try them tomorrow night after school. The boys say there is good skating down by the river where we skated first. I have got a patent stop when I am skating fast. The other night I was skating a race with Jule Brown and was going like lightning and was [with]in only a few feet of the fence. Glidden, the boss skater and a stranger to me, was sitting on the fence. I knew if I went on I would go head first over the fence which was low, so I just let my feet slip out from under me and sat down, yelling "look out for your dog," and shot right on. Glidden looked simply amazed. I won the race, however.

Wed. Jan 25th

It was cold all day yesterday, but last night the weather changed and it has rained most all day to day. If it only freezes soon we will have good skating. I went to school yesterday afternoon with the intention of going after school. Jim Boon had told me in the morning that there was good skating. I found out the boys had been fooling me and there wasn't a bit.

I feel very important, for I am aunt to a young nephew, born Jan. 24.[28]

George spent the evening here last night. Had a very pleasant time and my lessons showed signs of it to day. We made plans for having a cribbage party tonight but the weather is so damp that Et can't come up. We talked of poetry and spoke pieces and were very literary last night. George told a pretty good story about Mr. Sheldon that the last named told him. It seems that he has a pretty good education, at least he went to school enough to have. He almost graduated at Olivet College and went to Ann Arbor awhile but one wouldn't believe it to hear the grammar he uses in conversation. Well, here is the story:

"When he was at Olivet College, which is a college for girls as well as boys, one night the girls determined to give the boys a bread and milk social, so they stole the milk pans and all hooked a lot of bread and chose the largest room for the spree, forgetting that the largest room was directly under the president's room.[29]

They boys and girls were cutting up and making lots of noise when they heard steps ascending the stairs and the president's wife knocked at the door. They locked the door and when she told them to let her in they said she couldn't come in. She went away and heavier steps were heard

---

[28]This was Addie's nephew Georgie, the only child of William and Laura Graham.
[29]"Hooked" meaning swiped.

on the stairs. The boys all crawled under the bed but Sheldon, and he was so tall he couldn't, so he sat on the lounge and blushed. The girls slipped the pans of milk under the top quilt of the bed.

The president came and said "Let me in this room." They let him in and he held up both hands and said "Mr. Sheldon!" for he was the only one he saw at first. Looking down, he saw the feet sticking out from under the bed. He pulled them out and gave them all an awful lecture and said he would expell them all. Meanwhile, his wife got tired standing around, so she sat down on the bed in a pan of milk. Well, the president laughed and said [if] they would behave and not say anything about it he wouldn't expel them.

Et came up after school tonight. George was here and had been ever since two o'clock. Instead of a rhetoric lesson today Mr. Bronson read us a story of the "Heroic Serf," and we were to write it down as well as we could remember and in as good language as possible for tomorrow.[30]

I'm afraid Jule Brown isn't keeping his leaf down. He was in town all day to day, but he was working in the printing office.

We are going to have a candy pull soon.

Chick Wilkinson* and John Reiber* have got home.

I haven't seen my nephew yet. They say he has dark eyes and lots of hair, which is a relief to me, for I can't abide bald headed babys.

We girls at school wrote a long piece of poetry on Clifford Benson. That is, Mate Reiter, Himes, Et, and I each contributed a verse or two. Here it is:

"Verses on Clifford."
"Clifford is a noble boy
He is his mother's pride and joy.
Upon his head there is one curl
And ain't we glad he ain't a girl."
Mate Reiter
"He minds his mother's slightest wishes
He wipes and washes all the dishes
He sweeps the floor and makes the bed
And follows meekly where he's led."
Mate Himes
"He has such a gentle voice
All members of the church rejoice

[30]Rhetoric was a class in speaking effectively.

When they hear a bass voice sound
At our Clifford, look around."
Mate Reiter
"Oh who will not sing bright Clifford's praise
Must be a sinner in all his ways
Clifford who is so gracefully slow,
That he goes by the name of "Poor old Joe."
He goes to church and meekly prays
For all his school-mates wicked ways
His stand up collar's a pleasing sight
So stiff and shiney and snowy white."
A. Graham
"Now let us all join in the song
And praise our Clifford right along
Till Earth and sky his name shall sing
And all nature rejoice and ring."
E. Murdock
Song
"Clifford, Clifford, happy boy,
Mother's pride and only joy
May you never sorrow know
And never more be called "Slow Joe."
(E M).

Sun. Jan. 29th

I'll begin with Thurs. where I left off before. All I remember about Thursday now is that Mr. Bronson hinted that he was going to make us each read our own composition on "The Heroic Serf" Friday. He hinted this much to Kit and I. After school we hinted back that we wouldn't do it. It was awfully muddy (Mr. Bronson don't like "awfully." I do.) but we felt real worried at the prospects ahead for the morrow and sending our books home by Pearl tramped off toward the Indian fields with some sort of indistinct idea of committing suicide. Felt better when we got as far as Mrs. Euson's. Stopped in and borrowed Harper's Bazaar to read the "Transplanted Rose" to Jude.[31]

Friday morning the Rhetoric Class held an indignation meeting around the school-house posts. Resolved to strike, and all shook hands

[31]*Harper's Bazaar* was a general circulation magazine.

and vowed not to read our essays what ever happened. If he sent us all home we were going up to Kit's and she said she'd feed us taffy. Luckily for our vows, Mr. Bronson didn't have the essays corrected and ready for us, so we didn't read them.

Friday afternoon Et invited Herm, Jim, Mate Reiter and I down to spend the evening. Mate Himes wanted to go dreadfully, but Et or George can't bear her and didn't give her any invitation. After school, Jim Boon, Et, Jude and I went up to the depot. Chick Wilkinson, John Reiber, Cora Nichols, Ella Graham, Carrie & Hugh Mars, and Fanny Bradley also went. Had a gay time and rode around on the turn-table.[32]

When I went home and told Ma about going to Et's she said I couldn't go because Kit was coming over. Went down town, met Mary Himes. She asked me if Jude was going to be at home. I told her she would. She said she supposed I was going down to Et's. Said I didn't believe I could go. Said she had been coming up to see Jude and if she wasn't going too guessed she'd come up that night. I said "all right." After that I saw Jim and Dutch and told them to tell Et I couldn't come. Dutch walked up as far as the crossing with me and I told him why I couldn't come. He said to bring Kit along. I said I guessed I would for I wanted to go so bad. I didn't suppose it would make any difference to Mate Himes for she had only spoken of coming up to see Jude, and knew before she spoke of it that I was invited down to Et's.

Kit and I met her at Bradley's corner as we were going down. Spoke to her and informed her that I wasn't going to be at home. Had a splendid time at Et's. We played cards and debated. George took Mate home of course. Jim took Kit and Dutch, me. When I got home I found out that Mate Himes hadn't been here at all, then it struck me all of a sudden that she must have taken Kit for Jude. I caught it all around for not stopping and speaking to her and telling her that Jude wasn't home. Felt kind of mean about it, too. So I determined to go down and apologize in the morning. I did go but Mate wasn't at home so I explained it to her mother. She assured me that Mate didn't take Kit for Jude, so I have come to the conclusion that the only reason she was coming up was to keep me from going down to Et's and she didn't want to see Jude at all.

---

[32]"Turn-table": The narrow-gauge St. Joseph Valley Railroad connected the towns of Buchanan and Berrien Springs. The line reached a dead-end in Berrien Springs, so the company installed a revolving platform with a track, used to turn locomotives or railroad cars around for the return trip.

Et came up Saturday afternoon, and with Kit we all started up to the farm to see little George Graham as they are going to call the baby. Jude thinks he's a remarkably smart baby for one so young. I think he's mortal homely but prophesy future beauty. He makes the most awful faces and wrinkles up his face till he looks like a dried apple.

There was a dance last night but none of us went, so George, Et, Aunt Addie and Frank and Mate Reiter came up and spent the evening. We organized a literary society to meet every Friday night. Jude is president, Et is secretary. George is the only boy in it.

The boys say there was splendid skating yesterday. I didn't go. It snowed all last night and this morning. The little Tudor children came over about half past three and stayed till eight. Will was down this evening.

Jude says for me to come to bed. Guess I will. Jude's eyes are much better.

                                                            Thurs. Feb. 2nd

Went skating Monday night after school. Ma wasn't going to let me go but Cousin Bob came along and was going, so she let me. Had a pretty good time. I can't talk to Cousin Bob, so we generally walk along in silence. Coming back I thought I had a bright thought and said "How is your musical getting along? Are you going to have it?" I thought perhaps this would start him to talking but he simply said "I don't know." And I kept still after that.

Tuesday night we concluded to have a cribbage party at our house. Told George to inform Jule Brown. When I went down to school at noon he met me and walked down to the post office with me. Said George had told him to tell me that they would come. He invited me to go to Buchanan with him on the excursion Feb. 1st to the grand concert they were to have there. I said I'd see about it.

Went skating with Mary Himes after school. The skating was very poor. Didn't stay long.

Had a very pleasant time in the evening playing cribbage, and euchre. Et wouldn't play. We beat George & Jude every time.

Ma and Pa didn't object to my going to Buchanan so I told Jule I'd go. His brother Harry is here from Arizona. Jule talks of going back with him. His brother is engineer on a railroad and he could be fireman.[33] It would

---

[33]Engineers run trains; firemen stoke the fires that make steam for the locomotives.

be a good thing for him if he could keep out of bad company. Cousin Bob asked Jude to go to the concert with him and her eyes were so much better that she went. The car was crowded. Et and I sat on the woodbox going up.[34] Bob and Jude sat just in front of us. George stuck our euchre deck in his pocket just at the last minute and we had a game of six handed euchre. Jule and George and Walt Kephart stood up and took part in it. George and Bob & I played the other four and got beat.

After we arrived in Buchanan we had to stay at the hotel about three hours before it was time to go to the hall. The concert was grand but I couldn't appreciate only one singer and that was a Frenchman—"Peter" we call him. His name is "Pietro Feranti or Stantini," I don't know which. He made such funny faces and said "ching, ching, ching." We sat right behind Walt & Cora and right in front of Cousin Bob, George, Jude, & Et. Carreño is said to be the greatest pianist in the world.[35] Her playing was grand, but I couldn't see much beauty in it. I always thought a musician should sit as quiet as possible and not move her arms from the shoulder at all. But she went through all sorts of motions and reminded me of our dog when he [charges] for chipmunks.

I was listening very attentively to one of the songs and thought Jule was too when he astonished me by making this remark—"Walt Kephart is getting bald. Just see how thin his hair is on top." Of course I told him to listen to the music and not notice the backs of people's heads. We got home at about eleven o'clock.

I got up at half-past six this morning and went at my lessons like every-thing. Mr. Bronson gave us a very serious talking to about obeying the rules and I felt real bad and have resolved to do better. I am awfully careless about minding. Just as I was feeling the most solemn I happened to look out of the window and saw a fat old lady toddling across the street. Just then a team came along and she started into a run.[36] She looked so funny that I laughed of course when I wanted to look most melancholy.

Mr. Bronson read us another story, "The Dream of the two Roads," translated from the German by Richter.[37] The language was beautiful and

---

[34]The woodbox was a box that held the firewood used to feed a heating stove, in this case in the railroad passenger car.

[35](Marie) Teresa Carreño (1853–1917) was a renowned Venezuelan pianist, composer, conductor and singer.

[36]"Team" here meaning a team of horses, probably pulling a buggy or wagon.

[37]Possibly Johann Paul Friedrich Richter (1763–1825), a German Romantic.

he wants us to reproduce it as near as we can remember. I can't remember but precious little.

I was studying my lessons to night when Mate Reiter and Himes came up. It is such a lovely night that we went skylarking. Serenaded Cora Nichols, Ann O'dell, Mr. Bronson and several others. As we went by Reeds we peeked in the window and there sat George, so we stopped and serenaded him. He came out and went with us. We called ourselves the "Night Hawks." We all took Mate Himes and Reiter home and then went home ourselves. Must go to bed now. George says there isn't to be any dance Saturday night.

Sun Feb. 5th 1882

I had an awful time Friday. At noon Mr. Bronson called me to his desk and asked me if I had my composition there. I told him I had not. He said I had better go home after it. I told him I wouldn't have time. He said I could go after school called. I was so provoked, for I had made up my mind not to read it. After school called I took my seat and didn't look at him, but he came to me and reminded me of it and I went. I walked just as slow as I possibly could and tried my best not to find it but of course it was about the first thing I came across. Well, I read it but rattled it through as fast as I could. I have the satisfaction of knowing that very few in the class understood a word I said.

Friday evening we were invited over to Kit's. Mr. & Mrs. Bronson and the babies were there. Had molasses candy and pop-corn. Et came up for us to go skating. We went to a pond in Aunt Hattie's field. The skating was very good, though there was no one there but about half a dozen little boys. We skated about half an hour and then went down to Mate Reiter's. She wasn't at home, was at Hime's. Went down there. Saw Mate R. home. Mate H. came with us and we went to the school-house corner with Et, where we met George. Mate H. stopped at Dixes and we went home. Jude and I each [received] a card of invitation to a masqureade ball to be given in Benton Harbor the 17th. It is to be a very public affair; of course won't go.

Saturday we were busy all morning. In the afternoon Et came up and we went up to the farm to see Georgie. Will is sick, has a bad cough. The baby is so yellow [?].[38] He's as good as pie and never cries a bit.

[38]Probably the baby was suffering from jaundice. Many newborns, before liver function is adequate, turn yellow from an excess of bile in their systems. Jaundice, which can cause mental retardation, is treated today by exposing the baby to special lights. It would have disappeared after exposure to sunshine—not a common condition in Michigan in winter.

We went riding after that. We rode by Bronson's and seeing Mr. Bronson by the barn thought we would ask how Lou was. He seemed to be just going to unhitch; but when he saw us coming he suddenly jumped into the buggy and drove [illeg.]. We got after him but lost him some way, and when we got round to their barn again there he was unhitching. We drove up and said "You needn't have been so scared, we only wanted to know how Lou is."

"Why, were you after me?" he asked, and as we went around the corner we heard him laughing all by himself.

We went down to Aunt Addie's and played a game of cribbage with George and Et. Our literary club was to meet there that night. Jule Brown is a member now also. It wasn't at all literary.

I'm so sleepy now I can't write a bit more. Will write about the meeting tomorrow if have time.

Feb. 6th 1882

Physiology class is reciting. I had my algebra and geometry lessons perfectly this morning.

Ma went with us down to Aunt Addie's Saturday night. Nobody had anything prepared to read, so we played games. George had a literary puzzle and Jule had a letter which was also a literary puzzle. It was sent by mistake to his brother and was written crossways and everyway. We played proverbs, scandal, and guessed riddles, talked about books. Jule has read "Little Women," "Little Men," & "Eight Cousins," "Rose in Bloom."* I am sorry to say he has a great admiration for "Prince Charlie."* I think he is too much like him anyway: good-hearted, generous, always ready to promise anything but rather weak about keeping a promise. We didn't go home till after ten.

Walt Kephart just rode by the school house on his bicycle and waved his hand at me.

Saturday morning when I was coming from town, I walked along with Bud Nichols. We talked about skating and then conversation lagged and we walked along in silence. Pretty soon he laughed and said: "Well, I can't think of anything to say. Can you?"

"No," I said, "that's just my fix," and we both laughed. I think boys are splendid when they are blunt and funny.

Sunday morning Mrs. Wilson came up. Ma had to go to the farm so she went with her. George came up after Mrs. McC.W.D.W. to go down to Mahews but of course she couldn't go very well, not being there. I went to Sunday school.

In the afternoon George came up again and stayed till dark. The big goose made me believe he was getting fond of smoking cigars (I don't believe he ever smoked one in his life) then he said if I'd never tell anyone he'd sign a pledge never to use any more. Of course, I was delighted to have a chance to reform anyone and he signed a pledge. After he got through he said he never smoked at all and made me promise never to sing "My last cigar" or "Bye Baby bye" again. I spent the evening reading "English Literature."

It's a lovely day and I'm going skating after school if it don't thaw to much this afternoon. This is the mildest winter I ever saw. I haven't had but one sleigh ride and that was mostly on gravel.

'''Night'''

Et ran away from school this afternoon. Al and her mother came home and Et strayed out to go and meet them. I think she was real mean not to let me know so I could have run away or been excused too. Herm brought his ball to school this noon and we played catch.

Everybody said there was no skating after school tonight, so I came home and went horseback riding. I tried to race with Walt Kephart who was riding his bycicle but Charlie commenced jumping and cutting up and making believe he was frightened so I had to give it up.

This book had a narrow escape. I forgot that I had it in my dress pocket while I was riding and when I did think of it and feel for it, it wasn't there. My stars, but I was scared. I made up my mind to ride everywhere I had been till I found it, if it took till dark. So I rode around by Vinton's and there it was in the middle of the road. I was delighted and hung on to it until I got home.

Jude and I got supper and then started off down to Al's. She and Fan came out to the gate and we talked quite awhile and then skipped back and ate supper. Mrs. Euson was here all day today, sewing. After supper, Et came with a letter from Uncle Nat saying that Grandpa is dangerously sick.[39] He has dropsy of the chest and may drop off any minute.[40] I wish I could see him again. He's the best and dearest Grandpa a girl ever had. Uncle Nat will write every day. He said there was no possible hope.

Et spent the evening and we studied at our lessons, but I haven't got them at all.

---

[39]"Uncle Nat" was Addie's maternal uncle Nathaniel.

[40]"Dropsy of the chest" is probably congestive heart failure. Dropsy referred to any of several kinds of edema, or swelling, due to the retention of fluid by the body.

I'm getting so I can't bear Cousin Bob. I used to think he was a gentleman and had some delicacy about him, but I don't anymore. The reasons
for my change of opinion I will not state. Suffer to say I changed my mind
the night of the excursion to Bu[chanan?].

The wind is blowing to night. I guess it will blow up a rain. Robert
says they are going to have a dance again either Thurs. or Wednes.

Jude says I must come to bed.

A.M.

Tues Feb. 14th 82.

It's a lovely day. I have only fifteen minutes to write before Philosophy
class and lots to write. A good deal has happened since last Monday.

I am disappointed in Jule Brown. I thought he was a gentleman. He
isn't. Wednesday afternoon Et, Cora Nichols, and some other girls went
up to the depot after school. Jule Brown and John Reiber went up too.
Coming home down by Bradley's, Et told Al to come on and go to town
with her. John Reiber and Jule Brown were behind. They rushed up, John
grabbed Cora's arm and Jule, Et's and said they were going to town too.[41]
They may have done it thoughtlessly but it was rude and ungentlemanly
anyway. Et is mad at him and Jule has got to apologise to both of them
before I will have anything more to do with him.

Thursday noon Jude and I concluded to have a candy-pull in the
evening. Et didn't tell me about Jule Brown's conduct until noon that day
and I made up my mind that he should have no invitation. But Jude went
to town that afternoon and not knowing anything about it, she told
George to ask him.

After school we took the buggy and did errands and Et went up
home with us, stayed to tea and all night. Walter Kephart, George, and
Jule were the only boys we had. There was besides Cora Nichols, Ella
Graham, Abby Gray,* Mate Reiter, Allie Brad, Et, Jude, & I. Cora Nichols
pretended to us girls that she was very angry with Jule Brown, but to him
she was good as pie and begged for his tintype as if she thought the
world of him.[42] I don't believe in that way of doing. Jude says that's right

---

[41]Such physical familiarity as grabbing a girl's arm simply was inappropriate for boys
to do in the nineteenth century. Physical contact between unrelated men and women or
girls and boys was frowned upon.

[42]"Tintype" would be a picture of him on a piece of tin. The process, called ferrotype
and invented about 1856, produced a positive photograph made by a collodion process
on a thin iron plate having a darkened surface.

though, to treat everybody as if we thought everything of them, but I can't see it. If I'm mad at a fellow I want him to know it. We danced, played cards and had a good time generally. Also pulled candy.

Must go to Philosophy.

P.M.

The grammar class is now reciting and I have half an hour before Rhetoric.

Friday, Mrs. Bronson was sick and Mr. B. only came to school the last half hour in the after and fore noon. Mate Reiter took charge of the school. The little Bronson's were to our house all afternoon. Jude and I took them home.

That evening there was a concert at the Lutheran church got up by the young folks for the benefit of the Sunday school. Cousin Rob [Bob] took part in it. George and Et came up after us to go, so we went. While waiting for the singing to commence, George and I played pin on a hat. He confided to me that Mate Reiter was mad at him. I asked him to advise me about Jule Brown, he doesn't know anything about the Wednesday night affair. He said if I would walk with him when we went home, he would give me some good advice, and he wanted to tell me about his trouble with Mate. I said I would and felt immensely flattered at being made his confidant.

The concert was good. Sadi Reiber spoke several pieces and did well.

George told me going home that something happened that night of our candy pull when he and Mate were going home that made her mad. He said that it was his fault but there was also a misunderstanding, that when they parted she was friendly enough but that night when he got home he wrote a letter apologising to her and the next noon when he walked to meet her she turned right around and walked back to the house.[43] He went in and pretended he was going to Perkin's anyway. He says he guesses she wasn't mad till he apologized and then she thought it over and got mad. He won't tell me what it is she's mad at, but he did something that she didn't like, I suspect. I told him that Jule Brown had done something mean and I didn't like it, and he advised me to treat him as if I didn't, then. He wanted me to tell him what it was, but I wouldn't. I promised to do my best to bring about an understanding between he and Mate.

Saturday morning I cleaned windows and worked. In the afternoon I took Mrs. Bronson riding, also took Mate Himes riding, then went up to the farm to see nephew. There was a dance and a concert in the evening.

[43]This is a classic example of "cutting."

I didn't go to either. The concert was given by some folks that were going to get up a singing class here.

Sunday I didn't go to Sunday school. George came up in the afternoon. He didn't stay very long. Jude took him home in the buggy. I was to [have] stayed at Bradley's till she came back, but she was so long about coming that Et, who was there also, and Al and I went walking. In the eve the singing school folks gave another sing. We all went with George. It was very good.

Must go to Rhetoric now.

Night.

Just got home from singing school. Don't attend, just went to night to keep Jude company.

I am mad. I got a valentine to day that was a regular insult. It was a picture of a girl dressed in bloomers, a derby hat, and a cigar in her mouth, and under it was "The way you would dress if you dared." I suppose I'm a big goose to mind anything like that, but it hurt me and I was so silly as to shed a tear or two. I am not fast if I am a tom boy and like boy's games.[44] I'm afraid if I found out who sent it there would be a fight. It was a mighty small, despicable thing to do anyway.

Monday night after school I had a lovely horseback ride on "Charlie." In the evening Ma and Jude went to singing school. Pa went to town and I was left alone till George came and stayed all evening. We worked algebra, played cards, and talked. He is very gloomy about the Mate Reiter affair. And don't know what to do. I advised him to go right down to the house and ask to see her and explain all. But he says he can't explain before her Aunt and Grandma. I don't know what the boy is going to do. He's got the blues bad. Everything I advise he takes exception to.

It has been a lovely day today. Played mumble peg with Jim Boon and Et this noon. Carrie Mars had a lot of snuff in a bottle.[45] We each took

---

[44]"Fast" means morally lax. Addie was also upset because the character on the face of the valentine was wearing bloomers. While bloomers were becoming more acceptable in urban areas in the 1880s because they could be used by women to ride bicycles more safely, they would not be in rural Michigan because of their past connotations of being worn by "strong-minded women," a term denoting a suffragist—not at all an appealing implication to Addie.

[45]"Mumble peg" meaning mumblety-peg, a game where players try to flip a pocketknife from various positions so it will stick in the ground; "snuff" was powdered tobacco people stuffed into their nostrils and inhaled, causing a great sneeze. Addie campaigned against the boys smoking cigars, but had no compunctions about taking snuff.

a lot to make us sneeze in school. I couldn't sneeze a bit and my nose felt as if it was full of red pepper.

Must go to bed.

Monday
Feb. 20th 1882

It has been a rainy damp day.

Word came from Mississippi to day that Grandpa is dead. He died Friday morning, and was buried Saturday. Uncle Nat says he passed away very gently.[46] Perhaps I am hardhearted, but I never can sorrow or grieve long. I am a shallow-hearted trifling girl. Life is so full of joy to me that it seems sometimes as if nothing could ever make me sad. I do not think Grandpa's death could be sad anyway. He was always so good, and kind. It must have been a great day in Heaven when he went there. His life was one of simple generous piety. And death was but a sweet and glorious entrance into a life of future joy and eternal happiness.

Last Wednesday was one of the loveliest days I ever saw. I did hate like everything to go to school. Ma and Pa both went to Niles, and at noon when I came home from school I went out in the orchard to catch Charlie and have him all ready for a horseback ride when school was out. He followed me clear into the stable owing to an ear of corn I had in my pocket.

At noon when we went to school, Et and I saw George and made him promise to come and call us out and get us excused at half-past two. He did so, and we all went up to our house and played 'duck' in the yard with two stones.[47] It was lots of fun. Jude wasn't at home, was down to Mrs. Dixe's.* Then at four o'clock when Jude and Et went to singing-school I saddled Charlie and had a glorious ride and raced with George.

Thursday morning I woke up deaf in one ear and had the earache all day as hard as I could. In the afternoon it was so bad that I had to come home from school. I didn't expect to sleep any that night and fortified myself with a stack of Harpers* magazines; but Ma pervailed upon me to go to bed and I surprised myself by sleeping like a top all night after I got

[46]Grandpa Garrow died on February 17, 1882.

[47]"Duck in the yard" may possibly be a form of duck and drake, a game usually played by throwing flat stones so that they skim or bounce along the surface of the water.

to sleep once, and in the morning my ear had stopped aching but was rather deaf and has been so ever since.

Friday we received our deportment cards.[48] I stood 8 1/3, the lowest I have been this year.

That evening was the concert given by the singing-school. We all went. I don't think it was so good as the one given by Mr. Straub when he held his convention here, but it was good enough. I sat with Mary Himes and the seat was just comfortably filled and just a trifle crowded when Cousin Rob came and crowded himself in beside me. I don't think he has the least grain of true politeness about him. He would keep his seat in a crowded car and let a lady stand unless there could be something gained by letting her sit down. That's just him, he's as stingy as he can be.

He said to me "Mr. Howe had a real good seat beside his mother when Mr. Mars* came along and asked if he wouldn't give it up to a lady and of course, he had to."

He spoke just as if it was a great imposition to ask Mr. Howe to give up his seat.

I said "Well, that was just right. I don't believe in gentlemen sitting down and letting the ladies stand." He didn't say anything more.

There was a mask oyster supper after the concert but owing to a general misunderstanding none of us went.[49] Saturday, the singing class went and had their pictures taken on the stage. In the afternoon Et came up and we went riding. We followed a band all around. It was to advertise a show that was to be given in the evening. I had to go to Mrs. Dix's to get a jacket fitted and Jude and Et took Cousin Kittie Kephart riding. In the evening, Mrs. Ewalt, Mr. Wheeler, and Sallie Tudor* came over. There was a dance but we didn't go.

Sunday didn't do anything of any account. Went up to the farm and saw "Nevvy." He is a wonderful baby, makes horrid faces. Went riding after that with Et and Jude. In the evening worked algebra examples.

I guess George's troubles are over now. He wrote a letter to Mate Reiter explaining everything and she smiles on him once more. Will has bought Cousin Rob's pony and is going to let us have Nellie to ride this

---

[48]"Deportment" means behavior, which students were graded on in the nineteenth and much of the twentieth centuries.

[49]The *Berrien Springs Era* reported the concert a success and that the oyster supper would be given by the young ladies of the Methodist Episcopal Church. "As an extra attraction the ladies serving the table will be masked."

summer. I am reading a story in Harper's named "Anne,"* an[d] one in Scribner's, "A Modern Instance,"* by W. D. Howells.

Mrs. Wilson, alias M. McC.W.D.W., has gone to Chicago. She is going to Washington week after next and says she is to old to travel alone and wants George to accompany her. She will pay all his expenses and it will be a splendid thing. I guess he will go. I hope so anyway. It will be just —— words fail to express it. I only wish she wanted a handmaiden and would let me go along. Wouldn't we have larks, though?[50]

Feb 21st 1882 Tuesday.

Stormy cold day. It begins to look like winter again. Has snowed all day.

Et cried like everything in school this morning and I wept a little while Mr. Bronson was praying. Et always seems to take things to heart more than I do. It troubles me. I am afraid I am a shallow, selfish pig. I'm sure I love Grandpa as much as Et does.

I have made up my mind that Lee Wilkinson sent me that valentine for the following reasons: On Valentines Day Walt Kephart got a comic, it was the picture of a dandy and under it was; "The loudness of your dress is only exceeded by the weekness of your mind." Rob sent it to him. Walt was mad and thought Lee Wilk. sent [it] so he sent it to <u>him</u>. I suppose Lee thought I sent it for he knows I am not an admirer of his, and so he picked out one he thought would make me mad and sent it to me. The reason I thought he sent it was that I met him to day and he didn't speak to me. I wouldn't care so much about it if I was sure he sent it, for then I could consider who it came from.

Tomorrow is Washington's birthday and a national holiday, so there is no school, for which, oh be joyful![51]

Jude and I sang most all evening. That is, she sang and I tortured the piano as an accompaniment.

Wednesday Feb. 22nd

Today is the anniversary of Will's wedding day. It is also Harry's birthday. One year ago tonight I was mad. Will had got married and never

[50]"Larks" meaning fun times.

[51]Since 1829, February 22 had been observed as a legal holiday in most of the United States to honor President George Washington.

asked me to the wedding. I remember just as plain, how I stormed around. The poor fellow was so scared he barely invited Ma.

No school today. "Genius burns" a little while this afternoon, and I scribbled. Jude made some molasses candy. About three o'clock we went down to Et's and stayed till five. Al was there and Bob came in just before we left. I then went to Mrs. Dix's and was tortured by trying on a jacket.

Oh yes, we went to Bronson's after we left Et's. Mr. Bronson has ordered seven new volumes for our school library. Among them are "Figs and Thistles," by Tourgee, "Life of Franklin," "Katherina," by Holland.*

I studied, scribbled and read this evening. I am trying to write a love story. I never wrote anything but children's stories before and I'm afraid the heroine's little brother and sister are more prominent in my story than the heroine.

Tuesday Feb. 28th

It has poured down all day. Went to school as usual. After school, Jude and I lunched on maple sugar cookies and cream. We went over to Kit's and got wet. Water all over the yard. I wrote in two autograph albums tonight—Mate Hime's and Jude's.[52]

Last Thursday night Et and George came up and spent the evening. We played cribbage. Friday, Aunt Hetty Stevens came down and stayed all night.[53]

I have concluded to go to Wellesly College next fall if I am not too backward and nothing happens to prevent.[54] Aunt Hetty is going to send me a catalogue in the course of time. She went home Saturday and I took cousin Kitty Kephart riding. She is much better, but cousin Emma gets worse all the time.[55] We rode down to the Shaker farm and Mrs. Howe insisted on our coming in. Had a very pleasant call.

[52]Autograph albums were plain paperbound books that friends would fill with poetry, sayings and their signatures for keepsakes.

[53]"Aunt Hetty" was her Aunt Hester B. Stevens from Niles.

[54]Wellesley College was one of the first colleges for women in the United States, located near Boston, Massachusetts. Unlike many other women's colleges, Wellesley prided itself on having not only women students but also women professors and a woman president.

[55]Cousin Emma Kephart would die of tuberculosis that same June at age thirty-two.

Saturday night Mate Himes had a little party. George, Et, Jude, and I didn't go on account of Grandpa.[56] Sunday I stayed at home all day except going over to Kit's a little while in the afternoon. Monday went to school and was vaccinated.[57] After school, worked on algebra all evening about. Awful examples.

Will Stem* is so sort of quaint. I like to hear him talk. He reminds me of the innocent German one reads about. He is part German, I guess.

I wrote a letter to Belle Sunday night. She thinks of spending the summer with us. Hope she will.

Weather very blue.

Wed Mar. 1st 82

March came in like a lamb. The weather cleared in the night and today was lovely and springlike.

It is all settled. George is to start for Washington Monday. I am so glad for him that I grin all the time. It will be lonely for us girls with no one to escort us around. He intends to visit Harpers Ferry, Mount Vernon, and Chambersburg, where his Aunt Rose is. It will be glorious. Congress is in session and he will spend half his time there. I will feel so grand with my Washington correspondent. It will be too comical to see him parade the streets of Washington with big Mrs. Wilson on his arm.

Jude and I went down to Aunt Addie's and spent the evening and Aunt A. came up and spent the evening with Ma this eve. We played cribbage and whist. George is so delighted with his good luck that Et says he does nothing but sit around and pick his pimples. I don't know of any boy that would receive as much benefit from such a trip as George.

Laura and baby came down and took dinner with us today. Georgie Jr. howled all day, colicky. We had company this afternoon at school, an everlasting book agent. Lu. Bronson came to school this afternoon and went to sleep. Kit had to take her home. After school, Et and I went down to Mate Himes'. She went home from school sick this morning. Was all right when we got there though.

[56]The Graham and Murdock families were in mourning because of Grandpa Garrow's death. Mourning for the dead was far more ritualistic and longer than it is today; limiting activities was one common way to show respect for the departed.

[57]Her vaccination was probably to prevent smallpox. Beginning about 1803, people were vaccinated with cowpox virus in order to produce an immunity to smallpox. Other diseases guarded against by vaccination today were not preventable until the mid-twentieth century.

Lee Wilk. has got him a Seventy-six dollar bicycle. I shall enjoy seeing him ride it. It is a new kind and hard to ride. It has the small wheel in front instead of behind.[58] Et and Geo. came home with us this eve and went home with Aunt A.

Well, I guess this entry is well mixed up. I'm going to study Latin with Jack Wilk.* as soon as I get time. Haven't got one of my examples in algebra but calculate on getting up early and doing them in the morning. So I must go to bed.

March 2nd 1882

I arose at half-past five this morning and studied my lessons like a good girl. It was a lovely day today, the warmest we have had this year. I wanted to run away this afternoon and would have if it hadn't been for being absent and low standing. Jude and Al came and called me out in the afternoon.

Perhaps Jude will go to Washington with George. Aunt Al wrote to Mrs. Wilson today that she wanted to and if Mrs. Wilson is willing to see after her I guess she will go. It does seem as if everybody had such good luck but me. It will be awful when Et and I are pegging away at musty old books to think of Jude and George going to Congress or seeing the sights of Washington. Well, my turn comes next year when I go to Wellesley, Mass., but I suppose that will be nothing but dig.[59]

After school today, Jude and I took a horse-back ride. Cousin Rob took Al buggy riding and followed us around most all the time. We wanted to get rid of him and have some fun by ourselves and at last we let him go ahead and we turned a corner when he wasn't looking and escaped. I dislike him more and more. He is going south soon, I believe.

Et and George came up and spent the evening. Played cards as usual. We went part way with them when they went home. It is such a pretty night.

I hope Jim Boon will hurry and launch his boat. He has promised to take us most every night after school.

Awful sleepy.

[58]Lee's bicycle was so expensive and unusual that the local paper took notice and discussed its arrival. A photo of Lee and his two brothers show that his brothers had bicycles of the Penny Farthing type—large wheel in front, small behind—while Lee's had the small wheel in front. This safety feature helped overcome the tendency of the Penny Farthing bicycles to pitch the rider over the handlebars. The "safety" bicycle would have both wheels the same size by the 1890s.

[59]"Nothing but dig" meaning nothing but hard work at the books.

Tues. Mar. 7th '82

I will commence with Friday. It was a beautiful day and after school Et went home with me. She and Jude took Charlie and the buggy and I rode Nellie. Walter and Cousin Rob were out riding, also Minnie McOmber.* We had a glorious time, raced and tore around in general. Charlie always came out ahead of the buggies and Nellie generally came out ahead of him. The boys were playing ball down at the Indian fields. I sacrificed my hair ribbon to decorate Charlie's bridle as victor.

In the evening, Et, Jude, George and I went to Al's. We played "[illeg.]," "Consequences and Truth."[60] I think the latter is a silly game. Didn't enjoy myself much at Al's.

Saturday was a cold dreary day. I took Ma up to the farm in the P.M. and we stayed about half an hour. Nephew howled with colic. It rained like everything in the night, but Sunday morn dawned bright and glorious. Twice I put on my hat and started for sunday school and twice I took it off and at last stayed home. Ma went up to the farm and in the afternoon Jude and I took a walk.

Must go to Rhetoric. (to be continued)

Thurs. Mar. 9th

As I last wrote, Jude and I took a walk. We went down [to] Mate Himes. She came back with us. Et came up and we started down to the river bank armed with Whittier and Longfellow. Cousin Rob met us, he was riding. We stopped and talked quite a while with him. He had the cheek to tell me that I ought to get a new riding habit, "a stylish one," he said, a short skirt and pants![61]

Al, Fan, Cora Nichols, Jude, and I went to church in the evening. John Boon preached. I don't go to church often and he don't preach often, but I believe every time I go, he preaches and I'd rather hear—well, most anything else.

Wednesday I spoke to Jack Wilk. about taking Latin lessons. He is going to teach me and we will begin as soon as I get a catalogue from Wellessly [Wellesley College] and know what books I will need there. He

[60]Truth or Consequences is a game where the players must either tell the truth or perform a "consequence" such as an unpleasant or embarrassing task.

[61]By the 1880s, fashionable women's riding habits consisted of a knee-length skirt worn over a pair of full pants, gathered at the top of an ankle-length boot.

promised to do an example in Algebra for Et, and as he turned around she saw a key to the algebra sticking out of his pocket, which explained his obligingness.

Tuesday night we all went down to Aunt Hattie's, to the great jollification of the people, much to my discontent.[62] I had promised to go down to Et's and had to trot down and tell her I couldn't come. Had a dull time down there, as usual. Ella wants me to ride her colt for her. And I am anxious to.

I am out of patience and disgusted with Jule Brown. Monday night after school when Et and I were going down town we saw him coming out of a saloon. He saw us and turned into a store to avoid meeting us. Going home he walked ahead of me all the way and went up to the depot. I was so provoked that I stopped and talked to some girls on the corner to avoid walking with him. He yelled and asked if George went that morning.

I answered "yes," short as pie crust.[63]

He asked me what I was mad at and I didn't answer but looked at him in a way that caused him to go ahead and keep still. Afterward when I went down town I scowled at him and didn't speak. Jude said he was laughing at me all the time, but I don't believe it. Tuesday night when we went down to Aunt Hattie's I saw him sitting in a saloon window surrounded by a gang of loafers. I wonder if there is any use trying to help him be good. There is lots of good about him and I know it, if I could only get at the soft spot in his heart in the right way. I had just been congratulating myself that he was getting along so well and I had heard only good reports of him until that night. It makes me discouraged and cross.

George started for Washington Mon. morning and didn't bid me goodby. I saw him Sunday and he said he would come to the school house before going to the train in the morning and bid good [bye]. There but for some reason he changed his mind and came up Sunday night when I was at church. I suppose he got into W. sometime yesterday.

Last night I spent at Aunt Addie's. We tried to do algebra examples but didn't accomplish anything. Et wasn't at school today. I don't know what is the matter. It was a rainy dismal day today. I made Kit laugh in the History class and Mr. Bronson changed her seat. I was so tickled I didn't know what to do. She is always so proper and good in school, and now I

[62]"Jollification" meaning merrymaking.
[63]"Short as pie crust"—pie crust is made with substantial amounts of shortening.

can crow over her.[64] We have examination in Philosophy tomorrow morning. Next week is vacation—hurrah!

I am reading "Without a Home" by E. P. Roe.* We have our new school library books. They are "The Knight of the Nineteenth Century" by Roe, "Figs and Thistles" by Tourgee, "Life and Letters of Lord Macaulay" by Trevelyan, "Katherina" and Titcumb's Letters" by Holland, "Life of Franklin" and "Uncle Tom's Cabin" by H. B. Stowe.*

Sunday
March 12th 1882

I've just finished a letter to Harry. Friday, school was out for a weeks vacation. I was examined in Philosophy. Stood 80, not very good but passed.

Yesterday, it snowed most all day. In the afternoon Kit, Jude, & I went up to the farm and stayed till five o'clock. Baby is improving in appearance. We went down to Et's this afternoon. Will expect a letter from George Tuesday.

"Genious burns" must go to bed and meditate.

Mon. Mar. 20th

Vacation is over and I have only about ten minutes before the Rhetoric class recites. We had a bad week for vacation, it either rained or snowed every day of the week.

Thurs. I sent "Fritz" to the Children's department of the Home and Fireside* magazine and demanded five dollars for it. Time will tell the result though I have my doubts.

Last Monday I sent for Aunt Jo's scrap bag No. 8. It came today. Jude got a letter from George today, a full sheet of foolscap describing the capitol; is going to write me soon.[65] Et spent the vacation down to Mahews. She spoke in a school exibition there, "Creeds of the Bells" and "Two Glasses."

Tuesday Mate Reiter invited eight or ten girls down to tea and spend the evening. We told awful stories all about murders, ghosts, and robberies until after nine o'clock, and then skipped home, many of us quaking at every step.

[64]"Crow" meaning to gloat.

[65]"Foolscap" meaning writing paper or stationery. Addie's reference to "Aunt Jo's scrapbag No. 8" may be in error; Louisa May Alcott's work, *Aunt Jo's Scrapbag* (1871–79), came out in only six volumes.

Thursday afternoon we spent at the farm. I rec'd the catalogue of "Wellesly College" today and am all discouraged about it. I can not presently enter the Freshman class as I had hoped to. I want to commence Latin now as soon as I can.

Pa has sent for a new side saddle for me. It has a leaping horn to it.[66]

Must study History now.

Tues Mar 21st '82

We have had the stormiest weather today that we have had all winter. The wind blew a gale all day and it has snowed quite hard. I saw John Wilk. this noon and told him about Wellesly and that I couldn't enter the Freshman class until I had had 3 yrs in Latin, though if it wasn't for that I think I am far enough advanced in my other studys to enter it. He advised me to go to some good high school, saying Ann Arbor was the best. I am to have my first Latin lesson Friday night, doors open at five sharp.

Have got to write an essay about a trip on the Hudson from Albany to New York. Don't know any more about the subject than the man in the moon.

Kit is here to stay all night. Mrs. Ewalt is up to Tudor's.

This is court week.[67] A lot of us started to attend the trial after school, thinking it was the Chamberlain murder trial. It wasn't, and Mate Himes and I left, the other girls stayed.

They have just completed the Telephone from Buchanan to Berrien. It runs to the Drug store and County Buildings.[68]

Thurs. Mar 23rd

The sun set clear last night but the weather wasn't so very pleasant to day although pleasanter than we have had for some time but there is a large

[66]A "leaping horn" was a horn attached to a sidesaddle that enabled the rider to leap fences. Sidesaddles were designed so that women could ride a horse not astride, which was much safer, but with both legs on one side of the horse, thus being able to wear a dress. The riding habit Addie's cousin advised her to buy earlier would have been one for riding astride.

[67]Most courts in rural areas were held for limited time periods, rather than all year round, which would be too great an expense.

[68]Private homes in rural areas seldom had phone service at this time. Instead, lines were run into town centers and into public buildings so that officials and the public had access to the service.

circle around the moon to night and it is very windy. The snow melted off considerably to day.

Last night Et came up and spent the evening. We worked Algebra and reminisced our trip to St. Joe when we were young and green as we are still. Laughed til we pretty near cried. I arose at 5.30 this morning and wrote my essay and studied my lessons. After school to night alot of us went to court; the trial was very interesting, what we heard of it. It was the Chamberlain trial. The prisoner was in the witness stand, is a young man apparently about 25 or 6 year of age but looks like a regular rascal.

Jude is here bolting. Must stop.

Wednesday
Mar 29th '82

Only two more days in this month and I am glad of it. I don't believe we have had more than three whole pleasant days all month.

I took my second Latin lesson last night. I take Tuesdays and Fridays and like it first rate. I believe I have a taste for languages. I take the third declension next time.[69]

Last Friday night I attended a temperance lecture by C. P. Russell. He is a very earnest speaker but I was impressed that he was extremely slow. His face had a heavy appearance to me but I guess he is sure if he is slow. He organized a Good Templars club. I am Treasurer. We are to meet to night but I don't know where.

Sunday morning, Mason Long, a reformed drunkard and gambler, spoke. I didn't attend in the morning. Jude and Mrs. Ewalt did and were so much pleased that we all went in the evening although it was raining. I enjoyed the lecture very much, for although Mr. Long never had but five months schooling in his life there was a certain simple eloquence of truth in his talk, moved many of his hearers to tears. He spoke again Monday morning, and Et and I wrote excuses after algebra when Mr. Bronson was downstairs and signed our own names to them and went.

Friday I got "Macaulays Life and Letters" out of the school library and have almost finished the first volume. It is very interesting and I can't bear to lay it down when I get to reading once. It is as interesting if not more so as any novel I ever read. I think I will enjoy Macaulay's the history of England more after this that I know more of the author.

[69]"Declension" is a term used in language and grammar.

Last night, Et wanted Jude and I to come down and spend the evening, but my Latin teacher gave me a pretty long lesson and I preferred to stay home and study it. Ma and Jude went, and Pa went to town, so I was alone all evening till after nine and had a splendid opportunity to study and read.

I got a letter from George Monday and must answer it soon. Jude wrote to him Sunday.

I went up to the farm Sunday. "Nevvy" is growing quite good looking.

Tues. April 4th

We are having an April shower. Saturday was the hottest day we have had yet. It was really quite uncomfortable. Jude and I took a horse back ride when it got cooler in the evening. I took Cousin Kittie riding in the morning. She is getting better but Emma looks badly and is very weak.

Et was up in the afternoon. We went down to the Indian Fields and hunted flowers. Got quite a many and took them in to the Kephart girls. I wrote a letter to George Sunday.

Oh yes, Jude and I went to church in the morning. We had a good sermon from [the Rev.] Mr. [A. M.] Gould of Niles, but when he got through preaching they began dunning the congregation for money to lift the church debt. If the Methodists would go to work and try to make money to pay their debts instead of coolly demanding five hundred dollars of their congregation I think they would be more prosperous. When they do get up a social or supper or anything of that kind, it is generally a one horse affair and not worth the price. By the time we left the church, the good effect of the sermon was all gone and I felt as wicked as a pirate.

It was a lovely day yesterday. Just before school was out we had a little thunderstorm. It rained about ten minutes and when school was out the sun was shining as bright as ever.

Mate Himes had a goose party in the evening. I think it was rightly named. It was about the most stupid affair I ever attended, though goodness knows they are always stupid enough. I hate partys where everybody is stupid and all wait for somebody to do all the amusing. We serenaded on the way home. Walt Kephart shot off some powder by way of applause when we sang "Golden Years" at Reibers.

I take another Latin lesson tonight. I must study my Rhetoric lesson.

My side saddle came yesterday. It hasn't any leaping horn at all and I was so disappointed.

Apr. 6th Thurs.

Went to Good Templars last night and took my office as Treasurer, learned the secret signs and pass words. Mr. Skinner, a great Templar from Buchanan was present to help us get started. I received $13.50 and a receipt for $7.00.

I didn't have a very good Latin lesson last Tuesday. My teacher seemed to be in a very good humor. I guess it has a good effect on his temper for me to have poor lessons. I take another one to morrow night and intend to have a better lesson.

Jude and Et received letters from George yesterday. He says he was to start for Chambersburg yesterday. He congratulated us on signing the pledge and joining a temperance society. He says that at last our future looks very bright and tears coursed down his cheeks when he heard of our reform. He wrote more nonsense than he has since he has been there, in Jude's letter, but in Et's it was very sensible.

He says in hers that he visited the Senate and one of the Senators went into the cloak room and returned with an old man leaning on his arm. He then spoke to one of the senators and they each went up and shook hands with the old man and spoke to him except Anthony. George says he thinks the old man was Bob Toombs, the next greatest rebel to Jeff Davis.[70] George was quite indignant about it and thought Anthony did perfectly right in not speaking to him.

Mr. Bronson gave me a not exactly compliment but it pleased me nevertheless. He asked me if I knew I did well on the essay about a trip down the Hudson. I said no. He said I did do remarkably well but not as well as I could do. He also said that I wrote easily and if I had anything to say I could always express it, but my ideas were not so good as my language, or something to that effect. It is rather a doubtful compliment, but I like it. He says I don't put enough time in my essays and I guess it is so, for I don't believe I put one half hour of solid work in that Trip down the Hudson. In my essay on the Missi[ssi]ppi River there was no mistakes in language and but one comma omitted in punctuation.

---

[70]Robert Toombs of Georgia served briefly as secretary of state of the Confederacy, but resigned to become a brigadier general in the army and served both there and in the Georgia militia. He practiced law after the war and never asked for a pardon under the Reconstruction laws that demanded that in return for restoring citizenship. "Jeff Davis" was Jefferson Davis, president of the Confederacy. "Anthony" was most likely Senator Henry Bowen Anthony, a Republican from Rhode Island.

It was raining hard when I went to school this morning. but has cleared off now and the sun is shining bright.

I have a little over two chapters yet to read in Macauley. To day is the day I should have returned it. Have enjoyed it very much.

Fri Apr. 7th

A very pleasant day. Finished Life of Macaulay to night. A remarkable man. I like it much, but think he was too apt to judge others by his own literary perfection.

Had a Latin lesson to night. A miserable failure. Thought I had it perfectly and could recite it quite well before my teacher came, but the minute he told me to recite I felt it all slipping away. Was uncommonly stupid today anyway on account of a headache, something I seldom have and consequently am not used to.

Last night Jude and I took a horseback ride on the new saddles. We had Ella's, too. Were caught in a little shower down at Aunt Hatties and rode under the shed. A pleasant time. Mate Reiter and Jude rode while I was taking my lesson this evening. Rode by Platt's barn last night. Jule Brown was looking through the slats of the door. Said he was seeing how it would seem to be in jail. A nice pastime.

Mr. Bronson read an article on "The Diamond" this afternoon and had us reproduce it as much as we could in a half an hour. Didn't get half, though. Want to have a riding party to morrow if the weather is pleasant.

Mon. April 10th

It has been a very cold day. A few flakes of snow fell but it is almost to cold for snow. I do hope it will soon get warmer. I have just got through studying my lesson and as there is no fire in my room am almost stiff, but thought I would write in my journal before I go down to thaw. I intend to have a better Latin lesson tomorrow if pegging away at all times will accomplish it.

John got a letter from George to day. He is at his Aunt Rose's in Chambersburg. I wish the blessed boy would hurry and come home.

Saturday morning I took Kittie Kephart riding and that same morning Cora Nichols started for Albion to attend the conservatory of music.[71]

[71]"Albion" College, in Albion, Michigan, was originally founded as Spring Arbor Seminary in 1835. The school moved to Albion in 1839 as the "Wesleyan Seminary at Albion," opening in 1843.

She does not intend to return until next fall. I hope it will wake her up for once in her life.

In the P.M. I saddled Charlie and went down to Ella Graham's to see if she was ready for a horseback ride. Her horse was in the pasture and we caught it after a great many trials. It is a colt and I believe never had a saddle on before although the men have rode her and she is very gentle. I rode her and Ella rode Charlie. Fanny (her horse's name) is the clumsiest colt I ever rode. Her walk is harder than her trot, which is terrible. I rode her until I was tired to death and as she was perfectly gentle Ella took her and I was glad to be on Charlie's back once more. Della Clarke was out riding. She has a perfect beauty of a little pony.

Saturday evening I took "Macaulay" down to Bronson's and paid my ten cent fine. Sunday I went to S. school. A dull time. After that I went down to Mrs. Euson's to look over some Sunday school books she had. I picked out "Gulliver's Travels"*—rather a queer Sunday school book. I think I have never read [it] but have heard much about it.

Laura and Baby were down all day. Will went to Buchanan.

This afternoon I felt too silly to do anything but giggle. Et and Kit were not much better off. In the reading class we were reading "Garnant's Hall." There was a misprint in the fourth verse of each book and it read in this way: "Reginald felt that somehow he was oiled." It should have been "foiled," of course, but this tickled us so we didn't get over it for some time, and Mr. Bronson gave a lecture after school.

Et came up to practice after school; Jude is going to give her lessons and Ma is going to pay her for it.

Am entirely stiff now; must go down and thaw out before going to bed. We got a letter from Harry to day.

Tues April 11th

A very cold day. This morning it snowed like everything but didn't amount to much. Is too cold to snow now. Got up unusually quick this morning; was smoked out. The chimney was all stopped up with soot and when they built a fire downstairs the smoke poured out into our rooms and we had to dress with all the windows open. As it was bitter cold, we didn't linger any.

Latin lesson after school to night. Teacher said I did very nicely. Teacher awful glum. Smiled about three ghastly smiles and laughed once. Is always glum when I have my lessons anywhere near decent. I do wish George would come back and study with us. He would liven it up a bit.

I have to write an essay for next week Wednesday in the reading class on any subject I please. How I hate it!

I guess I will get a letter from George tomorrow. In his letter to John he said Jeanette (Aunt Rose's daughter) is about seventeen yrs old and a fit companion for Et and I. We judge from that she is a kind of tom-boy, especially as her forte is horse-back riding. I am so glad. I was afraid she would be very proper and lady-like. If she had been, Et and I would have Jeanette preached to us on all occassions by George when he comes back.

Jim told us the question for debate Thursday night. It is "Which has caused the most misery since 1861—War or Intoxicating drink?" I can't see anything to debate in that. Of course intoxicating drink has. The widows and children of the soldiers have pride mixed with their sorrow. But the widows and children of the drunkard have nothing but disgrace and shame. Rather a one-sided question, I think. I commenced to give Jim some convincing proofs of my view of the question, but as he is to be judge he stopped up his ears and wouldn't listen.

Thur. April 20th

It is after nine o'clock, but I must take time to write in this now or never.

Attended lodge meeting last night. Had a good time. Jule Brown has applied for a membership and I am so glad that I fairly float on air, though no one would think it to see me stub my toes. I was almost completely discouraged about him last week. On Wednesday Jude, Et, and I went down after bread and there he was sitting in a saloon window and what hurt me most Will was sitting with him, and after we had gone a few steps farther we met Pa coming out of the other saloon. I was completely dazed for a minute and didn't know whether I was on my head or heals.

Coming back, I met Jule coming out. I looked him right in the eyes and didn't speak to him. I went home and cried like a baby. Here I had been trying to keep that boy straight all winter and my own brother was sitting in a saloon with him. I didn't speak to him for two or three days and when I did at last it was very coolly, so I was surprised and no end delighted to have him come into the lodge of his own accord. I only hope he will stick to it and have some decision about him.

Mr. Laur, the financial secretary, and I sit at a little table by ourselves and have no end of fun. At least we did last night. He is so jolly and funny that we sit and laugh and talk all the time. Last night was the night for nominating new officers. The old ones were all chosen over again except the Worthy Chief. He says he cannot serve another term.

I got a letter from George last Thursday and would have written Sunday but Jude wrote to him and I wrote to Harry. Friday I took a Latin lesson as usual and mustered up courage to ask my teacher how much he charged for Latin. It is 15¢ a lesson. I think I have taken eight lessons.

Saturday Jude and Pa went to Niles. In the afternoon Et came up and we went horseback riding. There were about nine or ten out. Had a jolly time. Started about two and rode till six.

Sunday I went to Sunday school and in the afternoon Et came up and we took a walk up the rail-road track and got lots of flowers.

Monday Et and I wrote a note to Jim Boon, saying

"James

If you will let us take your boat key we will take you boat-riding this evening. Of course it will be a great condescension on our parts but I guess we can stand it for once.

A. G. & E. M."

He accepted the invitation and after school we started. We went down to Sulphur Springs. I rowed most all the way down, and it is at least two miles, and over half way back, while Jim and Et talked and squabbled. It was muddy down at the springs and we got our shoes just covered and had to sit down and wash them off before starting back. We got back about sundown. We had a jolly time and I had a pair of blistered hands for a while.

The other girls rode horse-back while we were gone. Mary Reiter rode Charlie and Mate Himes rode Nellie and Jude rode Ot Statler's horse. She intended to break it so Mate Reiter could ride it. It went splendidly and kicked up down near the Brethren Church and she went over its head. It didn't hurt her any and she immediately got up and on again.

Tuesday another Latin lesson. I had to have an essay for next day and didn't even have a subject picked out so I asked my teacher to give me a subject. He told me to write about "Bicycles." I took his advice and wrote as hard as I could all evening and by ten o'clock had quite a respectable essay. Ridiculous, of course, like all the rest of my essays, but it did first rate for the time I took to write it in.

To day was cold and cloudy in the morning. Mr. Bronson gave us a lecture that lasted a full hour. Of course we all deserved it. Yesterday when he was absent from the room we had a high time and Miss Howe told on us. Mighty mean of her, I think. She'd better make her own scholars behave better before she attempts to reform us.

Mr. Bronson said, "All those who did what they know they ought not to have done while I was absent from the room yesterday please stand."

About twenty-two rose up. He took their names and told them to be seated again. Then he began with the first on his list and had each one arise separately and tell what they did and why they did it. Annie O'dell did a mighty mean thing. She acted as bad as any one in the room, but she tried to shove the blame off on to Carry Mars, who was absent. All the girls are down on her. I always despised her for a meddlesome sort of back-biter and now I do more than ever. It was mean of us to cut up behind Mr. B's back. And I am ashamed of myself. To day when he left the room every body sat as quiet as mice and looked as solemn as a cemetery.

Et came up and practised to night. Jude and I went down with her. Got some "'lasses candy" and sat on the M. E. church steps and ate it.[72]

Jenny Boon has got home. After supper to night, Jude and I ran up there bare headed to see her. Made quite a call. The Presbyterians had an ice-cream social to night. Rather cool weather for it, but they made a hot fire and after their customers stayed in the room five minutes they were glad to get hold of anything cool. Kit, Jude, Ma, and I went.

Must go to bed.

April 27th Thurs.

A week since I last wrote. I have been studying my Latin Lesson for to morrow. Have to take the 1st conjugations. I got rather discouraged last lesson. It seemed as if the more I studied the less I knew. Teacher said I musn't be discouraged, for I was getting along as well as anybody ever did and better than most people. I don't know whether he meant it or only said it to cheer me up.

I went horse-back riding this afternoon with Ella, Dell Clarke, Jude, and Bert Tudor. I thought I'd never get started. I went up to the farm with the children to get Will's colt to ride and left Pa putting on the saddle and ran in to dress when lo! and behold! there sat Mary Himes. Well, I thought she would never go. She knew I wanted to ride a[n]d stayed and stayed out of meanness, I guess. Next Aunt Addie and Mrs. Hoyt came. Poor Et had to endure a visit from Grace this afternoon. After they left, Mrs. Mason, Laura, baby, and the children came. I didn't wait for them to go, but considered them Ma's company and got away as fast as I could.

I never rode Will's colt before and liked it very much. Mr. Brown got a new piano to day and we all rode down and saw them take it in. It is to

---

[72]"'Lasses candy" meaning molasses candy.

be a complete surprise to May and Susie,* who were over the river when it came.

Attended the Lodge last night. Had a good time, but was disappointed that Jule Brown didn't come to be initiated. I guess he didn't know they did it so soon after application.

Last Monday I wrote a letter to George. Jude and Et each received one from him this week. He said he was going to Mt. Vernon soon and didn't know when he would come home.

To day is Arbor day and a national holiday.[73] The boys got up a petition and had it signed by the board that we have no school to day. We had none. Kit and Mate Dunn and I went down to Mr. Bronson's after going to the school house and sitting on the steps until most frozen trying to work a contrary example in Algebra. Mrs. Bronson is sick abed and I guess Mr. B was glad of a holiday.

Last night after school, Jude, Et, and I went up to Jenny Boon's after some flowers. Got quantities and had a jolly time. Kit gave me all she picked and I had both hands full, to the great envy of the girls. I had to walk either behind or ahead all the way home to keep them out of their clutches. Sunday we three went down in Kephart's woods and got lots of flowers and bur[r]s. Went to the Lutheran church in the evening.

I must write oftener for I can't tell half the things we do if I don't. I'm too tired and sleepy to write a bit more.

I read two Sunday school books last Sunday: "Three People," a temperance work by "Pansy," and "Daisy-Hank."* I am reading several continuing stories: "Donald and Dorothy" in St. Nicholas, "A Modern Instance" in Century, "Anne" in Harpers and "Transplanted Rose" in the Baza[a]r.[74]

My eyes won't stay open any longer.

Monday
May 1st 1882

Had a thunder-storm to day. Haven't had much spring weather yet. Went to school to day as usual. Didn't recite in geometry. Mrs. Bronson is sick and Mr. Bronson didn't come to school until too late for geometry.

[73]Arbor Day is a holiday, begun in 1872, to celebrate and plant trees.

[74]"Continuing stories" refers to stories or novels printed in installments in popular magazines such as the ones Addie lists. Serial novels were popular among readers and authors such as Charles Dickens, who published many of his novels first as serials, then as regular books.

Went to church last night. Had a beautiful text and a miserable sermon. The text was "And God so loved the world He sent his only begotten son that they that believeth on him might not perish but have everlasting life."[75] It's a blessing that Mr. Wilson cannot spoil his texts though it seems as if he tried his best to some times.

It is after ten and I am so sleepy that I will write no more to night.

Wed. May 3rd '82

Have just got home from the Lodge and it is nearly eleven o'clock. Had a jolly time. Jule Brown was initiated and the new officers installed. I am to be treasurer for another term and "Jumbo" Laur (named after the baby elephant) is to be F. S. for the ensuing term, for which I am glad.[76] We have such jolly times. "Alacrity" is to be W. C. T. I wish he wasn't, am afraid he will fall to pieces some night before the business of the Lodge is settled. Made no end of mistakes to night. I'm so glad that Jule is really in and do hope that he will keep his vow to the letter. He walked home with us to night.

Et received a letter from George to day. Says he weighs 175 pounds more or less. Is getting so fat that the people mistook him for Barnum's baby elephant. He is coming home next week, expects to be in Chicago on the 12th of this month.

It rained to night as it always does when the Lodge meets. It has met five times and it has rained every-time. We are bound to have lots of cold-water.

Took my twelfth Latin lesson yesterday. Must study harder. It bears lots of solid digging.

I expected a letter from George to day but didn't get it. I suppose he's mad because I teased him about Mate Reiter and hinted "Valerian" in my last letter. I begged his pardon directly after though, and hoped he'd bear no malice.

Last Saturday after noon Jude, Et, and I went horse-back riding about five or six miles in the country. Had a glorious time. Explored new roads and followed them till they ended in a barn yard or something of the sort.

I got a letter from Belle last week. She expects to start for Mich. in June.

[75]John 3:16.

[76]"Jumbo Laur" refers most likely to Jacob Lauer, a farmer from Oronoko Township. The mention of Phineas Taylor (P. T.) Barnum that follows refers to a showman and promoter who opened his circus in 1871, then merged with a rival to form the Barnum & Bailey Circus in 1881. "Jumbo," an elephant imported from the Royal Zoological Society in London, was one of his star attractions.

We have a hired girl now. Jim Steffy* went after her Sunday. Her name is immense: Victoria Vibla Brown.* The first two had to be something remarkable to balance the last.

I must go to bed and arise at five if I want to get my lessons before school. The Lutherans are getting up a little entertain[men]t for a social and invited me to help. Don't know whether I will or not. Et wants me to speak. I would like to. I love to speak in public on the stage.

Saturday May 6th

This after noon Et came up and took our breath away by saying they had just received a telephonic dispatch from George. He was in Buchanan and was coming on the four o'clock train. We were all so excited we had to dance the Racquette to calm our feelings and as soon as we saw the Bus go by started for the depot.[77] There he was as large as life if not larger. Et wanted us all to especially come down this evening, so Ma, Jude & I went. Spent the evening listening to George's adventures. He thinks Chambersburg the nicest town and Chambersburg people the nicest people in the world. Jennie Senseny* is about the smartest girl that ever lived, writes for newspapers occasionally and is 18 1/2 years of age. The Chambersburg boys are models of propriety and a young man comes to see Jennie who has had his hair cut with a bowl on his head, and they sing hymns all evening for amusement.

George brought home a pair of indian clubs and a piece of Martha Washington's wedding dress, also a facsimile of the bullet Mason fired at Guiteau and which flattened into the shape of Guiteau's profile.[78]

[77]The "Racquette" was a popular dance; the "bus" a four-wheeled carriage for public transportation, known formally as an omnibus. A telephonic dispatch was most likely similar to a telegram: a message written down by a telephone owner and sent to the intended recipient. Since the only telephones in town were at the drug store and county buildings, George probably called ahead and had someone take a message to his family.

[78]"Indian clubs" may have been souvenir weaponry; "Guiteau" was a reference to Charles Guiteau, who assassinated President James Garfield in 1881. On the evening of September 11, 1881, one of Guiteau's guards, Sgt. John A. Mason, fired his rifle at the prisoner through a cell window. The bullet missed Guiteau and hit the cell wall, the impact flattening it into a shape that supposedly resembled the assassin's profile. Both the bullet and the "piece of Martha Washington's wedding dress" should be regarded as relics with the same verisimilitude as many of the pieces of the True Cross. These kinds of collections are examples of the Victorian mania for collecting and classifying relics and curiosities of all kinds. Another example is Silas Mosier's acquisition of a hedgehog quill, mentioned in the July 18, 1882 entry.

We are trying to get him to join the Lodge. Says he won't, is afraid of the goat.[79] Mrs. Martin* always starts the hymns at the Lodge and last time she commenced and sang quite a ways and just as the rest got ready to start in she stopped and said "Oh that ain't the tune. Wait a minute, I'll get it pretty soon," and started out again. The W. C. was absent last turn and W. V. C. took his place.[80] She didn't feel competent to give Jule the secret signs so she asked Paddy to give him the signs. He gave all he knew of and asked if there was any more and jerked off his coat as if getting ready for business. It looked so funny that everybody laughed. Jule said he was just getting ready to run. He thought Paddy was going to thrash him or lead in the goat. Jude laughed aloud and Carrie Mars asked what on earth was the matter with her. Jude said she had the hiccoughs and looked solemn. Jude is Alacrity's W. L. H. S. and don't like it.[81] Thinks she will resign.

George is going to study Latin with me for which honour I am duly grateful. He thinks the Wilson College at Chambersburg just perfection as everything else is and intends for Et to go this fall. If she does I shall go there too, and so will Jude.

I had a good Latin lesson yesterday, the best yet. Have finished the four regular conjugations of verbs. Last night we went over to Kit's. May Brown and Mate Dunn were there. We worked about two solid hours on an example in Algebra and didn't get it.

Kit, Mate, Jude, and I intended to go to Niles to day but it rained so we didn't. Had a splendid game of ball at school yesterday noon. It is a sort of a grub game we have got up ourselves. Have two sides and play catch, each side using all their ingenuity to keep the ball.

Jule Brown was in town all day yesterday. If he don't stay at home more he will get into bad habits again and I shall tell him so if he don't stop. I wish he would go to work at something. I detest laziness.

I got me a Latin reader of my own day before yesterday. Am reading "Vicar of Wakefield."* Finished "Love's Labor Lost"* to day. It is very entertaining and humorous.

[79]Addie's reference is probably to a Judas goat, a term used to describe a goat used to lead sheep to a slaughter. George is likening the Temperance Lodge initiates to sheep being led to their deaths.

[80]Possibly "Worthy Chaplain" and "Worthy Vice Chaplain."

[81]All of these nicknames, initials, and secret signs were part and parcel of the temperance movement and other voluntary associations in the nineteenth century. The insider knowledge made membership a commitment that could be taken less lightly than a membership which required nothing of the joiner.

Tues. [May] 9th '82

I just got back from taking a walk. I walked down to Aunt Addie's with Jude. She and Et went to singing school and I came back to study tomorrow's lessons. I had a good Latin lesson to night and quite a jolly time reciting.

It has been very warm to-day and yesterday. Is preparing to rain again tomorrow night, I guess.

We are trying to get George to send in his name to be proposed for membership tomorrow night, but he is contrary as usual. Says he's afraid of goats.

I read "Talbury Girls,"* a book I got at Sunday school. Began and finished it Sunday. It is very interesting and bright.

Yesterday after school I went out in the field to catch my pony to go horse back riding. She is the colt that Pa bought of Cousin Rob. I give her a new name about every day but generally call her Nixie or Trixie. I guess I worked two hours trying to catch her. She would come up and eat out of my hand and the minute I tried to slip the halter on she would jerk away. At last Ella and Pearl came and we drove her in the barn. Had a pleasant ride, only Ella and I went. Jude had to give Et a music lesson.

Last evening all those who were going to get up the Lutheran concert met at Et's. Jude and I are going to help. It is only the young folks getting it up. I am going to speak "John Burns of Gettysburg"* if they have it. They have not decided yet whether to have the concert or an art gallery. Didn't come to any understanding last night.

Jude and I went over to Tudor's a little while this evening. I played a game of croquet and Bun beat me. When we came home from Et's last night we found George and Aunt Addie here.

I have about six hard examples in Algebra to do yet to night and must get to work. We begin to review in Geometry tomorrow and began in History to day. Only four weeks more after this until vacation. The Rhetoric class has to write an essay on "Saloons" for day-after-tomorrow.

Tues. May 16th '82

Last Wednesday night when the Lodge met it rained like everything, it fairly poured all day. Just a little before dark it stopped raining for a little while, so Jude and I seized the opportunity and went down to Et's. It commenced to rain shortly after we got there and rained until Lodge was out. We were all astounded to hear George's name proposed for membership.

Jude went resigned her office as W. L .H. S. She went down to Mr. Spark's* this afternoon to help on regalia.[82]

Friday afternoon Mr. Bronson had Lena Martin, Mina Slade, Et, and I stay after school and talked to us about graduating. We all made up our minds to graduate, that is write an essay. We have only about four weeks until school is out and will have to dig with our examinations coming on and an essay on our hands. I'm in an awful state of mind. Have had at least ten distinct subjects since Friday but have now settled upon "The Milestones of History." Et has chosen "Earth's Battlefields." George selected the subjects for us. He and Et were up last night and spent the evening.

Pa, Ma, and Jude went to Minnie Mae's, his wedding.

I have chosen for my milestones "Creation," "Birth of Christ," "Discovery of New World," and "Universal Nation." Jude and I went down to Et's to night. Et and I wanted to write but Jude and George acted so we didn't get much done. He is such a fellow to tell big yarns. I didn't have a very good Latin lesson to night, but had a jolly time reciting it. Teacher gets more and more good-natured.

Jude, Et, and Mate Reiter went horseback riding to night. I expect to go tomorrow night if it doesn't rain.

We will initiate George tomorrow night at the club. We have been trying our best to scare him with awful and mysterious hints about the initiation and think we have partially succeeded. Fletcher Farley* and Charlie Turner* will also be initiated if present.

Had company at school this morning, Mr. McCord and another gentleman. No one but Mina recites in geometry now as she is reviewing plane geometry and we have all passed it. Et and I have dropped out of the History class and are going to prepare to be examined before the rest of the class.

Finished "Vicar of Wakefield" Sunday. Admire the old Vicar's philosophy of always getting some good out of every evil, very much.

I went to church Sunday morning and have discovered that Mr. Wilson's sermons are not so very poor in themselves; it is his mode of delivery. I listened to his sermon for once quite attentively for the first time and concluded if some other minister would take his sermon word for word and deliver it, it would really be good. It is so comical to see him preach to the floor and make all his gestures to it. At the very point where one would think he would naturally look at his congregation and address his remarks to them he turns his attention to the floor and it looks so funny that I always laugh. He has an unsympathetic expressionless voice

---

[82]"Regalia" meaning commencement robes and hats.

that makes everything that comes out of his mouth as dry and uninteresting as saw dust.

Sun. May 28th 82

Nearly three weeks since I wrote last in my Journal. Have been so busy with my essay and studies that have had no time and really ought not be writing in it now.

Last Tuesday Ma and Jude went to Chicago to be gone until yesterday. I was left to keep house and go to school. Et stayed all night with me Wednesday and Thursday nights. We went to the Lodge Wed. Had an unusually good time. Jule Brown brought an immense orange and gave me half, then he and I divided with George and Et. We administered the second degrees to those wishing them. George and Jule were among the number. The W. Chaplain was absent, so John Jacobs* was appointed in his place. He had to read a lot of stuff which the next day I found out was a prayer. He can't read very well and every little while he would stop and say "I can't make out this word," and Charlie Watson* would yell "Skip it," and the prayer would go on. I was blissfully unconscious that it was one and was having a good time with Jumbo all the time. He took my led pencil. Wouldn't give it up so I took the cork out of the ink-bottle and inked his face all over. He soon gave in.

Jule walked home with me. He wants to take Shakespeare. I told him to come and get it whenever he wanted it. Will be glad to lend it to him if it will keep him out of bad company, though I don't know how I can stand it to be parted from it so long. I read "Caesar" again the other day and liked it more than ever.

Last week Friday evening I spent at Et's. Coming home Et and I were singing and George uttered an exclamation that broke the third commandment.[83] I was so shocked and disappointed in him and didn't speak to him again until Tuesday night. Saturday evening Jude and I went down to the drug store after stuff to make washing fluid. He came in and I left him talking to Jude and went over and talked to Walter while he mixed the stuff.[84] He said that some day he and George were coming up

---

[83]"You shall not take the name of the Lord your God in vain," Exodus 20:7 (i.e., no profanity).

[84]"Washing fluid" was the Victorian equivalent of laundry detergent. One cookbook suggested using a pound of brown soap, a half-pound of soda, and three ounces of unslaked lime, mixed in a gallon of boiling soft water; or a half-pound of brown soap and two tablespoons each of turpentine and alcohol in a quart of hot water.

to take Jude and I fishing. George acted silly and talked so nonsensical that I had to laugh. Tuesday night we made it up.

Et and I were examined in history Friday. We both passed. I don't know how high I stood yet, but hear I passed. A splendid examination. It was very easy.

Saturday I made a splendid cake. Tried a new recipe. It just poured down all day. Saturday the folks came home. Was glad to see them.

Friday afternoon I waited and waited for my teacher to come and give me a Latin lesson. At last it got so late that I knew he couldn't be coming, so about six o'clock I went down after bread for supper. He came out and walked down town with me. Said he went fishing and forgot all about Latin and didn't get back till after five. As I passed Kephart's dry good store I heard someone yell "Hey!" and looking across the street saw Bob D. sitting in the Drug Store bowing and smiling. I had to laugh.

Tuesday when I was taking my Latin lesson Mrs. Dumont and Mr. McCord called. There was no one at home but me and I detest Mrs. Dumont so and was so provoked at having my lesson interrupted that they didn't tarry long. She is such a talker. I acted dreadfully stiff and was blunt and short as I always am when I don't like anyone. When I went back to the parlor Jack Wilk was laughing as if something tickled him immensely and said she [is] an awful one to talk. Oh dear, I can't act as if I liked people when I detest them and there [is] no use trying.

Laura and Baby were down to day. He is getting so fat and cunning. I have finished my introduction to my essay and have written about "Creation" but it don't exactly suit yet. I have been writing a little on "Birth of Christ" to night but it doesn't gow very rapidly.

Prof. Smith was in town to day.

My Journal is done and I must get me another to morrow.

Martha sent me a novel "Mademouselle de Mersae." She wants me to come visit her this summer. I want to go very much. She is better than she has been but very delicate.

❧

Volume 3

June 14, 1882–June 2, 1884

Berrien June 14th '82

The graduation is over and the first three days of vacation are gone. Our graduation passed off splendidly. Our essays surprised everybody, they were so much better than they expected. We all received quantities of flowers. Et and I each received a lovely hot-house bouquet from Cousin Kitty.[1] I received ten or twelve in all and a basket and a house [illeg.]. Jule Brown gave me a lovely bouquet almost as handsome as Kitty's. Such weepings and wailings as we had over our examinations. Nevertheless I passed splendidly in every thing but Geometry and I don't know what I stood in that, but I thought I would have to give up at first. Got along all right though after all.

The night before our commencement Lillie Howe,* Gene, Et, Jude and Slade and I went to Buchanan to hear their excercises. They were not nearly as good as ours. They only had two graduates and one of the essays was like none of our school essays and sounded very much like the encyclopedia. The other essay was "Success," and was splendid. A lady recited the poem called "The Fall of Dumberton Mills." It made me so sick I though for a moment I was going to faint. I never had a piece affect me so before in my life. I was in the awfullest pain all the time she spoke and thought it would never end, but about five minutes after she stopped I felt as well as ever. We didn't get home until one o'clock.

Saturday evening the graduates were given a reception at our house. Et and I flew around all evening inviting people. I didn't want one abit and thought it was nonsense. Felt tired enough to rest after the hurry and worry, but the folks were bound to have one. Over eighty were here and I guess they had as good a time as possible under the circumstances. I had a good time anyway. After the minister and old folks had gone we had a

---

[1]"Hot-house" flowers were from a greenhouse, or store-bought.

nice little dance. It was after twelve when they had all gone. Mina Slade stayed all night with me.

I took a latin lesson yesterday and have begun to take longer lessons. I want to get to the fifth chapter of Caesar by the first of Sept. and have got to dig to do it. [2] I didn't do any thing but study all day to day, that is hardly anything else, and I played four games of croquet—got beat three of them.

Went to the Lodge to night—business rather dull. Ed has the mumps and Jumbo is at St. Joseph. The committee who were to have an entertainment for this evening didn't have any thing prepared and it is postponed until next time. Had two new proposals for membership. Howard Ewalt and Gus Dudly.*

It has been a very hot day but is much cooler this evening owing to several showers that we had. I was out in the cherry tree studying during two of the showers. I got a Roman history from George which I am going to try to read between Latin lessons this summer. I feel the need of some knowledge in that direction. Et, Jude and I went up to Buchanan on the six o'clock train with Lora Howe* Monday eve and back on the eight. Free ride. After we came back went down to Et's and from there we four went down to bid Mate Reiter goodby as she left on the train next morning.

I got the first strawberries off of our vines sunday. Was up to the farm a few moments this evening. Georgie is getting so cute and fat. Laura is going to put short dresses on him the first of August.[3]

Dutch took Et and I boating last week. We went up the river and around the island; had a good time. I don't expect to get time to write much this summer. Our dresses and hats came from Chicago to day. I haven't had a horseback ride for a long time; am waiting for my new habit.

We xpect Belle this month some time and Mollie is coming in August with grandma.

I guess Et, Jude and I will go to Chambersburg to school this fall, at least that is the talk now. No larks for me this summer. My teacher says I musn't miss a lesson and I'm sure I don't want to if I can only learn to swim without going to Sister Lakes. Expect to go to Niles tomorrow to get my teeth fixed.

[2]"Fifth chapter of Caesar" refers to Julius Caesar's *Commentary on the Gauls*, one of the most famous and popular texts to use to teach students Latin. The Gauls were the French.

[3]Children in the nineteenth century wore dresses, regardless of sex, since it made it much easier to change their diapers. Boys were kept in dresses till they were toilet trained, then were put into knickers (pants gathered at the knees), and, finally, about age seven or so, into long pants..

Sunday
July 9th 1882

I hate to write in my journal to night. It is so long since I have written and I always have so much to write that I hate to begin for the simple reason that I don't know what to write first. I have put it off as long as I can and that only makes matters worse.

Well, George and Jude are mad at each other and have hardly spoken for the last month, and they are mad at some ridiculously foolish little thing concerning the lodge entertainment which by the way has not come off yet, and is not likely to. I suppose they will stay mad. I think George is acting very foolishly. I shall see him and have a long talk with him if I ever get a chance and try my hand at peacemaking. I make a very poor one for I always get mad myself before I get through, but I will do my best. George is editor of the Journal now and is very busy, has everything to do himself.[4]

I am just recovering from a cough and ague; was layed up for about a week. Was just sick enough to be awfully cross and disagreeable. Ma lays it to my studying but I think differently.[5]

Gertie Stevens was down last week and is very enthusiastic about Wellesley. She wants me to go back with her next fall. I can take a special course and study anything I please and will not have to be examined in anything. I like that idea first rate. I wrote an application for entrance to the president thursday. If any one wants to enter they have to apply in advance and it doesn't make any particular dif whether they go or not it does no harm to apply.[6] I don't think there is any hopes of my going there. Pa says it is to far. I know I shall go someplace this fall and that is all I do know. Et is almost sure of going to Chambersburg.

Belle is in Niles. We expect her down next week or soon. We expect Mollie and grandma almost any day now. Daisy is in Niles also.

I have real jolly times with latin, am getting better acquainted with my teacher. It has taken us a long while to get acquainted; he isn't as easy

---

[4]Addie's cousin, George Murdock, Jr., was editor of the *Berrien County Journal,* one of the two weekly newspapers then published in Berrien Springs.

[5]Nineteenth-century parents worried greatly over whether too much intellectual exercise would harm girls by weakening their reproductive systems, since the blood flowed to the brain during study. Much of the opposition to women's colleges came from people who feared that education would lead women to neglect their roles as wives and mothers.

[6]"Dif" meaning difference.

to get ac—d with as Lee. Page Boon* and Lee Wilk were up last night and we sang and played cribbage all evening. Each side beat two games. We didn't expect them at all until they suddenly walked in. Lee has just bought a piano.

I have my new riding habit. Dark blue lady's cloth, a regular beauty. I ride almost every night now. Lize is getting to be a splendid riding horse. Will sold Nellie the other day and that spoils a good deal of our fun.

I spent a very quiet fourth; fired a few crackers to distinguish it from other days, and that was all.

Judes eyes are bothering her again. She has had to wear a shade and bandage them for the last two or three days, but they are better now. I have been so hoarse I could not read aloud to her much, so Et has come up and read to both of us. She is reading "Figs and Thistles" by Tourgee now, it is splendid. We are reading another book "The Villa Bohemia" by Marie Le. It is a wishy washy book, the characters are simply characterless. It is about four silly girls—but enough; I have quit reading the "The Modern Instance" by Howells in Century in disgust. It is altogether too modern. While I was sick I read "No Gentlemen" by an unknown author. I don't know when I have enjoyed a book so much. It is written in a crisp fresh way, thickly sprinkled with drollerys and original ideas. It reminded me very strongly of "One Summer." I had an inspiration last week and in about five minutes got up the following nameless verses. I haven't had one before for almost a year:

> The dusky faries of twilight
> Are tripping through the gloom
> I catch but the gleam of their faces
> When they vanish in the gloom.
> All day they have caught the shadows
> As they crept along my floor
> And as the daytime passes
> They let them go at my door.
> There is a constant flutter flutter
> Of the little dusky hands
> Setting free the captive shadows
> With the glasses wasting sands.
> My room is full of these fairies
> As falls the dreamy night
> That is why I am never lonely
> Between the dark and the light.

It stops rather abruptly, but I think I will have more of it some day when I receive another scintillation on the subject.

It [is] oppressively hot tonight and looks like rain. Graham is here; has been here for about a month. I have planned to take a tramp with Jenny Boon on Wednesday.[7] Jude and Et are taking drawing lessons of Mrs. Jones. I think that is what hurt Jude's eyes again. Allie B. has gone to Valpraiso. Jude received a letter from her last week.

Must go to bed now. I shall endeavor to write less and oftener henceforth.

July 10th 1882.

Wonders will never cease. Here I am writing two nights in succession.

This morning I worked sweeping and fixing up stairs. Graham and Pa went to Niles. This evening Jude, Mate Dunn and I went horse-back riding; had a very pleasant time. Charlie lost two shoes. This eve. Jude, Graham and I went down town, bought a cribbage board and a pack of cards. Played two games of cribbage this evening: tie. Ella and I have planned to rise early and take a horse-back ride tomorrow morning. It is half past ten.

Graham says Belle is not in Niles and is not expected as she is taking music lessons in Chicago. I think it is downright mean of her not to write.

Latin tomorrow. A hard lesson and very little of it learned as yet.

July 11th 1882

I just wrote a letter to Belle demanding an explanation of her silence. Ella and I took our ride this morning. We started about 5-30. I got up first and went down after her. She wasn't up yet. We rode until 7-30. We went over to the Sulphur Spring. I forgot to write before that a Sulphur Spring has been discovered over on the poor house road and promises to be a great thing.[8] A new road has been made around the hill that leads to Tates. The hill is washed in places and not considered safe.[9] The new road is right

---

[7]"Tramp" meaning hike or walk.

[8]"Poor house road": the Berrien County Poor Farm was located across the St. Joseph River a few miles east of Berrien Springs. It provided a place for the homeless where they could work for their food and lodging. The sulphur spring's water was valued for its supposed curative powers.

[9]"Washed" meaning the soil had been eroded by rain.

through the woods and is simply lovely. I am in love with Lize. She is such a dear affectionate little thing.

About nine Jude and I went up to the farm and brought baby down. About dinnertime he began to cry and go on so that [we] hurried through dinner and took him home.

Had a latin lesson this afternoon. It was hard, and I had it very poorly. Jude and I played three games of croquet, I beat one, and a game of crib[bage]. Got beaten.

Fan B. went by and said she had got a letter from Allie. We understood her to say that she expected Al on the train so we walked up to the depot followed by our white cat and looking like a pair of old maids with our tabby. Of course Al didn't come and we learned of our mistake. Saw Jen B. and asked her down to play cribbage. She came. We played three games. Ma and I against Jen and Jude. They won the rubber,[10] and Jude and I saw her home.

There, I think this is a pretty fair ac't. of to-day's doings. It is after eleven and I must snooze.

Thur. July 13th 1882

Jude and George are friends again, for which I am eternally grateful. Yesterday I went down to Aunt Addie's intending to stay awhile and then walk down with George when he went to town. Et wasn't at home. She was taking her drawing lesson. Aunt Addie said she thought she would go up to our house afterwards. So I concluded to go home. But Aunt Addie stopped me and talked about George and Jude. Well, we talked it all over I defended Jude's cause and she George's.

We talked a long time and when we got through each held the same opinion we had when we began, viz. we each thought they were both to blame but she thought Jude the most and I thought George the most. She said she thought it had been so pleasant the past winter for we four to be together so much like brothers and sisters, and she didn't think this ought to go on. George had made a vow never to come to our house again until Jude asked him. She said George had tried several times to get a chance to have an explanation with Jude but he couldn't find an opportunity. I said if George would come to the Lodge that night I would try to make peace. George didn't come to the lodge—had to work.

[10]The "rubber" was the deciding game when there was a tie between players.

The lodge passed off very pleasantly. Had one initiation—a stranger. We had also two visitors. One a book-agent from New York and the other a member of the St. Joseph lodge. Gene Howe's name is proposed for membership. He came up to the lodge at recess with Jim Boon. He came into the room which was all right as it was recess, but Jim just to have some fun turned and said "Gene get out of here." How he did fly, he looked as scared as if the goat itself was after him, and Jim laughed for 15 minutes steadily.

This morning Jude and I arose at five and took a long horse-back ride. We went the same road that Ella and I went the morn we rode. Had a delightful time. About noon we drove over to the Spring and got Sulphur water. Saw a wood chuck and a turtle.

Jen and I had set apart this afternoon for one of our good old tramps. Et went too. Went on the railroad track to Farley's crossing then we struck off through the woods feasting on wild raspberries, which were plenty. Jen jumped over a fence into a field and almost jumped on the tail of a big blue racer.[11] None of us saw it but her. I fell over the fence and skinned both legs and my arm. As we went on through the woods we came to some sheep and a half grown lamb was fast under a tree trunk and was kicking like all possessed. It was a very heavy log and [all] we could do to lift it, but Jen and I managed [to] lift it a little and Et pushed the lamb out. It jumped up and scampered off without a word of thanks.

At last we came to a ravine with the lovliest little brook running through it. It flowed into the river. We sat on the river bank and rested. Then we thought we would follow the brook and see where it led to. It was full of large stones and so we walked right in the stream, stepping from one to another. We decorated our hats with ferns, daisies, wheat and anything that took our fancy. We soon looked like wild indians on the war path. The brook at last led us to the fence of an oat field. Here we picked a great many berries in our hats. We went through the field and again found ourselves on the railroad track. There we sat decorating our hats until the engine and flat car came along and picked us up. We rode down on the engine and Et and I made the acquaintance of Harry Sterribb, son of [the] engineer. He boards at Jen's and gave us a lot [illeg.] of berries. Reached home at last.

Et asked Jude and I down to spend the evening and play cards. We went and Jude and George treated each other the same as of yore. I guess both were heartily sick of being mad. Anyway they played partners at

[11]A "racer" is a snake.

cribbage and Et and I beat them. So all is once more serene for Jude invited him up.

To day is Ma's birthday. She is fifty-two. Jude and I gave her a silk necktie.

Walt. Kephart started up north this morning for a vacation.

Latin again to morrow, have an immensely hard lesson. I studied a good hour on one sentence alone and knew no more when I got through than when I began. I wrote for price list of archery [?] to day.

Sat. July 15th

It is late and I must be brief or I will be asleep before I get through. Yesterday afternoon Jude went to take a drawing lesson again. She and Et brought the Bronson babies back with them and took them riding while I stayed at home to prepare for the coming latin lesson. Two little boys came up with an invitation from Lee Wilk. to go boating that eve. and requesting us to set the hour. Ma was away and I had to act on my own responsibility so I wrote a short note accepting and set 5-30 as the time.

I had a poor Latin lesson although I had spent six hours of solid study on it. Teacher said that was about the length of time to spend on it. But I had such a poor lesson I shall try to put eight hours on the next. I studied an hour and three quarters on it to day.

We had a delightful boat-ride. We went up a ways and then floated down. We rode until about half past eight. I steered and Jude and Lee rowed. We talked of books coming back, and my cup of happiness was brim ful of enjoyment. Lee kindly told us we could take his boat at any time we wished to either with or without him.

We have planned to go very early some morning. There was a social at Reibers that evening. After we got through boating we went around to the social for a few moments and had some ice cream and then came home. Lee came in. We sang and waltzed for about an hour.

Uncle Nelson came down yesterday. He says I am studying too hard. I guess if he was my teacher he would tell a different tale. He took Graham home with him to day. The poor boy didn't want to go a bit and begged hard to stay longer.

This P.M. Jude and Et took a drawing lesson and I went around there when it was most time to be out to go down to Et's and read "Figs and Thistles." I had to wait about an hour, then we went down to Et's and read quite a while. Came home, played five games of croquet with Jude, got beaten three.

Then we went up to the farm and had a frolic with baby. He is just getting a tooth. He is the best baby. Will romps with him as roughly as if he was made of india rubber. Stands him on his head and throws him around and he just laughs and is tickled almost to death.

When we came back George and Rob were here. They stayed long enough to play three games of euchre. Geo. and I got beaten twice. Then Jude and I sung about an hour and now I must go to bed.

                                                        Tues. July 18th '82

I will try to hurry through with my report of the past few days, for it is late and I am sleepy. Sunday I went neither to church nor Sunday school. I was in the parlor drumming on the piano when to my horror I saw a double carriage full of folks draw up at the gate and cousin Rob alighted and came in. He inquired if we were at home.[12] I told him we were. He said he had brought some folks up to call. So he brought them in. They were Will D.,* Grace Hoyt, and a Dr. Smith from Chicago. I was completely muddled by the sudden invasion and when Bob asked me how I had rested after being so badly beaten the night before I replied "Very much." They departed finally to my intense relief. I don't like Dr. Smith. There was something decidedly "loud" in his actions at least I thought so.[13] George don't like him either.

After dinner we took "Figs and Thistles" and went down to Aunt Addies. Swung in the hammock and read. George caused the hammock to break down with Et and I in it. He and Jude played mumble peg. Say they are going to get a nice pine board and introduce [it] as a parlor game.

Silas Edward Mosier stopped in and talked in his intelligent way for a long time. He had been to hear the African preacher who had given him a hedge-hog quill. He says he is going to build him a brick house with a marble front, and have all the doors double so he can carry in as large an armful of wood as he wishes to. He has promised me his picture.

Grace wanted Et to go home with her and spend two or three days. She went. George came home with us and had some ice-cream. He stayed two or three hours until dark.

---

[12]To be "at home" in the nineteenth century meant you would be willing to receive company that had come to call. It was an insult to be "not at home" to someone; that meant you were cutting them socially.

[13]"Loud" meaning obtrusive or obnoxious.

Monday was a busy day. Jude is going to take care of household affairs this week and have Ma sew. About six, Lee came up and invited us to go boat riding—his boat was down by the Indian fields.[14] We started at 6-30. Got there and he had hidden his oar locks and forgotten where he hid them. I guess he hunted half an hour for them; he handed Jude and I his revolver and we shot at mark during the search. Of course we didn't hit any thing. At last we found them and when he threw them into the boat one went into the river. So we fished for that with the oars. Luckily the water was shallow at that place so we at last started. We rowed up a ways and then floated down etc. It was nine when we stopped. Quoted Tennyson, made fun of folks, in fun of course, talked, sang, ate delicious candy and in fact had a delightful ride.

Lee wants us to go to Sister Lakes with him some day. He is getting overwhelmingly kind and we rather dread the return of Miss Howe, when all those jolly times will probably vanish. He asked if he might come and take us boating any or every evening. Of course we were delighted to go. He expected to go to Ill. to day but I saw him this eve so I guess he hasn't gone yet.

This morn. I ironed some, studied some, rode some and to sum it all up did a little of every thing and not much of anything. This after noon I began reading "Through One Administration"* by Mrs. Burnet, aloud to Jude. Lee praised it so last night we concluded to read it. He says he is going to bring up his "Atlantics"* for us to read a story called "Doctor Zay." We liked "Through One Administration" very much so far.

I took a lesson as usual this after noon. Mr. Wilkinson is in the drug store now until Walter gets back. I had a pretty good lesson. Studied six hours and a half. We each got a postal from Belle saying she would start for Niles Saturday.[15] So she is in Niles now. Jude and I expect to go up to morrow and if she is there will bring her down. Aunt Addie was here to night and spent the evening. Expects Et back tomorrow. George is sick.

July 19th 1882

Went to Niles this morning. Started at 8 and got there a little after 10. I went directly to Dr. Rowley's office, got one tooth filled and one taken out.[16] I

---

[14]The "Indian fields" refers to a wooded park area along the St. Joseph River on the south side of Berrien Springs.

[15]"Postal" meaning post card.

[16]Dr. Clark Rowley would marry Addie's cousin Georgianna "Daisy" Holmes in 1884.

wanted to impress him with my grit and bore it without a murmur; it came hard and broke off and he left a little piece of the root in for me to remember it by which I undoubtedly shall if it aches as it has to day. He said I had grit enough to carry me through. Went to Aunt Judes and Belle came running out to meet me. She is just the same and not changed in the least unless she is a little fleshier than she was.

Took dinner at Aunt Judes and after that went over to Stevens'. The whole family are sick abed except Uncle and Franky, who have just recovered. They have a fever and hard cough the same as I did. It seems to be a sort of epidemic going around.

We all wanted to hear Belle sing so we went over to Mrs. Miley's,* the only person that on that street that owns a piano. She has improved wonderfully in singing, has a sweet clear voice and seems to have good control over it. We told Belle we wanted her to go back with us. At first she said she couldn't, she expected Carl Burton to night and he was coming down to Berrien with her to visit us a few days and he wouldn't like to come alone. Well, we were in despair awhile. And at last after a great deal of meditation and persuasion we planned to take her down with us to day and Friday or Saturday drive up and bring Carl down.

Carl is her cousin. I never saw him but Jude and Ma met him in Chicago, took a fancy to him and invited him to visit us. He is a musical genius. He never took but two lessons on the piano and plays like a professor and reads the most difficult music at sight. He plays on the violin in the orchestra of Haverly theatre in Chicago.

We went over to Belle's aunt Mrs. Smith and she packed her trunk. Minnie Smith acted perfectly shameful because Belle chose to go home with us instead [of] visiting her. She actually got very angry. Selfish old thing. She is going to be in Chicago all winter and so is Belle and I'm sure she might let us have her a couple of weeks.

There was quite an accident in Niles today. The engine ran off of the trestle work of the new railroad built across Main street. The engineer jumped but the fireman got his leg crushed.[17]

We started home about six. We were so hungry that we stopped at a restaurant and bought rusque and butter, crackers and cheese, cake, plums and candy.[18] Had a delightful ride home. Ate so much I won't be hungry for a good while. We drove slowly for we didn't want to get here

[17]Local accounts tell of a locomotive and tender which jumped the tracks in Niles and fell twelve feet down an embankment.

[18]"Rusque" is a sweet, hard, dry bread like crackers.

in time for lodge and being out of town afforded us a good excuse. Got home about 8.

We had hardly got into the house before Lee Wilk. came and talked a whole rigamarole about a picnic Saturday. Where, when and why we do not know, all we know is that there will be a picnic and we are invited.

I heard more about that Dr. Smith to day which seems to show that we were about right in our opinion of him. Daisy saw him in Chicago and Cousin Frank Young wouldn't introduce her to him because he didn't consider him a fit person for her to know. I don't know why.

Belle and Jude are in bed. I spilled nearly all my ink a little while ago. Baby is getting the same epidemic the Niles folks have. He is better to day.

Aug. 16th 1882

I have been waiting for the spirit to move me before I wrote. It has moved me at last.

Belle stayed a little over a week with us and we endeavored to crowd a whole summer into that week. Succeeded very well. Fred Dougherty* was in town the same week and took a great fancy to Belle. They carried on a kind of flirtation all the time she was here.

Lee took we three to Sister Lakes. We went early in the morning and got home at about two the next morning. Had a delightful time. Rob and Fred were there. I do dislike them both so much. In the afternoon went boating. Lee took Jude, Fred, Belle and Rob, me. I was rowing and Rob sat in the bow. I wished to change places with him and intimated that fact to him. He said it was so dangerous for two to stand in the boat at once so he said I should come and sit down in the bow before he got up. As the bow was just large enough for him I had my doubts as to where I should sit and told him as much, but he insisted that there was plenty of room so I [illeg.] attempted to sit down in an inch space. The result can better be imagined than described. Suffice to say that the curtain next arose upon a boat half full of water, a sadder and wiser young man with very conspicuous wet feet doing duty at the oars. Dark and gloomy melancoholy sits upon his peaked face. A young lady in the bow who is consumed by a burning desire to laugh but who has an inward consciousness that she ought not. Never-the-less she is happy because of the misery so near. Scene III. a lonely island. Melancholy young man wringing out his stockings and hanging them on bushes to dry, while placid young lady looks on with solemn eyes. But enough of this. . .

After tea I went out with Lee and had a real good time. I always do with him, he is such a relief after moping around with silent melancholy Robert. There was a dance in the evening; we started home at eleven o'clock.

The next day Belle was to start to Buchanan. We arose at 11-30 and got down in time for dinner. Belle went up on the 6 o'clock train. George, Jude and Lee went up with her intending to come down on the eight o'clock. But they went up to Fox'es* and got to waltzing and train went off and left them. They telephoned down for a team and got home at 12.[19]

A week ago Sunday Lee spent the evening with us. Jude walked down to the gate with him and there he attempted to bid her a <u>very</u> affectionate good night. She was very angry and the walk was very slippery and she sat down with a vengeance. Of course she was indignant and was never going to have any thing more to do with him. Tues. night he and Jenny Boon, George and Et came up to have a euchre party. Jude didn't speak to him all evening until she was playing the piano. He stood beside her and begged her pardon for what he did, said it was momentary insanity, said he'd never do it again and was exceedingly humble. George and Jen. were in the sitting room and I diverted Et's attention, for I confess to have a weakness for Lee in spite of the many times I have been mad at him and vowed I would never speak to him again. Well, he said he'd never do it again and Jude said she would certainly never give him another opportunity.

She finally forgave him but in a grudging sort of way and he said "all right Miss Julia" and went away much hurt. Well he didn't come near us again until to night. We missed him like everything and Jude rather repented of her hard-heartedness and thought she might have forgiven him with a better grace after he had been so good to us. Well, I set my wits to work to get up some way to make peace that would be original and not require much humbleness from either one. For if there is anything I dislike it is humbleness.

At last Sunday night at midnight a bright idea struck me. I immediately arose, woke up Jude and confided it to her. She was to make a little wooden hatchet and put it in a little box for a coffin and send it to him requesting him to bury it and put off the fight until the weather got cooler. Jude wouldn't here of it at first but after while when I had skilfully reminded her of the boat rides and pleasant times she would miss if she

[19]To "telephone down for a team" meant they called for a horse and carriage, in a nineteenth-century version of a taxicab.

neglected this golden opportunity she gave in and sort of half promised. I whittled her out a hatchet the next day but she couldn't get up courage to send it until yesterday and then she did it a little different from the original idea. She decorated a sheet of paper and envelope with a gorgeous sunflower and wrote the following little note enclosing the hatchet.

Mr. Wilkinson

If you are willing we will bury the hatchet or at least suspend hostilities until the weather is cooler.

J. Graham

I wanted her to send him a candy or ginger bread hatchet so he could bury it on the spot but she wouldn't.

I must go back a little now in my record. Grandma and Mollie arrived Sat. Jude, Et, and I went up to Buch. on the 6 train and met them and rode down with them on the 8. Grandma seems much feebler than she was and thinner. Mollie is a tall dark girl, not pretty, decidedly southern, slow and, to tell the truth, rather tiresome. She is quiet and contrary, a sort of a dead weight, won't play any thing, won't dance. She joined the Baptist church just before she came up. Perhaps when she is better acquainted she will be different. I hope so.

I applied to the Kalamazoo Female Seminary for entrance and was accepted.[20] I leave three weeks from today. Jule Brown says he is going to Kalamazoo to the college this winter. I take three lessons a week now and take my first lesson in Caesar tomorrow.

Jude and Ma went to Niles to day. Jude went on to Chicago with Mary Gould* to have her eyes examined by Dr. Holmes. She had them examined by Dr. Avery in Niles and he said it is the muscles of the iris become weakened and the pupil admits more light into the eye than it can stand. She will be back tomorrow night I think.

Lee didn't know she had gone and having received her note came up this evening. Mollie and Et were also here. Jude is treasurer now at the Lodge and I am minus an office. I haven't been for two nights.

Grace Hoyt is in town. Rob has gone to Pennsylvania. Wirt Stevens is here. Jude and Et visited the Stevens in Niles last week, only stayed two days.

[20]The Michigan Female Seminary, its official name, was incorporated in 1856 as an educational institution for young women. Opening after the Civil War in 1867, the three-story brick structure was located on a bluff on the east side of the Kalamazoo River. Its program was designed to educate girls in the liberal arts as well as religion and physical training; in 1880 the student body consisted of 37 students.

Night before last we spent the evening at Reeds. Cash and Kit Van Riper* of Buchanan were there also Grace Hoyt, Mollie, Et and Geo. Had a dull time. Spent last evening at Aunt Addies in the same comp. minus Cash and Grace. Took a delightful horseback ride this evening on my Liza.

Campmeeting has begun. Don't think I shall go up this year. Baby has a short dress on and is cuter than ever.[21]

Friday Aug. 18th 1882

I am tired and sleepy. I wouldn't write to night only I want to keep up my Journal pretty regularly now until I go and keep it up all the time I am away. I took a Latin lesson again last night not a very good one but pretty long. I think I shall like Caesar.

Mate Hoyt came up yester-day morning and wanted me to go to the farm with her. It seems she stopped for Et and Mollie to go up with her but they managed to hide from her and so escaped. I was less fortunate. I had just got on my habit preparatory to doing an errand and taking a short ride. She took no notice of my apparent haste or of my riding habit but mercilessly pounced upon me as the doomed mortal who must accompany her. I did my errand and then succumbed to the inevitable.

Mate Himes came up about dusk and stayed until eight and went up to the train with me to meet Jude. She brought me a new dress ox-blood in color, a fine woolen stuff, which is to be my best dress this winter, also stockings, [handkerchief], collar, stuff for a [illeg.] and the flannel for my gymnasium suit. They thrashed up to the farm today and will thrash all day to morrow getting throug to morrow evening.[22] Jude and I went up to help this A.M. Molly and Ella were also up a while. Molly had never seen 'em thrash before.

I studied some this afternoon. Dutch came in and played me eight games of croquet. I beat the first and last games. Jude stayed all night at the farm to night. Jule came and got the cribbage board and chatted awhile. Says he has a circular of the Kalamazoo College he wants to show me. Spent the evening ripping my old blue dress to pieces. Pa has a very sore throat. Thinks it is something like diptheria.[23]

---

[21]"Campmeeting" refers to outdoor religious services; the "short dress" baby has on refers to the garments small children wore after infancy.

[22]"Thrash" meaning to thresh the wheat, separating the grain from the straw.

[23]"Diptheria" was a contagious bacterial infection, usually of the throat characterized by difficulty swallowing and breathing and possibly affecting the heart and nervous system.

The doctor in Chicago says it is the optic nerve of the ey[e] that is affected with Jude. She got some glasses and a perscription.

"Farewell dere diary" . . .

August 20th 1882

I stayed at home all day yester day. Devoted most of my time to Latin and managed to scare up quite a respectable headache by lesson time. Had about as poor a lesson as usual. Managed to get about 2/3 of the sentences twisted so they mean something entirely different from what Caesar intended. After my lesson we talked sometime about school and studies; he doesn't approve of the Kalamazoo school. He believes in schools where girls have lots of liberties and can learn something else besides what they learn from books. He says I have done splendidly in Latin and am better prepared to begin Caesar than he was when he began it. I have a sort of inward consciousness that I know precious little about it. I told him I was going to study medicine. Said he thought I would make a success at it. I intend to be either a first-class-high-notch physician or I won't be any.

Jack brought a letter to Jude from Lee. Jude wast at the farm yet so after my lesson I walked up to come down with her. She intimated that she wasn't coming back that night and I concluded to stay too. I helped her read her letter.

Lee said he was mighty willing but he would never bury that particular hatchet. That he would call to night which, by the way, he did. We stayed all night, played cards, euchre, three games. Will and I, Jule and Jude. We won the rubber. We didn't come home until three this P.M.

I read a little of Mrs. Southworth's novel "The Changed Brides."* I never read any of her writing before and I don't think I ever will again. Such an unhealthy sickening thing as it is. We went down to Aunt Addie's about five. Molly, Et, and George came up to spend the evening. Lee came about eight and stayed until ten. He and George talked political economy a great deal. I don't understand it. The conversation was mostly of whether it was wrong to say "Damn" or not and about smoking cigars. I would like to put it all in but lack of memory, not of space, prevents.

Lee stayed awhile after the others went and we sang some. George, Et, Molly, Jude and Jule expect to go to camp-meeting tuesday after-noon, take tea and come back in the evening. I am happy to say that Latin prevents my going. What would I do without Latin? It has saved me from many a similar trying situation!

.I wish I was going to Ann Arbor instead of K-zoo.

Baby is not feeling well, has a terribly sore mouth he is remarkably good and patient under the circumstances.

Aug. 26th

My birth-day. Eighteen to day! Et was [eighteen] yesterday. It seems awful to be so old. Et, George and Allie came up and spent the evening. Grandma and Mollie have been here since Wednesday. We had ice-cream and "old maid." I got the [old maid] many times but it didn't make me feel bad and only strengthened my conviction.[24] Mollie gave me a shell jewel box, Et sent me a lovely birth-day card, and Pa gave me a lovely little gold pen.

My blessed teacher came at three today and stayed until six. Three hours lesson instead of one and one-half. Have had an awful head and eyes ache ever since. Everyone says I am studying too hard. I am getting big black rings under my eyes but I don't think they are caused by too much study.

Mrs. Euson has been up all this week making my under clothes. They are all done now and my dresses will be commenced next week. I go to Niles Monday to have a dress cut.

Lee invited Jude to go to Sister Lakes with him to day but she refused. She says she won't go any place with him again.

Took a horse back ride last night. Mother doesn't want me to study any more until I go away. I have a great notion not to but dread stopping.

We had a hard rain this after noon and will have some more to night, I think. I hope so. My eyes ache so I must go to bed. Only a little over a week until I go. I am both glad and sorry.

Kalamazoo Sem.
Sept. 11th '82

What an awful responsibility it is to keep a journal. Here I haven't written for nearly a month and I intended to write every night.

I am in the third story of the Kalamazoo Female Seminary. I came last Wednesday with Pa. The night before I had a tea-party. Et, George, Mate Himes, Mollie and Kit Ewalt were all [text ends here]

---

[24]"Old maid" is a card game that requires players to match cards. The loser ends the game when left holding the old maid card, supposedly predicting spinsterhood.

I must practice now.

Just back from practicing.

We spent the evening very pleasantly. Et wept when she said good by and we coaxed her to stay all night and see me off in the morning and so she did.

We started at about seven. Got to Niles about 9-30, waited an hour at the depot and then started. I saw a girl and her father on the train and made up my mind they were going to same place we were. I told Pa what I thought and he spoke to the gentleman and sure enough they were. There names were Sherrill.* Winny Sherrill had never been here before and so we soon got acquainted. There were very few here when we came only the Matron, Mrs. Safford, and two girls.

Got to go to bed now; all lights have to be out at 9.30.

Kal. Sept 13 1882

I am homesick. I guess I don't know what else to call the the desperate feeling I have.

Last night as I was sitting in my room about four o'clock Miss King sent word up that I could ride to town with her if I liked. Of course I liked and was surprised at the invitation for I hear from the girls that it is no common honor. So we started in the "chariot" accompanied by little Miss Skinner and Clara Matthews, one of the girls.[25] Almost the first carriage we met contained Lee Wilk and another gentleman. I knew he was in the city from a letter I rec'd yesterday from mother. She also returned my list of correspondents so I could send the letters I had written to Mate and Et. I was pretty glad to see someone from home.

Miss King got out in town to do some shopping and little Miss Skinner took us riding all over Kalamazoo. It is a lovely place. I saw several girls out horse-back which made me a little homesick. When we went through town again I saw Lee and he motioned for me to have Miss Skinner stop.

Just got back from practising. Well, I asked Miss Skinner to please stop a moment, which she did, and Lee came and talked to me quite awhile. Said he would call to day and take me riding if I could go. Just then Miss Skinner turned around and said "Miss Graham, I think it

[25]Caroline E. Skinner was the music teacher.

would be better to drive on," or words to that effect. Then Lee stepped up and began talking to her and I gave them an introduction. It is against the rules for the pupils to stop and talk to friends on the street and why she stopped is a mystery to me.[26]

After my ride I moved again and am now with Miss Clark again. I roomed with her when I first came and then Little Miss Schofield got so homesick that she wanted to move down on the same floor with her sister, and so I moved up with Lizzie Anderson and she went in with Miss Clark. Yesterday she concluded to room with her sister and so I came back to my first roommate. She is very pleasant and I like her much. Carrie Roberts is the object of my admiration. I don't know why I like her so much but I do.

To day was recreation. A little boy with a basket of pop-corn balls sits on the steps of the Sem. and is patronized daily by the girls.

Lee didn't come until nearly four to day. Couldn't get off any sooner. I was walking down the walk with another girl and saw him driving in, so I waited and rode up to the Sem. with him. We marched in outwardly brave but inwardly quaking to ask Miss Sprague's permission to go riding. She said I couldn't go!! because didn't happen to have a note from either of my parents giving me permission. He stayed and talked quite awhile and after he left I was more homesick than I have been since I have been here. I wrote a letter to George to day.

The retiring bell has rung and I must go to bed.

Sept. 30th 82

The last day of Sept. and only about eleven weeks until Christmas. I have been here nearly four weeks and have only had one real homesick time and that was the next night after Lee called. My room-mate went to prayer meeting and when she came back was desperately home-sick and that got me started and we had a regular time for a while.

Last Wednesday I was sitting in my room reading a letter from George and Ma when Miss Rose came and told me some one wanted to

[26]Such restrictions on casual interaction would be unthinkable in the modern era, but in the nineteenth century, schools were particularly careful to protect their students from any possible criticism from outsiders by limiting their freedom. This was particularly true of women's colleges, since the fear of young women being corrupted in a faraway place would keep many parents from sending their daughters to school away from home.

see me in the parlor. I was surprised to hear it and went to the parlor and there was Pa and Ella Graham. Ella had come to stay and I moved that day up [to] the third floor and we room together. It is nice to have some one I know here. She is through bathing now and I must go at it. She just spilt a wash bowl full of water in our closet.[27]

Have finished my bath and have ten minutes yet before lights are out. Jude is in Chicago having her eyes attended to. She intends to stay a month. She stops at Mrs. Wood's with Belle. Belle is coming over to spend the Christmas holidays with us.

This morning we had to hand in our account books to Miss Sprague. I take German lessons of the nicest old German. I take all alone for the others that take are ahead of me, having studied it before. He says I do remarkably. I am trying to work ahead in Caesar, but have stuck fast in the middle of the 14 chapter. Miss Sprague thinks I can graduate next year if I work hard.

I have physiology. We have a splendid skeleton to work with, a perfect beauty. It is the skeleton of a peasant girl 18 years old and is perfect in form and every other way.

I detest Miss Safford she seems to be always sticking her nose into everything. I do believe she is a crank. I used to whistle in the domestic hall but she has shut down on that and to night I was singing and she invited me to stop. Shoot her.

Sunday Oct. 1st 82.

We have just returned from Bible class and I feel as if I would like to be desperately good. Our Sunday evening bible classes are so pleasant. We have begun in the first part of the Bible and are studying about Abraham, Sarah, Rebekah and Isaac. Miss Sprague is our teacher and makes the bible peoples seem so real and so like the people we see around us every day. We all marched to church this morning as usual.[28] Ella and I walked together.

---

[27]Students' rooms had few luxuries. Bathtubs were shared, and a washstand which held a large bowl was used in the room to wash faces and hands.

[28]Marching to church in order and together built a sense of camaraderie among students and kept them under control as well. While the seminary was not a religious school, it did have a religious component, as most schools did, and students were expected to attend religious services daily or weekly.

Our text was the tenth verse of the thirteenth chapter of St. John.[29] Mr. Hunting is the minister and is splendid. There somehow seems to be something so solid about him and everything he says is right to the point. Oh dear, I always feel so good here Sunday nights but how it does vanish in the morning! I suppose it is better to do that way than not to feel good at all.

I wrote my sermon this afternoon or as much as I could remember of it.

Mon. Oct. 2nd Sem.

It is the silent ten minutes before retiring. I got a letter from Et this noon. She says Jule Brown and another young man start for the Kalamazoo business college this week.

My domestic work was changed to day from washing dishes to sweeping the domestic hall and walks.[30] It is awfully hard. I work right after dinner and as Ella practises then neither of us got our half hour excercise in the open air, so after school to night I asked Miss Sprague when we could take it and she said we could go the first half of silent hour and keep the last half together in our room.

We went off in search of fruit. We received directions from some of the girls before starting to go to a little white house on the corner. We couldn't find any so we knocked a[t] several houses we thought might be the right one and they sent us somewhere else. At last we asked some little boys and they directed us to a little yellow house which was not on a corner. There we got three musk-mellons and one water melon and three pears for 20¢. Had a feast in our room tonight and didn't keep study hour.

Oct 30th Mond. '82

I have been reading over some of this Journal to night and am sorry that I haven't kept it up better since I have been here, but I don't seem to get any time to write and when I do I generally have to write letters.

---

[29]"Jesus saith to him, He that is washed needeth not save to wash his feet, but is clean every whit: and ye are clean, but not all" John 13: 10 (King James Version).

[30]In order to control costs and to instill the sense of discipline that comes with hard work, many schools required students to perform domestic duties as part of their education.

It is the last half of silent hour now. I spent the first half in the chapel reading aloud to Miss Kate Inglis while she knitted.[31] She is one of the seniors and has washed dishes with me ever since I have been here. She is lovely and yet so homely, and she is as smart as she is good. She is about the only girl here that I really love to talk to. She is so sensible and talks so well. The other girl in my circle is Lena Clark, a little brown-eyed freckled girl always jolly and always getting off some bright saying and keeping us laughing all the time.

Harry came home from Kansas about the 4th of October and I was almost crazy when Ma wrote it to me. Jude and Harry came to see us last Tuesday afternoon, also Uncle Nelson. I got a postal from Jude that morning saying they would either be here that afternoon or Wednesday. I was sitting looking out of the window after study hour had begun after dinner. Edith Mizner had just come and told me that she was going to ride to town in the chariot to take a telegram for Miss Sprague and that Miss Sprague had said I might go with her and I was waiting to see the chariot drive up when I saw Jude, Harry and Uncle Nelson coming up the walk. I didn't know Jude or Harry but I did know Uncle Nelson and so I sat waiting for them to send up after us, with a calmness that was surprising. Well, Jude stayed all night and we all slept in one bed. (I mean Ella, Jude and I.) Jude brought us a big box of candy.

Louise Perrin was just in to say that Miss Sprague has given us permission to have a candy pull tomorrow night as it is Hallowe'en and we can dance in the dining room. Each girl contributes five cents toward molasses.

Well, Jude and I wanted to go to town on Wednesday and wanted Ella to go to but feared she would not be allowed to without her mother's permission in writing, so Jude wrote a permission and signed Aunt Hattie's name and I signed Pa's also to make it more certain. Jude had permission to do so if necessary so we didn't feel so very guilty. We had a gay time, went to town about nine in the morning. Ella and I each got us a hat then we all three got tintypes taken in group then we met Harry and Uncle on the street, went to a restaurant and had a splendid dinner and the most delicious fried oysters I ever ate. After that we bummed around a little more and then they went to the depot with them. Ella and I got four cakes of sweet chocolate and a bag of ginger cookies and came back to the Sem. There was a concert that eve here but we were so tired and sleepy we were glad when it was over.

[31]Kate Inglis was Catherine M. Inglis.

Harry expected to go back to Kansas today. Sade Reiber and Will Hall were married last Wednesday the 25th. We had a terrible wind storm this afternoon.

Nov. 5th Sunday

My ink has all dried up so I have to write with led pencil or not at all.

Went to church this A.M. as usual. Mr. Hunting preached a splendid sermon from the 28 chapter of Proverbs and 20th verse. I have just finished writing my abstract of the sermon but have no ink to copy it with.[32] Ella is asleep on the bed, is not feeling very well. Harry went back to Kansas last Monday. I received a letter from Jude saying that Pa had rather we would not go home Thanksgiving on account of Ella and because it is so short a time from then to Christmas. But just seven weeks from next Wednesday I will go home. I wrote and tried to persuade Jude to come Thanksgiving and stay a day or two. Have not heard from her since.

Lu Brown has gone home. Miss Sprague found out that she and Fanny Cameron had been skipping out nights and told her father she would rather he would take her home. All the girls who did so have been found out. Wini Sherril and Lizzy Anderson owned up to it and were forgiven.

Night before last Miss Sprague called a meeting of the Seniors Middle class but didn't call my name. Yesterday noon she sent the "rare bird" to tell me to come to the office. I went and she asked me about my studies and told me I belonged to the Senior Middles and would be a member of the Clio Society. Every few weeks Miss Sprague calls me to the office, asks me about my studies and informs me that I am a member of the Senior middle class. I am getting so I believe it now.

Well, when she got through talking about that she asked if I was a member of that foolish society. I knew of course that she meant "Satan's Angels" and promptly answered yes. She exclaimed and I grinned. The "Angels" only met once, were found out and broken up. But we had fun that one night and elected the officers. We met one Tuesday night or

---

[32]"A faithful man shall abound with blessings: but he that maketh haste to be rich shall not be innocent" Proverbs 28:20 (King James Version). Nineteenth-century pencils were made of lead, not graphite; this was before the dangers of lead poisoning were known. Students would do their work in pencil, then copy out a finished product in ink to hand in to the teacher.

rather Wednesday morning for it was after twelve o'clock up in Fan and Lu's room on the fourth floor. We elected officers and caroused all night, eating apples, grapes, melons and candy. Fan was president, Sue Munson Treasurer and I was secretary. Miss Sprague said she didn't consider it wicked only it wasn't orderly and was foolish. Then she asked me if I had ever left the Seminary after night. I said "No, nor Ella either," and we separated in peace.

After dinner I learned that it was reported that Ella and I had skipped out nights and some of the girls said they could swear they had seen us. Oh, I was mad. It was study hour when Ella told me. I announced that I was going right down and speak to Miss Sprague. Ella went with me. Miss Sprague was in the Chapel. I went in so angry and excited that I didn't care what happened.

Se'z I, "Miss Sprague, did you hear that Ella and I had been out nights since we have been here?" and I bit my words off as short as pie crust.

She looked at me kind of funny and I didn't know whether she was frightened at my terrific "mean" or was going to laugh. She said yes, she had heard it.

"Do you believe it?" I asked again, as if I was a prosecuting attorney and she the prisoner. She said no, not after what I had told her that noon. Then I felt relieved and as a natural result I cried and made a fool of myself generally, and blurted out "Well, I didn't anyway."

She told me not to be troubled about it for she wouldn't believe we had if every girl in school said so. We went back to our room quite comforted.

The Clio met last night and elected officers. Bert. Harpham president, Emma Kuhl secretary and myself treasurer. It is a literary society. We are going to meet for about half an hour every Tuesday evening and Miss Sprague is going to read something nice until after Christmas, and then I suppose we will do great things in the way of entertainments. Next Tuesday evening Mr. Hunting is going to address the school on the subject of Charlotte Corday and we will probably not meet until a week from Tuesday.[33]

I have caught up with the other class in German.

---

[33]"Charlotte Corday" was a French patriot who assassinated Jean Paul Marat, a French revolutionary, in his bathtub. Her act was made famous in a portrait by David.

Nov. 7th Tuesday

It is the silent ten minutes. Mr. Hunting gave his lecture tonight. It was perfectly grand, all in rhyme and some of the prettiest ideas. I really believe it was worthy of Longfellow.

Last night in the first half of silent hour Miss Sprague met the Clios and read us a sketch of Charlotte Corday and all day today I have heard nothing but discussion as to whether she did right or wrong in killing Murat, and we all waited with a considerable suspense to see the view Mr. Hunting took of it. He thought she did right.

Ella has been sick for the past few days but is better. I got a letter from Et to night saying she and Jude will probably come and see us Thanksgiving. Only three more weeks till then. Miss Inglis has gone off our circle and Sue Munson has been put on. Miss I. has care of the sick now.

Nov. 18. Saturday

All hopes concerning Thanksgiving are blighted. Jude can't come here or we can't go home.

The Clio are considering the subject of a literary entertainment to be given after Christmas. We met last evening in Bert. Harpham's room, minus Miss Sprague, to consider and decide what to have. We had a jolly time and after much discussion and many proposals decided to have it anonymous. The Seniors Society is going to take Tennyson for the subject of the entertainment they give before Christmas. The Clios and Seniors are going to have a debate sometime between now and Christmas. Subject: Is capital punishment justifiable? We take the side that is.

The subject of our compo's the time before the last was the biographical sketch of some historical character. Edith Mizner and I took Alexander the Great. She proving that he was great and I the opposite. We are to read them next Saturday in rhetorical and it remains to be seen which side will triumph.

Night before last I went and spent the evening with Cameron. We met for the purpose of studying Caesar but did more talking than studying. I never saw a girl change so much in so short a time as she has since Lu was sent home. Lu had an awful influence over her. Fan is desperately in love with little Miss Skinner and confided to me all her hopes and fears as to whether her passion was returned. She says that she believes if any thing should happen to make Miss Skinner dislike her she believes it would kill her. She has sworn off using slang because Miss Skinner doesn't like it. She studies five times harder on the lesson she recites to Miss Skinner than on any of the others and is in the height of bliss if Miss Skinner smiles upon her. I have been there myself and can sympathise with her.[34]

Four weeks from next Wednesday I will be at home. Oh bliss!

The girls all sneer at Fan's sudden change for she was the worst of all the "Angels" and swore like a pirate when she got a little mad. She don't care for their sneers, though, as long as she pleases little Miss Skinner. I admire her pluck and stand up for her on every occasion.

Mon. Nov. 20th

Second half of silent hour. To day I rec'd a package from home and enclosed in the flannel suit Ma sent was a bag of candy. Maybe it didn't taste good!!————

First term of German is over. I took a music lesson to day. I hate to take music lessons and I am sure if I keep on it will lead to St. Vitus' dance.[35] It makes me so nervous I can't sit still for an hour afterward. I have such miserable lessons. To morrow we are examined in Ancient History. I don't dread it much. right after silent hour to night I have to go down to Miss King's room and she will correct the essay I am to read at rhetorical next Saturday. I have not had much time for any reading since I have been here. I have finished Katrina which I began before leaving home. Oh dear, that reminds me of how I used to lie in the hammock up at the farm, read Katrina and eat pears.

By the way, Jude said in her last letter that Georgie could stand up by holding on to a chair and that his big grey eyes have changed to big brown eyes. Et said he was the prettiest baby in Berrien. I want to see him so much. Only twenty nine days and I will see him!

I have also read "Undine and Sintram."* I enjoyed them so much, "Undine" especially and "Aslange's Knight." Rare sweet Undine and

[34]The phenomenon of schoolgirl "crushes" on teachers is well-documented. In the nineteenth century, the rigid gender-role differentiation fostered an emotional segregation between the sexes, often leading women to form intense same-sex relationships of love and devotion. Expressions of their emotions in letters and diaries appear homosexual or incestuous to modern readers, given our more restricted sense of acceptable kinds of sexual and emotional expression, but in the historical context, these nineteenth-century relationships were seen as socially acceptable, entirely proper, and emotionally supportive.

[35]"St. Vitus dance" is a nervous disorder, or chorea, the popular name of which refers to the irregular jerking movements over which victims have no control.

pale sad Sintram. I have wanted to read them both so much, and they were even better than I anticipated. I am reading Goethe's "Sorrows of Werther" now. Think Werther was extremely silly and effeminate and cannot imagine what sensible Charlotte could see in him to admire and like. He was always on the verge of despair and could not appreciate his blessings. He was always trying to analyze his feelings, and his efforts to grasp the unattainable were really painful.

Silent hour is over and I must go to Miss King's room.

Sat. Nov. 25

Rhetorical this afternoon and our essays on Alexander the Great read. I have been complimented and flattered until my head is fairly turned. Miss Mizner and I walked upon the stage together and made our bow to Miss Sprague, then Edith advanced to the front and read hers while I took a seet in the back-ground. She was very much embarassed and showed it although her essay was good and had some pretty hard facts in it. After she finished I read mine. I don't believe I was ever so embarassed before, not even at my graduation where the crowd was five times as large. There was no umpire to decide which side was victorious. A great many say that I beat, but they probably tell Edith the same. I had the advantage of her by being able to conceal a great deal of my embarassment and in having committed the most of my essay and in speaking last, so upon the whole it was nothing very remarkable after all.

Werther has blown his brains out at last, much to my relief. I thought he would never do it. I think that parody on the Sorrows of Werther by Thackeray very good. The lamp bell will ring soon. I will copy the parody in here tomorrow if I have time.

Sund. Nov. 26

Sorrows of Werther
"Werther had a love for Charlotte,
Such as words could never utter.
Would you know how first he met her?
She was cutting bread and butter.
Charlotte was a married lady
And a moral man was Werther
And for all the wealth of India
Would do nothing for to hurt her.

So he pined and sighed and ogled
And his passion boiled and bubbled
Till he blew his silly brains out
And was no more by them troubled.
Charlotte having seen his body
Borne before her on a shutter
Like a well conducted person
Went on cutting bread and butter."
Wm. M. Thackeray

When I woke up this morning I saw the ground all covered with snow. It had snowed all night and was about three inches deep. No one went to church so we all met in the Reading room and Miss Sprague read a sermon on the ninth commandment. I have thoroughly enjoyed this day. I always feel so happy when I don't go to church Sunday. I think there must be some defect in my nature, for I'm sure I ought to be happier after going to church; all good girls are. I wrote a letter to Marmie this P.M.

Lee is extremely attentive to Jude I hear. He is reading "Doctor Zay" aloud to her evenings. I don't see how anyone can help falling in love with Jude. I fell desperately in love with her myself about a year ago and I fell in even more deeply that time she came here with Harry. There is a kind of irresistible charm about her. I don't know what it is. I used to try to analyse it but have given it up in despair. She pleases without trying to.

I have been congratulated to day on my essay. It seems to have made a great impression. Miss Marmi Clark congratulated me to day. She said it was splendid, that I brought forth such good arguments. Even Miss King told me I did "so well." It makes me so happy. I had determined to do well if possible but I never dreampt of such a complete triumph.

Sat. Eve. Dec. 2nd

Just returned from silent hour. Miss Skinner read to us to night. She is reading "The Life of Josephine."*

Thursday was Thanksgiving. The day before, Ella and I received a box from home containing turkey, celery, mince pie, cake, dough nuts and crackers, also a great quantity of candy. Almost half of the girls were gone home. We had a candy pull that night. We invited eight girls in to have a feast. Anne and Gussie Taylor, Fannie Little & B. Adams, Lena Clark and Carrie McKee, Clara Sumson and Em Mooney.

Wed. Dec 6th

I stopped writing rather suddenly last Saturday eve. Ella wanted me to talk to her. She was sick. Was in bed. Sat. Sund. and Mond.—too much box. We got the pictures of the horses and of Jude Thanksgiving day. They look as natural as life. I haven't accomplished anything to day but write a letter home and I had to do that being clear strapped with only one copper left.[36] I got a letter from Jude yesterday. She attended a Thanksg ball in Niles last Wed. attended of course by the devoted Lee. He has invited her to attend every ball given in Niles or Buchanan this winter. Just <u>two weeks from to night I will be at home</u>! ! !

The Clios met last night. We decided on a Bryant entertainment, or rather Miss Sprague decided on one. We are going to read Shakespeare's Henry V. at future meetings. Miss Sprague made out a kind of rough programme for the Bryant. I am to speak "Thanatopsis."* I am to be in a tableau in the Tennyson entertainment.[37] Wish I wasn't.

Miss Ella Platt and Mr. Morton were married today. There is a glorious cold snow storm going on outside. Jude said there was skating on Boon's pond in her last letter. O————————h!!

Thursday Dec. 7th

With the help of our Father I make a resolution this night to henceforth be thoroughly honest in everything that I do and say.
    Addie Graham,
    M. F. S.
    Kalamazoo
    Michigan.

Monday
Jan 8, 1883

. . . We returned last Wednesday, I should say Thursday, after two weeks spent at home. I wish I had written some while there but couldn't bear to

---

[36]"Copper" meaning penny.

[37]"Tableau" was the representation of a scene, usually literary or historical, by a group of people in costume who would assume an appropriate pose then remain silent and motionless while the audience appreciated the setting. Tableaux were very much in vogue in the Victorian era and were a party game, as well as a school pastime.

take the time. I didn't go skating once while I was home and only attended one party, which was at our house. I went out to tea three times at Mr. Bronson's, Himes and Et's. Ella & Mollie and I went to Niles intending to return the same evening, but Charlie was taken very sick and we had to stay all night. That night there was a surprise on Ella and of course we missed that. Poor old Charlie hadn't quite recovered when I left home and I am afraid will never be real well again. We had two splendid horse back rides while home. We had a masquerade at our house the Tuesday evening before we left. I dressed to represent a gypsy. Jude represented art[?]. It was quite a success I think.

Wednesday evening my old Latin teacher came up and spent the evening. We had taken tea with Et that night and Geo. came home with us and also spent the evening. Played euchre. I was quite surprised when tutor said he was coming up to see me. I didn't know he ever went to see any one but Clara Reiber.

I got a good many Christmas presents. First and foremost a little gold watch just what I have long wanted, three books, "Dr. Zay," "Old Fashioned Girl," and "Shirley,"* a photograph and autograph album, a handkerchief, bag for darning cotton.

I am studying English History and Literature, astronomy, Caesar, German twice a week, and French History & composition Saturdays.

Jack Wilk can't read Virgil with me next summer, shall have to wade through it alone. Miss Sprague is reading the "Schonberg Cotta Family"* to us in silent hour. Like it very much.

Thursday Feb 15—'83

It is silent hour. Miss Sprague has finished the Cotta Family and is now reading "The Life of Washington."

Yesterday Miss Lottie Skinner departed for good. She is going to start to Europe in three weeks. It was like a funeral here yesterday. Weeping and wailing sounded from one end of the house to the other. Fan nearly went wild over it.

It is thawing very rapidly and the sleighing disappeareth, for which and other blessings I am extremely grateful. Was very home sick last week. I didn't get a letter from home until Saturday night. It had been six days on the way.

The 10th of February I would have gone home if Ella would have gone with me, but she backed out at the last moment and that eve I got a letter. Sunday night we had a picnic. Gussie was not able to go to Bible class and Ella didn't feel very well, so Gussie came up here and Ella had supper brought up. I concocted some wonderful oyster soup and toasted a liberal supply of bread, coaxed from the philanthropic Miss Inglis. Emma Kuhl heard our Latin class to day and Miss Sprague spectated and scared the few remaining grains of sense out of my sievelike numbskull.

I received a long letter from Martha and wrote a longer one in return. Jude expects to go to Albion next term. I am reading "The Monastery," "Miss Jameson Warren," "Through One Administration," and "For the Mayor," "Shirley," and "Little Men."*

March 1st '83

It is a lovely day, snow is going fast and I am very glad. Jude is in Albion taking music and painting and having a good time generally, I should think from her letters. She stays at the same home as Cora Nichols does and is gracefully receiving attentions from a Mr. Seamore. She has only been in Albion about a week and seems to be getting acquainted at a lightning speed.

I got a long letter from Martha yesterday. She wants me to come and visit her next summer and I want to very much.

It is just 4-15. School will be out in five minutes. Ella has just gone out for a walk. She and I took a long walk this morning before Chapel.

Yesterday there was lovely skating in the morning just across the road and I wanted to skate very much. Mabel Thayer and Maude Hoag skated but of course I left my skates at home and couldn't go. In the afternoon Maude was going down town and offered to lend me her skates and as heel plates were necessary I had to wear her shoes too.[38] She wears fives. But I stuffed rags in and wore my leggin and some [illeg.] and thought perhaps I could skate a little, but the ice was all slush on top and my feet turned upside down in side the shoes and I had to give it up after several (un)graceful plunges.

The teacher who takes Miss Skinner's place is Miss Starkweather. She is very pleasant and I suppose we might like her if we didn't compare her with Little Miss Skinner (bless her heart). Gussie came up and studied Latin last night and we didn't go down to the singing. We want her to go home with us in the summer and make a visit and perhaps she will. I have had quite a mania for drawing lately and have been drawing heads.

[38]Ice skates in the nineteenth century strapped on to shoes, rather than being a shoe-type skate.

Clara Sumson and Emma Mooney have separated and Lizzie Anderson rooms with Emma now and Clara rooms with the tomcat. I think Emma treated Clara shamefully and always did detest Lizzie Anderson with her snakey little eyes and snakey little actions.

March 28

At last we are on the way home. We are on the train. Ella, Win and I. It is a lovely morning. It is only about 6-30, and I am so sleepy. Jude went home yesterday. We have a horseback in prospect for this afternoon. Examinations are over and I stood well in everything.

Kalamazoo
April 14, 83

Arrived here last Tuesday, was almost a week late. Had a glorious time at home, rode horse back every day but two, went to four parties and had one ourselves. Got photos taken in Niles. Started back on Saturday and again on Monday, but narrow gauge prevented. Nearly went to sugar camp.[39] Had tintypes taken and all sorts of larks. Rode to Niles Tuesday morning in lumber wagon with Pa, Jule & Ellie. Got here at noon. Miss Sprague lovely & amiable. Ed Helmick is here attending the business college. Hope to see him to morrow in church.

This morning I arose a little while after the hour bell, dressed, went down and helped about breakfast because Miss Milham was away. Miss Sprague changed the table all around this morning. Miss Reed has gone home with the measles so Miss King took a table. I sit a[t] hers between Louis [?] and Miss Long. There are six new girls. After breakfast did the room work, and then went to walk with Anna Taylor. Went to the bridge and back in time for Chapel. Ma Sprague didn't call report for study hour, so was all right. Miss King met me after chapel and said I might sit at the end of the table because it would be pleasanter for me!! That woman is made of strawberries & cream she is so good.

Have to write a review of the "Psalm of Life"* for our next essay. Oney is going out to milk in his shirt sleeves. It is hot today, looks like thunder.

---

[39]The "narrow gauge" referred to the St. Joseph Valley Railroad, which opened between Buchanan and Berrien Springs in 1881. As Addie suggests, the railroad suffered from notoriously unreliable service and finally closed in 1886. "Sugar camp" may have referred to a sugar bush, where maple sap was boiled into syrup and sugar.

Chemistry recited today. Miss Schereezy came up from town she is going to perform experiments for us ever[y] Saturday. She looks interesting and picturesque, as if she had just escaped from one of Mrs. Burnet's novels.

I have started the thumb to my mitten. Didn't have any dessert for dinner. After dinner went into Taylor's room and studied prose until study hour. Went to class. We were all stupid. Ella is talking to me and I can't write. The five has rung.

Wed. April 18, 1883

Sunday I went to church. Ed wasn't there. A man with white eyes tried to flirt with one of the girls. Saw a girl there with lovely hair, the color of Miltons.[?] Think it made more impression on me than the sermon. I walked to church with Anna. Wrote my sermon in P.M. Was promoted to Miss Skinner's Bible class. Monday Ma Sprague told us we must all pay ten cts. [a] week and take lessons in voice culture from Miss Hewitt Tuesday [40]...

Sharky just came in and asked me to go get her some water.

Tuesday morning took our first lesson in voice culture. Learned to wiggle our fingers and make graceful motions. Voice is much culturated.

Tuesday night Anna and I cornered Ma Sprague and asked if we could go down town to day to do shopping. She said we could if we could get a Senior or Senior Middle to take us. Drew my self up and said "I am a senior middle, Miss Sprague." She said we might go. Anna came up and we wrote on our compositions. Bought ten cents worth of popcorn and lent M. Thayer 2 cents and payed for our voice culture. Anna, Gussie, Ella and myself started for town about nine this A.M. Washed out some hdkfs first. Got me a pair of slippers 2.25 3 1/2 C. Kid 2.00 gloves 6 1/2 Lisle gloves .50 very long wristed, a corset 1.25 collar 12, Maple sugar, Bananas, Oranges, candy & Pickles 84¢.[41] Had a good time. Came home tired and hungry, late to dinner. Miss Chane [?] gave us some and we had dinner for four on little table in dining room. More tomorrow.

---

[40]"Voice culture" would be lessons in speaking with well-modulated tones.

[41]"Kid" gloves were made of leather; "lisle" ones from a smooth cotton.

Thurs. April 19

We get up 15 m. earlier now so we can take voice culture 30 min. in A.M. Miss Hewitt came and taught us to wiggle our wrists. Can see wonderful improvements in my voice already.

Took a German lesson. Herr L. don't know when novel will be here. Studied Latin this noon and went to walk with Nellie Ransom, Anna and Fanny. Found quite a good many little wind-flowers.[42]

Didn't pay attention in Latin. Was drawing Mell Findley's picture. Miss Starke called on me three times to recite and twice didn't know where the place was. I have Anna's, Gussie's Fan's & Mell's pictures drawn on the margin of my Caesar and I'm going to make all the class. Gave my flowers to Miss King when I went to Chemistry. We all had an awful Chem. lesson. Went walking with Anna. We studied and practiced holding our breath. Held mine 80 sec.

Silent hour doesn't begin until 5 anymore. Miss Sprague is reading the "Letters of H. H."* to us. They are very interesting and lively, but contain little real information.

It is five minutes of six. I have some gum. Ella chews it as much as I do and I have to take my chances if I get it at all. Silent hour is over and here she comes with her shawl. She got 10¢ worth of onions yesterday and her breath smells like————————

Friday May 11

Scarlet fever in school.[43] Leta Slocum has it. Great excitement, a great many of the girls are going home. I am worried about Ella, she does take things so and she kissed Leta last night, not knowing, of course. Her throat is so tender that if she gets it it will probably go hard with her. I don't know what to do.

Thurs. May 31

It is the loveliest day imaginable and to morrow the 1st of June!!! Three weeks from today is commencement! The scarlet fever scare is over. Leta

---

[42]"Wind-flower" was an anemone, one of the crowfoot family.

[43]"Scarlet fever" was a very contagious infection with a red rash, inflamed throat, nose and mouth. It is a complication of strep throat, and in the days before antibiotics, could be fatal or lead to heart problems.

is almost well. Over half of the girls went home, Ella among them, so I am alone. A great many have come back again and more come every day. It rained all day yesterday. Anna and I went out in the yard to write letters and watch the procession go to decorate. I wrote a letter to Martha and didn't see much of a procession. Also wrote a letter to Marmie. She is lonesome. This morning got up a little while after the hour bell and tried to do "Trig." examples until breakfast.

Fan stayed all night with me. Set right beside my adored Miss King at table. Worked trig until chapel. Didn't have anything to report for handed in my "May morn in Venice." Miss Sprague changed the time of trig so now I have two divisions for it before recitation. Studied Caesar this noon and played with Duke. We got him to chase us. Came up stairs and Fan & I showed each other how we walked.

Talked to Edith Mizner. She says Miss King wanted her & me to read our Alexander essays the eve before commencement. She declined. They are going to have a little entertainment that evening. I am to be Cleopatra. Had a pretty good Caesar lesson. Drew pictures of children and owls in the class. Had a horrid Chemistry lesson.

Went to walk with Anna. We went down to the bridge, talked to some little boys who were fishing, came back, picked some flowers, saw the "irresistible" of course.

"Friend Maud" was just in.

Anna and I took our time to it and when we got back were informed that silent hour had begun. We were so hungry that we went in and teased Miss Chamberlain for something to eat. She gave us each a large slice of bread and butter and a little piece of meat. Went around on the back doorstep and ate it. Miss Sprague was down town so didn't go into silent hour. Went to my room and soaked my head with camphor for head-ache and here I am.[44] Most time for supper. The birds are singing in to the loveliest day.

Supper bell.

Friday, June 1st

Silent hour. Just ten minutes before supper. A lovely, lovely day. Last night Anna came up and stayed through both study hours. Emma Kuhl came up and read a letter from a Mr. Lax. She expects him here next

---

[44]Camphor, a compound from the camphor tree, has been used since the 1600s as a mild painkiller and liniment.

Wednesday. She gave us a slice of cake. We didn't study at all. We were so tired and my head ached so we lay down on the bed and pretended to go to sleep. Demonstrated to Anna by means of its shadow the reason why every one steps on my heels. We had a good time playing circus. I would toss Anna up on my feet and she would fall with her whole weight on the bed. The bed groaned all night.

I smell fried potatoes.

Fan stayed with me all night. Looked at the stars. I got up at five this morn and had my domestic work all done when the rising bell rang. Copied my part as Cleopatra and did room work before breakfast.

After breakfast, Anna and I walked down to the gate and back. Studied on Trig. Miss Chamberlain had me build a fire in room B. Paid my wash bill and Ella's too. Reported for being late to silent hour in Chapel. Anna & I sat together and laughed all through chapel. Mizner came in and worked Trig second division. At noon we studied Latin as usual.——Maud just came in and borrowed glycerine.[45]

Anna & Gussie are going home with Lizzie Anderson to spend next Wednesday. Ironed after school. Crocheted and wound yarn. Supper bell.

Monday June 4.

Rose at five this morning and rewrote my "Castles in Spain." I had my domestic work done before the hour bell. Laughed a good deal in chapel at Help-and-Comfort's sermon. Am reading in German "Die Müfler ons [illeg.]" It is very warm to night and the mosquitos are very thick. Had a bad Trig. lesson as usual. Miss King told a good story at dinner of how she dreamed out a story which she wrote for a literary paper. It was really wonderful. After dinner studied Latin with Help-and-Comfort.

Went to walk alone, carried "Shirley" for company. Made the acquaintance of a little boy whose first name is "Freddie." A nice child. He came over in the yard and we picked flowers to gether. He seemed very fond of flowers and birds and seemed to think the flowers and birds at home in his own yard were best of all. I left him with his two hands as full as they could be and still searching for more. Fought 'squitos all during first half of silent hour. I hope Miss Sprague will soon finish Hawthorne's note book. Here is a memento it tells of suffering too deep for words.

---

[45]Glycerine was used as a solvent or cleaner.

Berrien Springs
June 27 / 83

Well, I'll be pegged if I dindent get ready for Niles this morning and sit around with my things on for nearly an hour and wait for it to stop raining. But it still continues to pour.

Thursday
June 28—1883

Well, its still pouring and shows no signs of letting up. I sent a letter to Anna this morning. Pa and I went to Niles yesterday. It poured down the last half of the way home. Got one tooth pulled and one filled. Took dinner with Aunt Ellie and afterwards went over to Aunt Julias and Hetty's. Daisy wants me to go to Chicago with her next Tuesday. Guess I will and stay until Friday. Paddled down town this A.M. to mail Anna's letter. Saw lots of men. Don't believe its ever going to stop raining. This is the 4th day it has poured.

Wirt and Graham are here, so is Mollie. Commencement passed off with much gusto. The night before, I read my musical composition and Miss Skinner kissed me. I also took part as Cleopatra. We had our Clio feast on the cake Bert sent. Wed. night I met Geo. Stanton and was invited to ride with Anna & Gussie to the depot.

Next day we had a good time. Got our tintypes taken. Mr. Stanton gave me an elegant bouquet and I lost my tintypes. Chas. Whetstone found me at the depot and trotted me in to Jude. We talked incessantly until we got to Buchanan. Every one looked then smiled and looked and smiled again. All the family including Cousin Bob met us at the depot, the latter immediately asked us to go horse-back riding, but we concluded to wait awhile.

I am going to study Botany this summer. Oh I wonder if you are!

July 29.

Just finished a letter to Harry. Belle is here writing to her mother. We have been reading Jude's Journal. Belle has been here almost a week. Rose at 8 o.c. this A.M. Jude & Belle went to church. I didn't. Jule came in after church. We, Belle, Jude & I read aloud from St. Nick and went buggy riding this eve.; drove our new horse, Fan. We want to go to Sister Lakes in a week. Belle wants us to go to Chicago with her and make a visit before school begins. I was in Chicago a week near 1st of July, stayed at Marthas. Bob has a friend from C., Mr. Miller visiting him. It is 15 of 11.

1884
January 8—

Got back to Seminary yesterday noon; was late on account of storm. Lots of fun at home. New Years calls, dance, etc.

Have been feasting since my return. Minnie More stayed all night here last night—three in a bed. Am blue to night. Gus is getting ready for bed. Fan is writing, Anna is off with the girls. Oh dear, it is oh such cold weather, snow awfully deep. Reported for study-hour this morning. Lessons middling. May Johnson threatens to go home, will be one less senior. Tried to reason with her, couldn't. Am going to read "Sultier lends."

Sund. Feb. 10, 1884

My Dear:
Oh, I feel so melancholy to night. What am I good for anyway? Weak miserable fool, never know my own mind. Shall I drift on this way forever? One day planning wonderful things and the next dashing all the bright castles to ruins. It is silent hour now and I have been staring out of the window at the grey sky indulging in sweet melancholy dreams. I guess I am on the road to home-sickness. Shall I be a physician and lead a noble life relieving suffering and doing good? Or shall I do as so many women do, drift on in the old way, marry if the chance is presented and if not living a lonely life for others. No, I will not be so commonplace and yet I fear I haven't the stern perseverance and concentration of all objects to become a truly noble physician. Oh, I don't know what to do. If I was only sure I was fitted for a M.D. I would not hesitate a moment but to make a mistake my whole life would be unbearable. Went to church this morning, the text was "That thou doest do quickly," appropriate for me wasn't [it]? What would you advise me to do? I wish I knew.

We are all going down to church to night. The five has rung. I must stop, dear.

Mond. February 11 1884

My Dear:
Finished "Hypatia"* yesterday, like it although it ends with horrors. The girls are studying Virgil diligently and I ought to be doing likewise. A letter from Jude tonight.

I Recited in Arithmetic to day. Miss Sprague gave out subjects for essays: "Trailing Arbutus or any flower," "A short story-scene Venice or Rome"
"The Skeleton"
"Waiting"
"Queen Elizabeth"
"Marie Stuart"
"Graduates and What then?"
are to choose our own.

Went down town to night in the big sleigh. Horrible weather, sleet and rain. Made bread to night.

Cousin Rob is dead.

Tuesday 12.

My Dear:

Whoever you are but it is so much more interesting to address my scribblings to someone. A cold rainy day turns to ice as soon as it falls, slippery out, I guess. Quite an exciting day: down town three runaways, church burned down and a boy killed.

Chose the short story for my essay.

Wish Fan wouldn't be quite so affectionate, between you and me, my dear unknown. I hate to be kissed by any but a very few. Fan is always saying how lovely I am and how she adores me. She thinks she means it, poor child. She is always asking me if I love her and I won't tell her yes, for I don't believe I do. I don't love many people. I am too fickle I suppose. Fan makes me tired sometimes. What treason I am writing against my roommate, but I know, dear, that you will never divulge any of the things I tell you. Have been reading "Life for a Life" to night, and that accounts for my mode of writing. Have been studying my Schiller to night, a lesson to morrow. The girls are all invited out to dinner and I will have the whole day to myself. Got Scribner with "Fair Barbarian"* out of Library to day.

Noon
Tuesday Feb. 19

My Dear:

I am so glad to tell you that at last my destiny is decided. I came to a firm decision Monday, Feb. 18, 1884 at about 2-30 P.M. I <u>am</u> going to be a

Physician. It will be a noble life-work to devote myself to saving lives. It is for two years now that I have been wavering between two opinions and it is a relief to have it settled. One cannot live long at best and surely a short life full of usefulness is to be chosen rather than a long life of worldly pleasure and of no good to any but perhaps a very few.

May I never falter or turn back from this on

Monday Feb. 25

My Dear:

Silent hour time. I have but 5 minutes before supper. Began "Unknown to History" this silent hour am reading "Judith Shakespeare" in Harpers.

The past week has been quite eventful. Tuesday Aunt Em came. Like her immensely. She takes delight in making startling statements which greatly shock Misses King & Sprague. We four went down town Wednesday with her, had our tintypes taken—a jolly time. Friday eve had a sleigh ride and candy pull. It being the 22nd, half holiday. Aunt Em came up from church yesterday and stayed the afternoon, took her departure from Kal. this morning, at least she is suspected to have done so.

Elocution at Academy to night, don't know whether Annie Laurie and I will go or not. Took a walk with Emma Kuhl the other day, planned the plot for my Venetian tale.

Supper bell—. . . . .

March 9.

Everybody abuses me. her I will not stand. Oh how I hate Miss King. She has insulted me and I will not forget it very soon, either. I want to go home and I will with just a little more provocation. I can't and won't stand it to be snubbed in this style. I wrote a terrible letter to Jude to day and she, Miss King, dared to write on my last Sundays sermon and ask me if I was a Christian. Oh, the miserable viper. I could have stood it if she hadn't done it before all the girls, and to have them remark upon it was unbearable. Oh, I will show her that I know when I am insulted. I haven't treated her decently since. Oh to be free from this place and its diabolical inhabitants. Oh for a good free ride behind Charlie. Oh for freedom and home, where somebody loves me a little. Two more wretched Sundays to spend here. I can't stand it. I wrote for Jude to come and see me. All through Mr. Huntings beautiful sermon I sat and thought how I hated her. Oh, I am getting so wicked. Last night we went into Miss

Sprague's room and demanded privileges, got the priv. of entering each others rooms and of not writing sermons next term.

Oh this horribly narrow little Seminary. How long must I endure its petty annoyances and insults, I wonder.

Recd $10 from home last night, am going to hear Thursby to morrow night. Oh what a day this has been.

Silent hour
April 6, 84.

Came back Friday noon; had [a] good time at home. Didn't go to church to day, neither did Anna or Gus.

Went into Miss Sprague's office to read our sermons at her request. Had a good time, no one there. Miss S. gave us each an orange to quiet the rage of hunger. Peeped into the back room. Saw that they do not practice what they preach about neatness. Looked at scrap books and autograph albums, I comfortably seated in an armedchair while Ann wrote the sermon. Ann & I took a walk. Love my new dress. We are to be separated Tuesday or Wednesday. Gus & Anna going on the wing second floor and Fan & I someplace not yet decided upon.

Miss Sprague kept me after composition class to talk about my final essay. Think I shall write on "The Master Waiteth." Suggestive! She was quite complimentary, says that I am deep, that while I am laughing & joking with the girls I have thoughts that they do not or could not understand. Thinks I should go on in a literary way. Poor woman, how she is deceived. Comes from my having such owllike eyes and solemn countenance, I presume. Supper summons me.

April 13 1884
Easter Sunday.

My Dear:
I haven't addressed you for some time, have I.———

Wednesday Annie Laurie and I went down town and had a good time. Fan and I moved to the fourth floor Wednesday. We <u>room</u> there but we <u>live</u> in Anna's room. Miss Wallace is so good to us and lets us go in there whenever we want to. Do you know poor little Gus has been sick again, but I think we have kept her better fed this time. She is better now. Macbeth is to be played by Keane Monday night. We are going, isn't that glorious? Miss Sprague gave her consent without a struggle; although we had letters from home requesting that we might go, we did not need them at all. I don't understand it. Went to church to day. Mr. Hunting preached a lovely Easter sermon. John 20—20. Walked with Fan, quarreled on the way back as usual.

I expected T. L. W. yesterday.[46] He didn't come but a note saying he would come some other day—didn't care much. My work is care of food after dinner and the mail. Stayed in Anna's room all last evening. Miss Wallace told us about opera and theatric. Fan said the other night that the girls were afraid of me. I don't believe it.

What's the matter with the weather? It isn't a bit nice. When are you coming, my dear? Oh hum! It's a dear, nice, weary, wicked old world. Silent hour over.

Mon April 21—

My Dear:

It is the first study hour and as I didn't want to study I thought I would devote a little time to you. I got a letter from Jude to night. She told me something about J. B. that raised my ire to a high pitch. The miserable [illeg.]. If I was a man I would thrash him.

Saturday my box came, clothes all fit nicely. Girls admired them much. Went to church yest.; walked with Miss Hogue—nice little girl. In the afternoon Gus and Anna came up and we boiled eight eggs hard, ate them and threw all the shells on the floor. Made Fan sweep them up. Composed an "Ode to our Mustard bottle" yesterday, began it at dinner while waiting for Miss Keith to say something. Also composed a "Jingle" with references to Starky. Had great fun, made believe to be mad at Annie Laurie because she didn't walk with me as she promised. We settled it after supper in the library. The dear child! She said she loved me better than any one else in school. She is my dearest here.

Edith and I are reading "Troilus and Cresseda." Read the the "Comedy of Errors" before.[47] Argued with Miss Sprague in "Evidence" about the vicarious atonement. She did not answer me satisfactorily at all.

Gus got a letter from Ella last week. She will be married the 14 May and will be in Berrien the 17. Is to be married in light blue satin; didn't think the sample very pretty.

Am reading "Minna von Barnhelm."*

---

[46]Presumably Lee Wilkinson.

[47]*Troilus and Cressida* and *The Comedy of Errors* were both Shakespearean plays, typically included in the kind of liberal arts education Addie was receiving at the Seminary.

April 28—

Have lost the outline to my essay. Can't write on it anyway. In the dumps. Got a letter from Jude to night, also one from George. Wish I was home. Daisy to be married 30th of June. Will be there if I live through the essay.

April 30

My dear: It has been a true April day, showery and warm. Its time we had some April weather. Wrote on my essay about all day, and only got about two pages of scratch block. Anna was up all afternoon, busy with her essay. Walked with her just before silent hour—hot!

Mr. Hunting talked to the school this evening about building. As we were going out of the chapel Miss Sprague said he wanted to see me in the parlor. Perhaps you can imagine my consternation, and yet I need talking to badly enough. I told Miss Sprague that I didn't want to. And she said he wanted to talk to all of our class, so I got Edith & Emma and we went. Bert had had her talk. He was lovely. Didn't ask embarassing questions but just talked himself, urging us to be Christians. What is it to be a Christian anyway, do you know? Is it to believe on Christ? I do, of course, there is nothing else to believe. I pray to God and try to do right—generally. I ask him to help me, and yet I don't believe I am a Christian. I am too—weak minded, to come out boldly and let people know that I am trying. Yes, I who have always prided myself on my strength of mind—blind idiot that I am—haven't enough of it to stand the—well, not exactly sneers of my classmates. This is ridiculous. I vow every day to do differently and yet I always know that I will come out just exactly as I started. I wonder if you have the same difficulty. But no. If you thought you ought to do a thing you would do it, though the heavens fell, or else I have a wrong opinion of you. Help me to keep this good impression.

May 3—1884.

My Dear:

Have got through with Phidias; intend to write on Michael Angelo to night.

It has been a lovely day. Am translating "The Famine" in Hiawatha into German. Have finished Hell (after having spent the whole term there) in Dante and am about to enter "Purgatory." Don't expect to reach "Paradise."[48]

Got up very early this morning, got room work all done and analyzed the "Sanguinary Canudenes" before breakfast. Ann is dieting but goes over to Mr. Humphrey's and fills up between meals. Miss Sprague is flourishing, has been known to help herself five times to beans, seven times to ham, three times to pickles and twice to cake in one day (fact.) All this has been vouched for by a careful observer. Think it a fact worth chronicling.

The baby over the way is howling. Mason just disappeared into the house, which probably accounts for it. Saw him kill a chicken Wednesday.

Read Judith Shakespeare 1st half. Anna is writing on "Longfellow and Evangeline." She gave a minute description of his symptoms in her life. Suggested that she end his life with a verse, something like this:

"He shuffled off this mortal coil
But sprang up tall in heavenly soil"

May 18

5 minutes before lamp bell. Had a spread in Bert's room to night. Cake, pineapple, radishes & dates. Animated discussion afterwards as to good things to eat. Tendency in Bert and Ede to get quite excited. Unanimous decision that dinner to day was gobby, to quote Mat. (Rhetoricals to day.) Em and I too _ethereal_ to care about such a worldly matters as eating. Think it almost a waste of time. Never intend to cook when we keep house. Live on cold victuals.

Stuck on essay. Life as hollow mockery. Stark has been in. Going to keep my lamp.

Fan is cutting her nails, has come to conclusion that if nails were let alone they would grow real long. Gives Susie Chamberlain's as an example of this. She is now impressing persistently on my mind that "moonlight will come again."

May 11—1884

Dear:
Went to church to day. Mr. Hunting didn't preach. A weak kneed minister took his place. Walked with Anna. Wrote a letter home this P.M.

---

[48]All references to Dante Algheri's _The Divine Comedy_.

Are going down to church to night, I guess. Jack Wilk. is married at last.

Sunday May 25.

My dear: Received Cora & Walter's wedding cards yesterday. Very neat and pretty. They are to be married a week from Tuesday, June 3—

Wrote a letter home yesterday and hinted that I would like to attend the wedding. We got our class pins Friday. Very much pleased with them.

Walked to church with Anna to day. Mr. Hunting preached to the "G. A. R." Academy crowded. Missionary meeting to night, subject Siam. Wish I was home.

My essay still drags along its weary length. Miss S. has looked over the first part, mangled it to the best of her ability and has left me what remains to put to gether again. It's worse than a dissected map puzzle. She stuck in some of her own old thoughts, but I scornfully rejected them and was ever so rude as to tell her that I didn't think they were pretty at all. Ah me! What a thing it is to have one's own cherished thoughts taken to pieces and looked at with a microscope and then jammed together again all wrong. It makes life, truly, nothing but one great discord.

My pictures will come Wed. Like them quite well.

Well, Cora and Walter are going to invest in matrimony. I expect Et will go next and then Allie. Fan is already engaged. Oh ye Berrien girls, what are ye coming to? Ella is now Mrs. Louis Walton. My! Jude and I will begin to be looked upon as venerable old maids. Well, well, I suppose we are. Here I am almost 20 and never had a lover.[49] What on earth could I have done with him if I had? he would have been a dead-weight no doubt, and I know I should have hated him. I have always felt and still feel that my life is to be one of single blessedness, for who ever would love me, I should hate and the one I love would hate me. Twas ever thus. You, my confidant, are the only one I have ever loved and you are—a mystery.

[49]To "have a lover" in the nineteenth century meant to have a boyfriend or suitor.

Sunday
June 1—1884

My Dear:

Rejoice with me! I go home Tuesday morning June 3. I am going to attend Walt's wedding. My essay is all done and ready for the final copy. Have all my [illeg.] analyzed but three _ _ _

Yesterday had a fall out with the rest of the class. Was high and mighty all day, went down town with Fan in the afternoon. Ede came to me for an explanation. Told her what [I] thought of her in pretty strong language. Explanations all around; made up.

Walked to church with Edith this morning. Lovely sermon. We are going out to night to a sabbath-school-concert I guess it is.

This P.M. Edith and I went out on Mt. Tom with books and had a lovely time. Squelched a pair of [binies] who dared to offer some of their impudence. They slunk off. We planned great things for the night of commencement which I am to talk up and arrange when at home.

Gussie is sick, poor child.

I must dress for church. . . .

June 2 '84

Going home tomorrow. Have got everything ready to put in my "grip." Oh, I can't wait . . . .

Adeline Eliza Graham,
ca. 1882

Julia "Jude" Graham,
ca. 1885

"Pa"—George Graham, ca. 1880

"Ma"—Mary Bacon (Garrow) Graham, ca. 1890

Adeline and Julia's paternal grandmother, Mary Kimmel Graham, ca. 1880

Adeline and Julia's maternal grandfather, John Garrow, ca. 1880

Adeline and Julia's brother,
William Holmes Graham,
ca. 1880

Adeline and Julia's brother,
Harry Kimmel Graham,
ca. 1880

"Aunt Julia"
—Julia (Graham) Higby,
ca. 1885

"Uncle Nelson"——Nelson Higby,
ca. 1885

"Cousin Bob"—Robert Dougherty,
ca. 1880

"Cousin Martha"—Martha Holmes,
ca. 1885

"Daisy"—Georgiana Loring Holmes,
ca. 1880

*"Et"—Henrietta M. Murdoch,
ca. 1882*

*"George"—George H. Murdoch, Jr.,
ca. 1885*

*"Belle"—Julia's cousin and fellow
homesteader, Belle Graham, ca. 1888*

Downtown Berrien Springs on a winter day in 1878

The village school in Berrien Springs, which Adeline attended, was built in 1873

Adeline Eliza Graham in the fall of 1885

"Lee"—Thomas Lee Wilkinson, Jr., ca. 1880

Julia's Diary

Julia Graham's Kansas Adventure: The Diary of Julia Graham

❧

In September 1885, Julia Graham, Adeline's elder sister, embarked on the greatest adventure in her life: homesteading on the Great Plains. During the next year, this young woman of a proper Victorian family endured blizzards, prairie fires, floods and droughts while she proved up her claim.to land on the Kansas prairie.

Julia was born at the Graham family farm in Berrien Springs, Michigan, on June 20, 1862. She was named for an aunt, Julia (Graham) Higby, her father's sister. She attended St. Mary's Academy at South Bend, Indiana, and Albion College in Albion, Michigan. On September 7, 1885, she and her cousin, twenty-year-old Belle Graham of Buchanan, Michigan, left for Kansas to homestead in Greeley County. Together with three other young women, Laura Rodman of Harper County, Kansas, Mary L. Campbell, and twenty-six-year-old Minnie I. Smith of Niles, Michigan (a cousin of Belle's), they lived in a dugout at the location of the future town of Tribune, then called Chappaqua. They called their dugout the "Palace Hotel" and offered meals and a place to sleep to travelers. The girls organized a club called the "Five Greeley Girls" with the intention of serenading all the newcomers to Greeley. It became successful and soon had a membership of seventeen girls. They organized euchre parties, dancing, ice skating and horseback riding, and they helped found the new church and school. In 1885, at the land office at WaKeeney, Kansas, Julia met a young attorney named Samuel Harlan Kelley, whom she would marry two years later.

Julia Graham was one of the many thousands of Americans who benefited from the Homestead Act of 1862. Passed in 1862, and taking effect January 1, 1863, the Homestead Act was supported by many as a boon for anyone desiring land in the great West. Any citizen, or any alien intending to become a citizen, who was the head of a family and at least twenty-one years old could acquire a farm simply by filing a claim from the vast acres of government land in states such as Kansas. After five years of continuous residence and after making improvements to the land, such as buildings, windmills (for water), barns, fences, and the like, and then paying a registration fee of $26 to $34, a homesteader gained clear title to the property. Homesteaders could file for up to a quarter-section—160 acres—of surveyed land. If homesteaders could not stay the full five years, they could pay $1.25 an acre after six months of residency in order to receive title.

As an unmarried woman of twenty-three when she arrived in Greeley County, Julia Graham had the legal right to acquire land under the Homestead Act. Why she chose to do so in an era when many women refused even to travel without a male escort is not clear. Certainly it was not financial necessity, since her father was a wealthy and influential farmer in Berrien Springs, and her diary makes no mention of any reluctance on his part to support an adult daughter. She was not alone in her adventure, however. Thousands of women homesteaded the Great Plains, either by themselves, with other women, or as part of families. For Julia, part of the reason she chose Kansas was probably because her older brothers William and Harry were living there temporarily. Most likely, Julia thought "roughing it" in the West would be a lark, and despite many privations, her diary shows that she and her women companions had a delightful time.

Greeley County, where Julia arrived in September of 1885, was named for Horace Greeley, the influential editor of the *New York Tribune* in the 1840s and 1850s, who had advised "Go west, young man." Julia took his advice to apply to her and claimed 160 acres in section 14 of his namesake county. The county enjoyed a population explosion by 1886. The 1880 census had found only three whites in the area, all hunting buffalo. The 1885 census found ten, most herding cattle and other livestock. In August of 1885, dozens of people came to settle the county; within four years, there were twenty-six hundred people. Most lived in dugouts, as did Julia and her companions. The autumn was delightful weather, according to the records; the winter was abysmal. The blizzard of 1885–86 was one of the worst on record, with a week of sub-zero temperatures and blowing snow. Thousands of animals died in the storm area, which ran from Montana to Texas. Six people died in Greeley County, most lost in the storm.

The "Greeley Girls" survived the blizzard, as Julia records in her diary. Julia took advantage of the Homestead Act's provision allowing her to purchase the land instead of staying for the five years, and she "proved up" her claim in June 1886, only eight months after her arrival. She left Greeley County in August 1886. On May 4, 1887, she married Samuel Kelley of Scott City, Kansas, at her family home in Berrien Springs. Family members later recorded a story of how Samuel and Julia Graham had met.

> "The four girls built their house so that it stood on a corner of each of their four homesteads, and they only had to stay in it one night a month.
>
> "After they had been there six months they thought they had proved up and got their trunks and everything packed up to go home. Went to the Land Office in WaKeeney where Papa [Samuel Kelley] looked over their papers. He refused to accept them, saying they must stay six weeks longer. They were much discouraged, very homesick and tired of it all, so they stood in a corner of the office by a big oleander tree and cried. Papa heard them saying they hated that young man with the big brown eyes who wouldn't let them go home. They went back to the hotel and Papa suggested to several other young fellows in the office that they go and call on them that evening since they felt so bad. They did and took them to a dance and it just happened that Papa was Mamma's escort."

Julia and Samuel Kelley moved to Scott City immediately after their marriage, then spent four years in St. Joseph, Missouri. In 1893, they moved to Benton Harbor, Michigan, where Samuel worked as a railroad company attorney, and raised three daughters: Mary Adelia (1888), Louise Graham (1890), and Julia Zerilda, or "Daisy" (1891). Julia never enjoyed good health, something apparent even in her sister Addie's diary while they were still in school. In 1900, her failing health forced physicians to "adopt measures that might be considered desperate" to save her life. She went to Chicago on October 1 to undergo surgery, performed two days later, for appendicitis. She died in Chicago on October 8, 1900.

The diary that follows is Julia's record of her adventures in western Kansas. As with Adeline's diary, the entries have been edited with additions only to make meaning clear where needed. Expository footnotes define historical terms and identify people for whom records were available.

Volume 4

September 11, 1885–December 31, 1885

September 11, Friday 1885 at 6.30

Belle + I arrived at Independence Kansas: started from Chicago Thursday noon the 10th left home Monday afternoon the 7th[1]

Kansas
Independence
Tuesday <u>September 15—'85</u>

I have just come from dinner at the Colwell House—and expect to have this afternoon to devote to my Journal and letter writeing we have been so busy since we came that our correspondents have been neglected. We arrived here on Friday eve 6.30 were met at the deapot by Mrs Crawford + Mr Harris took tea at Hotel. Mr + Mrs Spencer called in the eve and invited us to ~~tea~~ 6.0 o'clock dinner next day. Take all our meals at the Hotel. I have met a great many pleasant people Belle has a great many friends here and all vie with each other in making it pleasant for her. Adam and I left home Sept—7. '85 for Buchanan.[2] stayed at Aunt F's all night in morning 6—o'c—started with Uncle John for Chicago.[3] Belle, Minnie + Charley met us at 22 St. shopped awhile there Adam + I went to Lake View to visit Martha spent a pleasant evening. started at 8- next morning for city Met Uncle John + Belle finished shopping spent eve at Minnie Smith Met Asa Mc + other invited company. At 12.30 Thursday said good bye to Charley, Will. S. & Adam on 22 St. and turned our faces toward the "far West."

---

[1]Independence is located in southeast Kansas, about fifteen miles north of the Oklahoma border.

[2]"Adam" is Julia's sister Adeline.

[3]"Aunt F." and "Uncle John" were Belle's parents, Frances and John Graham.

Charley introduced us to James Smith who prooved an agreeable traveling companion. he lunched with us and we dined with him in the car. we took a <u>section</u> in the sleeper,—quite a joke, but we vow secresy on the subject.[4] Were awake when we crossed the Mississ.—River at 1 a.m. It was very star light + the train rumbled slowly over the bridge. ~~as the new moon~~ The morning found us very sea-sick + all that day we suffered volumes

Mr Smith was very kind + helped us to change cars at Kansas City our tickets from there to Independence. were 4.90 from Chicago to Kansas C— 10.50. The expence of a section, we ascertained was 5.00 &.&.

At K. C.—we met Mr Stich and little daughter who went with us the rest of our journey.—I am staying at Mrs Crawford's + takeing meals at the Colwell House. She is very nice + kind to me so are all the people in fact and I am having a very pleasant time. The floods are so bad west of here that the train is not running on the direct rout, so probly will not leave untill Saturday morning for Harper.

Sat for my pictures yesterday. at Al Brown's, 5.00 per doz. Sunday we went to church at the Presbiterian. in afternoon + eve we had 14 calls + water-mellin for refreshments. It is very warm at least it seems so to us but the people here say it is nothing compared to what they have had. We fan generally with one hand and write with the other. We can hardly find anything cool enough to put on. We have had several hard rains here + the mud is dreadful—it is almost as bad [as] banana peeling to step on + almost impossible to get off but the one redeeming feature of the roads they dry off in a half a day + are already getting dusty. We have a delightful breeze all of the time. Bed-bugs are simply awful.[5] I spent a few prescious moments in cracking bout a doz this morning so they wouldent be <u>quite</u> so thick to night still I left hundreds of them walking over the mattress.

Sept. 18—'85
Wednesday

Got a letter from Adam. Mrs. C. and I got our breakfast this morning. she went to the store + I did up the work—Belle came over from Mrs. Spencer + we decided to lunch instead of going to the Hotel went down town.

---

[4]"Section" here referred to the berth in the railroad sleeping car, but also to a 640-acre "section" of land that Julia hoped to acquire.

[5]"Bed-bugs" are a wingless, bloodsucking insect which infests houses and particularly beds.

~~got~~—rested made calls—went out for the afternoon, eve. + all night. Belle got a letter from Sedan inviteing us to visit there as soon as convenient for us.[6] We had a call last eve from Mr McDonald, after which went to a church social and spent a very pleasant eve.

Thursday 17. 85

Got home from Mrs Calks where we spent the night. Made call untill noon got home here in time for a lunch, then Bub + I wrote letters.

Took tea at the hotel. Bub went rideing with Mr McDonleigh— expected a call The Dr. Turner called + Mrs. C. and I went rideing with him in the eve but "he wasent himself"—(joke) we three, B—, Mrs. C. + I sat + talked it all over untill after 12 o.c.

Friday 18—85 September.

We got breakfast at Mrs C's Belle + I did the work + packing. Got dinner for Mrs. C at 2 -o-c Went to the Fair in a Barouche with Mrs Spencer + Mrs. C.[7]—Bub + I had a good time it was about two miles out on the prairie. The grandstand was in the sun with no top and was very warm pumpkins were very large—painting display was much better than I expected to see. met a great many people—bummed around—got home in good season were invited to Mrs S- to tea with other company. Went down town in the eve—packed untill late.

Saturday 19. -85

Rose up at 4.30 made preparations for our journey were at the deapot at 6.30 on our way to Elk Falls.[8] Took breakfast there at 8.30. At 9- took the stage with two other gentlemen besides the driver for Sedan—a distance of 25 miles over the worst roads immagionable—all solid rock in some places + most of the way our little ponies wound in + out or climbed over the rocks as best they could, leaving the stage to jolt along it best could + keep right side up. We were dreadfully shaken up + feel as tho we had

---

[6]"Sedan" is the county seat of Chatauqua County, in the southeast portion of the state, not far west of Independence.

[7]A "barouche" was a four-wheeled carriage with the driver's seat in front, two double seats inside facing each other, and a folding top.

[8]Elk Falls is a small town in southeast Kansas.

been rideing horseback for weeks—we arrived here 1.30 all were very glad to see us. A little dinner party of Michigan people were waiting us 3 young gents are stopping here also in a home dramatic play "A Soldier of Fortune." Mr Dod and Mr Barnes also little Fred—we went to the theater in the eve + saw them play.

Very pleasant. Our trunks have not come yet, so we stayed from Church and I wrote letters to Adam + Lee + Mrs Crawford are so tired, took a sleep in the afternoon went to church in the evening.

Monday 21—85

We have been helping Mrs M. with the work. it is very warm. we have all the peaches we can eat + they are very nice. Mrs. Bins + Nannie came in this morning to talk of a picnic for tomorrow down in the nation. They stayed to dinner. My trunks came this afternoon but Belle's will not be here untill to morrow. I have been trying to find something to fit her so she can have a change. she is now looking very sweet in my blue dress. After tea Belle + I went down town. Stanley spent the evening with us and we sat out on the rocks in the moonlight talking over old times. The Misses Shipley and Sayre called in the afternoon.

Tuesday 22—'85

We started this morning on what the settlers here call a "jant" but what northerners would call a picnic. We at 9 o-clock started in two lumber wagons + two carriages. our wagon had hoops + a genuine canvas top + gipsy rig. 8 of us on the three seats, but the roads were simply Kansas— such mud, rocks, high stony hills + jumping-off places, it had never before been my of misfortune to witness.

We had such a jolly time. went six miles into the Indian Territory after leaving the state.[9] we passed near Artillery Mound + foarded [forded] the big Cana [Caney]. We did not stop our wagons until 2 o-c + then found a pretty place to camp on the bank of said river.

Near Conners Stanley shot two birds + we had them cooked on sticks. Belle and M. Sayre went in waiding to the great ammusement of the rest of us. in their haste to be ready for the wagon, they were obliged

[9]"Indian Territory" referred to present-day Oklahoma. In the nineteenth century, Oklahoma was territory set aside for occupation by various Indian tribes driven out of the southeast United States in the 1830s.

to put on their shoes and carry their stockings in their hats. We came home a different road + a very dangerous foard We drove quite a way in the stream with the water to the bottom of the wagon-box. The carriages being lower were partly filled, but after much excitement all got safely through + up the long rocky hill.

We stopped at the famous Chautauqua Springs.[10] After refreshing ourselves with the water, we ate water melons + played around for nearly an hour. Got home in Sedan at 8.30 We had just gotten in the house + read our letters when a tramping was heard out side + a large Surprise party of young people came in arrayed in party attire, all strangers to us, and spent the evening we were rather tired but let them take us as they found us. Went into it + had a jolly time. We took time to in the middle of the eve to steal into the kitchen one at a time + to refresh ourselves with our supper. We did have a lovely time, retired, quite tired, at 11.30. I got two letters from Adam. We also heard from Mrs C. We rode about 45 miles in all.

Wednesday 23—'85

We feel quite fresh after the "jant" of yesterday. Belle + I took old Prince + drove over to Mrs Bins Mad[e] a very pleasant call. Stanley thought if not too busy he would be up to take us a horse-back ride but he did not come. We took a nap, dressed + called upon Misses Sayre + Shipley. More letters in the eve. Also called on Merrile, got a letter from Adam the third in two days.

Thursday 24. '85

Belle + I had old Prince in the carriage and drove to Mrs Stars after appels. when we were turning around the buggy box got loose + one side came off but we fixed it up + got home in safety. Went to a Progressive Euchere party at Mrs Davis.

Friday—Made a few calls. the Stars, Bins and Merrills were here to dinner. In the eve we went to a euchere party at Mrs Turners.

Saturday—We helped Mrs M with the work I painted. A surprise euchere party on us in the evening.

Sunday—Mrs M + I went to Church. B was not feeling well—so did not go. Stanley took dinner + spent afternoon and eve. Mrs. Davis and Lyster called.

---

[10]"Chautauqua Springs" lies just north of the Oklahoma border.

Monday 28—85

We did house-work all morning. Rosa went to Topeka for a week. I painted all afternoon. B + I went down town shopping got letter from Adam. rained hard this afternoon + all eve. B + I went to town.

Tuesday 29—85

Showery this morning. We helped do house-work and painted. This afternoon Craig took us all over to Mrs Bin's. B + I stayed all night.

Wednesday 30– 85

We did a lot of fancy-work. Mrs. Bin + Nannie are very pleasant—they have a nice piano + I practised at the "Wilde Waves" and finished my lamberquin for Mrs Matthews.[11] After dinner Craig came after us. I had a very pleasant time. all around learned a new receipt for pie-crust.[12] It is very windy today and smokey, but warm.

October 1. '85

Thursday—Painted. Were all invited to dinner at Mrs Merrill's. B did not go but the rest of us did and had a lovely time. In afternoon finished up our calls. Mrs. Bin and Nannie came + we talked up our scheme for the winter. Wrote to Adam.

Friday 2 '85

We started this morning at 10.15 with Craig in the lumber wagon with our three trunks for Moline only 25 miles. The country is very beautiful + hazy. We had a nice lunch + stopped near a farm house for water + refreshment. Got in Moline at 4- o-c. Went to the "Southwestern Hotel" a little room with turkey red calico curtains. The sun shineing in on them with such a dazzeling effect that we retreated to the parlor. from there we started out + in a few minutes did the town. This is the most civilized place we have been in for some time. for two weeks we have been 25 miles off of a railroad. at the welcome sound of the supper bell we

[11]"Lamberquin" meaning lambrequin, a piece of drapery hanging from a shelf or from the casing above a window.

[12]"Receipt" is the nineteenth-century term for recipe.

repaired to the dining room + partook of hotel fare with an appetite whet-
ted by long fasting which truly does justice to our returning health.—a
scene with the tall dark man.— we threaten to supply ourselves with
insect -powder. We sit at our little stand + write letters + tell fortunes
untill late. Both are dreading to be the first to retire + be the food for the
countless number of lean + hungry bed-bugs that were disclosed to our
view on examining the abode of rest. **** We are rather tired after our ride
+ conclude that rest is sweet, bugs or no bugs.

Saturday Oct– 3– 85

Took breakfast and started for the train which was due 8.15. Ticket from
Moline to Wellington 2.00 hack + trunk .50 c.[13] Got into W. at 11.45 found
Mr. Dye + family expecting us. They are very pleasant people. after dinner we went down and saw the town it has from between 7 + 8000 inhabitants its the nicest + most civilized place we have been in since we came
to Kansas. in the eve Dr. Burton called—he is an interesting young widdower with two bright children.

Sunday 4. '85

Very cold nights + mornings but warm + very windy during the day. We
went to the Presbiterrain Church. Mr. and Mrs. Dye are members of the
same. After 2 -o-clock dinner retired to our room to nap, and write letters.
We talk over with Mr. D the prospects of taking up a claim. We think that
we are in every town. B- has made a deep and lasting impression on this
one we fear. We went to church this eve with our party. all took a lunch
of bread + milk before retireing.

Monday 5– October–

Belle + I walked down town to mail a letter. after dinner recd- calls and
went down to see the town stopped at Mr. D-'s office. Miss H. went with
us + we went through the court -house, which is a very fine affair. Mr.
Wallace came in + we had a 4 hand game of euchere until late. also told
fortunes. We seem to have quite a reputation in that line. This has been a
lovely day but very cold in the morning and evening.

---

[13]A "hack" was a nineteenth-century version of a taxicab.

Tuesday 6– '85.

Last night was the first frost that Kansas had this fall. Went to town made calls. We took a lovely ride with Mrs Maggaird to Piety Hill, Saints Rest + saw the most of Wellington. Had calls when we got home. played euchere in the evening.

Wednesday 7–85.

Started at 11.40 for Harper fair from W $1.06. This after noon Mr. Walton, Ella + Jessie + we took a lovely ride over Harper. went to the fair grounds. Spent the eve at Jessie's.

Thursday 8. '85

We all went down town this morning. I mailed a letter + picture to Adam. Got weighed—weighed 122 1/2. Belle 120 Ella 119 1/2. Had calls at noon + evening.

We spent the day at Jessie's and part of the eve at home visiting.

Yesterday I mailed a letter = $4.00 to A.H. Abbott's 50. Madison. Chicago for tools and brass for Repoussee work.[14] A Kansas zephyr took the chimbney off of the house while we were at dinner.[15] Got letters from Adam and Lee to day. This evening played whist it is warm + we wore our lawn dresses but the wind + sand blow very hard.

Sunday.11. 85

Threatened rain + blew dreadfull. so we did not go to Church—but stayed home + wrote letters to Adam + Mrs. Crawford.

---

[14]"Repoussee" meaning repoussé; decorating metal by hammering a design on the reverse side.

[15]"A Kansas zephyr": a zephyr is a soft gentle breeze. There is seldom such a thing as a true zephyr in Kansas, where the wind comes sweeping off the Rockies down the plains.

Wednesday 14. '85

Belle did not go to Anthony as she intended. it is quite pleasant + warm.

Monday + Tuesday was so cold + windy that we wore our winter cloaks. painted crotcheted, had calls, ducks for dinner + Mr Hackley the gentleman that says !! <u>but</u> !! This eve I went with Belle to practis singing at Mrs Moffit's + I think I have secured a pupil. I got a letter from Adam + Bob's picture, also brass and tools for hammering. Wrote to Adam.

Thursday 15—1885

It is very warm to day Belle + I wore thin white and were uncomfortably warm. Jessie came up + spent the day. calls in the afternoon. B. + I went to Moffits again to sing.

Friday 16, October

"We toiled <u>on,</u> and <u>on.</u>" B. + I started about 8.30 + walked the town over in search of a boarding place where we might at last settle down + feel at home but all of our efforts were fruitless. We felt very blue + discouraged + spent the day at Jessie's we were offered board + rooms at $5.00 a week but it's too much with our washing, + piano rent. the ammount it would make ~~by~~ in 9 mo. seemed enormous + we gave it up. Jessie went with us in the afternoon as our last resort to Mr Warrens. The clouds immediately showed up their silver lineing to a good advantage + the light that broke over our clouded pathway was at first dazzeling + left us speechless with Joy. Evry thing worked like the last chapter to a novel We walked in + were introduced, made known our errand the lady was ready to accomidate us, + walking across the parlor threw open the folding doors + shewed us a lovely parlor bedroom 1st floor, which is to be our own at $3.00 a week—including board + piano rent. We went down town in the afternoon with Jessie visited Mr Cs office + other places of interest got home about 8.30 Mr. W. taught us to play "<u>Blue Pete</u>."[16]

Saturday 17. 85

Another lovely day Mr. W. has gone off for a week on a business trip. B. Ella. Baby + myself went down town shopping. We bought rugs, + carpet + made it in the eve. as it threatened rain so that we could not go to choir

---

[16]"Blue Pete" was probably a card game.

meeting. called at Jessie, got letter from Adam + postal from Abbott's. had a call in the afternoon Friday I weighed 125 lbs. gained 2 1/2 since I came to Harper.

<u>Sunday 18., 85</u>

Raining hard, cold and windy could not go any place. packed up our trunks to move to morrow. wrote to Adam. Mr C. + Jessie came up

October
<u>Monday 19. 1885</u>

We got our trunks off at noon but did not get them until eve. Some missunderstanding, I suppose. took dinner + supper in our new home. Ella wants us to spend the nights with her while Mr. W. is away. she is cleaning house. we sewed carpet all eve.

<u>Tuesday 20. 85</u>

We unpacked + arranged our room. Took dinner + supper here + spent the night at Ellas. it is <u>very</u> cold. got the curtains made.

<u>Wednesday 21—'85.</u>

The ice is nearly an inch thick in the rain-barrel.[17] We got down from Ellas at 8.30 I went to hammering brass + kept at it all day. B- practised and gave a music lesson I got a letter from Lee. spent the night at Ellas + took tea there.

<u>Thursday 22 '85.</u>

Got back from Ellas at 9 o-clock. both went to writing letters. wrote to Adam + Lee. went to Mrs Moffits after scholars, found one at Mrs Clark's, Mrs Dickson at the Eagle House. Got letter + picture from Adam.

---

[17]A "rain barrel" was a wooden barrel often placed at the end of a roof or downspout to catch rain water for washing or bathing.

<u>Friday 23. 85</u>

I hammered brass this morning until noon finished the head, it is the best I have done yet. went to see Mrs Dickson at the Eagle House in regard to takeing lessons, but was not successful. walked untill dark with no better. but I think . . . I lost nothing by advertising my work. we five girls did fancy work this eve while we visited + got better accuainted. I found time to practis some but was very tired after my walk. It is very warm + lovely to day + the birds are singing.

<u>Saturday 24.—85</u>

Warm + pleasant this morning I found time for a good practis besides hammering brass. Very cloudy this afternoon + we decide not to call. B gives a lesson + I call for went to Ella's it is getting dark + raining hard the lightning is very bright. Too teachers with their long slickers (gossamerrs) fluttering in the wind, the rain pouring in torrents on their sun umberellas + running into their shoes, but they "toiled on + on" for more than a mile. they were not discouraged. (Oh No, + they smiled at each other as they were heard to murmer "Ah, this is Kansas.") A hot supper awaited the weary pilgrims + they were soon in dry clothing.

I got a letter from Abbott's. B. got one from Will, + the excitement was all most too much for her frail nature. she is now lying on the bed wrapped in her shall [shawl] (for the nights are cool) while her face shines with surpressed emotion. While I take up my pen + endeavor to settle the boy for her, which together we do to our satisfaction. a dance next Thursday eve.

<u>Sunday, October, 25.—85.</u>

Very pleasant + warm. we went to the Christian Church this morning. Went to Church this eve with Mr. [George B.] Campbell + Miss Mollie

<u>Monday 26—1885</u>

At 8.30 B + I started out + made a few business calls. Went to Ella's, she went down town with us. all stopped at Jessies. This is a lovely day + for weeks we have not worn wraps everything is like an eastern May morning. Ella went with us + we made 6 calls this afternoon. B trimmed my black hat with a canary colored silk h[an]dk[erchie]fs—+ and it looks very stylush.

October
Wednesday, 28.—85.

This is Belle's birthday. we dident do very much. Went to Ella's + Jessies. Got our home letters.

Thursday 30, 85.

This day we painted + practised. after—dinner lay down to rest up for the ball this eve. Mr C. + Jessie came for us to ride + we went all afternoon to his farm + around the country had a lovely time. We limbered up after tea by waltzing in the parlor. Hooper + Ella danced a quadrille for our bene-fit. Mr Walton + Campbell came after us + we went with the two family's and had a lovely time. we met ever so many nice young people, + danced nearly every set. came home at the intermission 12. o-clock. Mr C. told us while we were rideing of the great scheme he had for our claims if we wished to take one and we are quite wrought up on the subject.

Saturday 31—85.

Practised, did our mending, received calls. Went to Ella's + all went down town. called at Jessie's. went to Moffitts + B resigned her position as organist for the sufferage entertainment.[18] Mollie C. went with us. I got a letter from Adam, a paper from Bob, + letter from Abbotts. Yesterday wrote a business letter to Pa about a Claim. This eve went to choir meet-ing. were to tired to go the rink with the girls. This is Halloween B + I invested in chocolate + pulverised sugar, which we partook of during the eve + imagined it was caromele.[19] when the three girls got home we sat up until 1/4 of 12—told stories, + fortunes + spent a very pleasant evening.

November 1st, 85.

Very pleasant and warm to day. B went to Church and played in the choir as is her want. I did not feel like it but lay down instead. we wrote letters.

---

[18]"Sufferage" meaning suffrage, or the right to vote. Belle was apparently pianist for either a suffrage society or a series of meetings where supporters attempted to convince voters to grant women the vote in state elections.

[19]"Pulverised" sugar was probably powdered sugar; "caromele" was caramel, a firm, chewy, brown sugar candy.

had a lovely dinner at 2.30. in the eve went to Church with Mollie. she + the Miss Bucks came home with us + called.

Nov 2. Monday 85

B. has the tooth ache and is feeling badly. I wrote to Adam + took the letters to the office. after dinner I took B to the dentists + after taking both either and cloroform, she had it extracted.[20] Dr Finch presided with his moustache + made me think of Dr Fox at home. it took all afternoon to have it out + cost $1.00. It is eve. B's in bed + to ammuse her I have been reading "Enoch Arden" and "Maude."[21] I got a nice letter from Harry to day and an express package of art materials from Abbotts. I fixed a frame for my picture + worked on my fringe. Also practised my exercises good. went to Jessie's.

Tuesday
November 3 85. ~~Wednesday~~

This day was particulary noted by B's having an original thought, but after enjoying it by herself half the eve nothing would induce her to ~~tell~~ part with it for an instant + it is dead to the world.

November 17, '85

Tuesday—Belle and I have been staying with Ella since Thursday afternoon. Mr W. has been on a hunt + Bessie was away. they both came home yesterday + we are staying over to day to help eat up the game. we were down to Jessie's this morning. the weather for a week has been lovely + warm. we ware no wraps + carry our parasols.[22] Wednesday 4th we started for Greeley Co with Mr Campbell his sister Mollie and Laura Rodman from Anthony. I never had a more delightful trip I don't think. we had 35 m[iles]. to go overland accross the prairie from Syracuse ~~from~~ to Chappaqua our new town. we had two double carriages + 4 in a carriage. we stopped an hour for dinner + made coffee. The plain was perfectly level + we dident see a tree from the time we started untill we got

---

[20]"Either and cloroform" were ether and chloroform, two common anesthetics of the nineteenth century.

[21]*Enoch Arden* and *Maude* were poems by Alfred, Lord Tennyson.

[22]"Wraps" being outer garments such as coats and cloaks.

back. We saw droves of wilde horses + antelope, one bear + a wolf. we stopped where three dugouts constituted the town.[23] 6 cow-boys were there preempting + helped to make it very pleasant for us. we stayed two nights there. at night we would take our lantern + climb up the ladder to the roof of the dugout. one old man did the cooking with the assistance of "the widdow" who made one of our party. we got land within a mile from the future town, Chappaqua. We made our improvements that is, started a well + threw up the foundation to our dugout. Monday morning we again started accross the plains for Syracuse. The boys brough[t] out their guns for us to shoot at mark. I got kicked in the head by a Colts revolver, but was very successful in hitting the mark.[24] the boys all crowded around us when we started + seemed very sorry. we were the first ladies, except one that had ever been in the town. we played euchere a greateel [great deal] + at Syracuse met to young gentelmen, Mr Saunders and Mr W. Larkins they were also very good to us. we were away from home untill the next Tuesday nearly a week. I have written several business letters to Pa, sent him a map of the township + a little bottle of soil from my land. Last Sunday we were invited down to Jessies to help eat Turkey + mince pie. Last eve we land owners of Greeley C.[ounty] had a meeting in Mr. C's office to talk business. I wrote to Harry Sunday sent pictures to him + Etta. wrote to Abbott's + answered two advertisments.

November 18. 85

I did not get my letter from home. finished my shirt. this eve after tea B + I went to town + invested in popcorn + H. nuts. came back + we girls had a good time dancing untill after 11. o-c it has been a lovely day.

Thursday 19, 85

I have been writeing off receipts to be used on our claim. wiped the dishes for May. I have a very bad cold just now wrote to Adam to day. it is very warm + pleasant. This eve we spent at Mrs. Thomsons, took tea +

---

[23]"Dugouts" are shelters dug into the ground, with log or sod walls and a sod roof. Since so few trees were available to use for lumber, most early settlers' houses were sod dugouts.

[24]"Colts revolver" was a handgun with a multichambered cylinder for bullets that revolved, enabling the shooter to shoot five or six shots in a row. It was invented and named by Samuel Colt in 1835.

stayed all night. had a very pleasant time. got a letter from Adam. very pleasant and warm.

Friday November 20—85

Left Mrs T's at 10:30. Went to Ella's for morning call then to Jessies. We painted this afternoon. I finished Jessie's pin-cushion. Just before tea we went down town for a walk. Wrote letters in the evening. So warm today, little boys were barefoot and men went in their shirt sleeves.

Saturday 21. 1885

Very pleasant but windy + dusty. B. + I made dough-nuts for May had good success with them. We hammered brass. Graham C came in the afternoon to say company would come in the eve. We purchased appels for refreshments. went to Ella's a little while she invited us to take Thanksgiving dinner with her. Mrs. Share Glenn Lacure + Molle Campbell spent the eve. with us. had a good time playing euchere, poker, + music. They did not go untill 1/4 of 2 o'clock. I got a letter from Adam and a check from Pa of $100.00.

Sunday 22—85

We did not breakfast untill 10 o'clock. cloudy + windy. stayed home + wrote to Adam. Just before tea we went to Jessies for a walk. In eve wrote letter + read.

Tuesday 24, 85

We went to Mrs Thomsons after tea. Grace had a little party + wanted Belle to play for them to dance. Mr T. was away from home so Mrs T. wanted B for company. had a very pleasant time. in the morning we went to Ella's + she wanted a cake made for Thanksgiving so B. made it with some small help from myself. we then got to Warrens for dinner

Wednesday 25. 85.

a lovely day. Mollie C came up spent eve + stayed all night all slept in our big feather-bed[25]

---

[25] A feather bed is a bed with a mattress stuffed with goose, duck or chicken feathers, noted for its comfort, softness and warmth.

Thursday 26. 85

This day is Thanksgiving for the first time in weeks it is storming. I has rained a cold wet rain all day, + is very dismall. Mollie C went home + B + I proceeded to dress. got started for union services at the Christian Church where B was to play. got as far as Jessies were so wet + cold thinking it would not be prudent as damp as we were, we went to Ella's. Mr C + family soon came, also Misses Zacharias + Wilson. we had a lovely dinner, turkey, plumb pudding, mince pie, cake, Calaforney [California] grapes, scalloped oysters, cranberries, potatoes, cabbage, &.&.&. to numerous to mension. Everything was served nicely the babies were all good + all was a success. after dinner we played 6 hand [in the original diary, "hand" appears as a picture of a hand] euchere untill nearly 4 o.c. dinner was at 2.30. B. went to the dance with Willie G. arriveing home at 1 o.c. I assisted her in a raid on the pantry.

Friday, November 27. '85

Very cloudy + misty. B was down town nearly all morning. I hammered brass, finished Jessies cushion + accomplished much. Mollie sent up a note, inviting us down to stay all night. Mr. Van + wife were there in the eve. + we talked of Greely. Got letters from Harry + Adam.

Saturday Nov. 28. 85

We helped with the work then with Mollie we went shopping + purchased the things that are to go overland in the wagons. Monday we made several great bargains. at 1.30 went to Jessies for dinner after which we again shopped. B. went to give her lesson. we purchased by the quantity beans, onions, dried fruits, sugar, coffee, rice, flour, &.&.& we ruled out canned fruits + meats instead took bacon, ham, and dried beef. we got a good cookstove and all the belongings, two bedsteads, 2 rockers, & & also eggs + lard, excelsior for our mattresses.[26]

Sunday 29 November

We had breakfast at 10.30 this morning to late for us to go to church. I wrote to Adam + B took it to the office. She went without her wrap +

[26]"Excelsior" referred to fine, curled wood shavings used for packing or stuffing upholstery.

came home with her umberella up, complaining of the heat. we dressed + at 4.30 went out to call upon our relatives. stopped first at Ella's, then took a long walk. went to Jessies + took tea spent the eve. The girls have company in the parlor, we retire to our room + write letters. As the hour grows late + their Pa retires for the night. Hark!! What do I hear? they are playing euchere. I repeat again + again to B. how shocked I am. she evidently does not think it anything to be surprised at. Ah, these western ways, I cannot understand them.

In regard to Greely the great question that we are now considdering is, whether to announce our meals with a dinner horn, or a cow bell.

Monday November 30, 85

We had an early breakfast then went to Mr C's to see about the packing of our goods on the wagon that starts to day for the overland trip to Greely 220 miles we got excelsior for our beds. were up to Ellas twice, and into Jessies four times. We told her we only regreted the days were so short that we might not come oftener. Mollie got news to day of the death of her mother. I wrote to Adam.

December 1st '85

This is a lovely day and to warm for a shawl. we were at Jessies also at Ellas this afternoon. I pounded brass and painted.

Dec. Wednesday 2—85

This day is noted for B's going to the minstrels with Willie Glenn.

December 3—'85

Very warm and lovely I have been obliged to stay in the house all day with my chillblains and cannot ware my shoes.[27] B. went after the mail + we each got a lovely letter from home. after tea we went to Mr Cs for an hour had a very pleasant time + talked + talked of Greely. I finished the bush broom holders for Pa + Will.

---

[27]"Chillblains" were chilblains, painful inflamed swellings and sores that develop in fingers or toes from exposure to cold.

December 5. '85

B. was taken sick yesterday afternoon and went to bed—this morning was worse with fever + sore throat + needed my constant attension all day. I sought my relatives for advise. Jessie, Ella and Mrs Thomson called this afternoon. this eve I went for the Dr, as B announced she had lost her appetite so I became fearful. I stopped at Jessies + Mollie went with me. Dr. Vandervogen came home with us. Dr. Martin was already here he is so nice + Frenchy, so delightfully polite—although his wife is as decidedly Irish and say "faith and begorry" when excited.

Dec. 6 Sunday '85

My patient is much better. Dr came this morning + visited. told us stories of his boyhood + how he started in life with 35 1/2¢. Mollie spent the afternoon with us. I got a letter + box from Adam. it is very cloudy + rather cold. We with a dictionary on my lap read several selections from Bacons Essays. I wrote to Adam. we keep our room this eve—the girls have company

Friday 11—85

It is now afternoon and nearly a week since I last took the time to write in my Journal + this week has been an unusually long one. it began snowing + blowing on the 8th the first Kansas snow that has stayed with us any time. I have been having the worst kind of chill-blains that ever effected mortal man or woman either. it has been impossible for me to ware even the largest kind of shoes. people may smile at chill-blains, and they often do, but indeed they are not to be sneezed at. yesterday the 10 was the first that B has been out. the weather varied but is still cold. maybee you think we havent been lonley, but we have done what we could to keep off homesickness. I read aloud each day at appointed times, as our mental food, several of Bacon's Essays, also for lighter "Tennyson's Princess."[28] Our board was not what we could wish it. still that is of small importance, while our kind + Joviel widdower has developed (on longer accuaintance) into a chronic grumbler and perpetual reader of trashy novels. moreover he does so rale against our friends + relatives while at the table as causes our ire to rise + we talk secretly of revenge.[29] Ah it were sweet!

[28]*The Princess* by Tennyson, written in 1847, was a long narrative poem about the founding of a university to which only women were admitted.

[29]"Rale" meaning rail, to revile or scold.

One thing though which we have both enjoyed has been the twilight. Just before the lamps are lighted, when the evening shades creep slowly over the land (like some truant child returning to its home when tired of wandering.) B would seek the piano and let her fingers ~~wander~~ stray over the keys, in search of the old familiar airs that brought back to our minds our home + friends. I paced up + down the room, as was my want in olden times.[30] frequently we stopped + remanisced, told little incidents, spoke of people whome we had not thought of for years and wondered what all were doing back in our dear old Michigan. "Alas for the days that are no more." A head is here thrust into the door + May announces "Supper, Girls." The allusion is soon dispelled. Fly away ye thoughts of the past—ye might well engrose the time of the homesick + bilious mortal! for us awaiteth the viands. the Bruin is in his place, our relatives are discussed with great ardor by "Pa + the Hopeful" while we quietly nibble at our hard Graham gems, inwardly thinking it were but to lower us to stoop to notice the conversation or deign to make reply.[31] But mind you in secret our comments are <u>great</u>.

Last evening W. Glenn and Mr McClure spent the eve with us. the cole was low and the <u>fire</u> <u>went</u> <u>out</u>. Alas it was cold—undaunted the boys suggested starting it up again. kindelengs were near at hand + unceremoniously all fell to work.[32] it soon rewarded our earnest efforts by a cheerful blaze. played cards, had a good time. Will said he was going into the country 10 miles tomorrow + wanted us both to go, but let us decide by <u>cuts</u> who it would be.[33] B was the fortunate one. She has gone—here I sit writeing + waiting her return.

Mr Walten drove up this morning for us to come up + spend the day, as it was Ella's birth-day.

December 23 85

We four girls, Mollie, Laura, Belle and I, are sitting in the Palace dug-out. the girls are at their fancywork, while Ham sitting on the trunks is trying his best to tease us.[34] We have been in Chappiqua since the 16th on

---

[30]"Want" meaning wont or habit.

[31]"Hard Graham gems" meaning either graham crackers or dried out graham muffins.

[32]"Kindelengs" meaning kindling, small bits of wood for starting a fire.

[33]"Cuts" as in cutting cards to pick a winner.

[34]"Fancywork" meaning embroidery or decorative needlework.

Tuesday afternoon we four with Miss Moffitt + friend + Mr Proctor
started. we had a jolly time, sat up all night met Mr Parsons, played
cards. at 7 in the morning were at Syracuse where we took breakfast—
then with 10 of us in two carriages with Mr Jackson + ~~another fellow~~
Combs, started over the plains. it was dusty + warm the snow in some of
the hollows was drifted, but fast melting away. reached Chappiqua safely
6 girls were obliged to sleep all in a row across the end of the room on the
floor. it was a cold night, + we rose early to start the travelers on their
way. the eve was passed in playing cards + telling stories. Saturday Ham
+ Mr Van left for Syracuse. Sunday the boys borrowed our glass and
shears and after shaveing + dressing up Mr Proffet, being the only single
one made an afternoon call.[35] then in the eve they all came over. Monday
we got opportunity to send letters home. Tuesday was a lovely day. Ham
got home at noon with our trunks. the boys presented us with a roast of
beef, so we unpacked our dishes, set the table very pretty, decorated our
rooms and invited all over to a 6 o'clock dinner they seemed to appreciate it very much. when the dishes were done the dictionary was led forth
a spelling match ensued. after playing a few games of euchere the boys
took their departure. This morning as I was looking at the mirage, I saw
in the distance a herd of over a dozen antelope they were within gunshot
for a short time we were all much aggitated the girls <u>begged</u> me to shoot
them some and I verily believe I would have <u>slain</u> <u>them</u> <u>all</u> if it had not
been that the boys had gone after water and taken the guns.[36]

Ham is such a mischeveous bright boy, so possessed is he with the
spirit that he can hardly contain himself. This afternoon we have had a
jolly time shooting at mark. Mr Profet, Mollie, Ham + I went hunting for
a wolf that was said to frequent a certain part of the bank. we tramped
about two miles but saw nothing. while we were at tea, Mr P. came over
to fill his lantern he seemed afraid to go home, so we arose from the supper table took him home + made a brief call on the boys then ran back
over the plains. Monday eve the boys had a euchere party. I got two letters from Adam heard from Harry + Lee before I left Harper. wrote to
Harry + Adam to day. was out all afternoon with my sun hat on girls
wore sun bonnets it is so warm + pleasant for December, while they are
sleighing at home. We have been reading aloud "Bacons Essays."

[35]"Glass and shears" meaning mirror and scissors.

[36]Since water supplies could be fairly far from living spaces, settlers would carry guns
for protection, mostly from animals, occasionally from Indians, who might object to their
presence.

Thursday Dec. 24. 85

We arose at 5 o-clock this morning, had breakfast at half-past, to get
Ham + a part of the boys started for Syracuse before day-brake. We left
our dishes seizing our wraps, we all climbed into the wagon, rode over
the river about 1 1/2 miles in all + walked back. We all felt so good +
had a jolly time we do as we like + there is no one to make remarks. we
think this the great advantage of ~~having~~ makeing a town ~~made to~~ to suit
ourselves. came home, did the work. I made brown bread + Mollie made
the first white bread that has been baked in the town. after dinner while
Belle did the sweeping, we 3 walked over the prairie in search of fuel—
for a source of profitable ammusement is searching buffalo chips to
burn.[37] it is the warmest day we have had for some time. thinner clothing was in demand shalls were to warm. I did an extencive wash of hdkfs,
but having no irons we are obliged to press them with our hands which
of course is a new ammusement. our fire has gone out + we sit with the
door open. Old Mr [Albert] Myers went to stay with Mr Wright + were
left alone in our glory.

Christmas Day
Friday December 25 '85

We got up this morning at 8.30 Mr Myers not being here to awaken us at
4.30 as has been his want for a week. he sleeps up stairs in our palace +
is a queer specamin of humanity. our up stairs is only loose boards laid
down over the rafters. he talks down at us, while we talk up at him. we
call him our gardian angel, because he hovers over us. we sound a gong
for breakfasts, said gong consists of the potato masher comming in brisk
contact with the dishpan. Before our dishes were washed B. + I went over
to the dug-out + invited Mr Wright to take dinner with us. he + Mr M. are
the only ones left in the town the rest are at Syracuse our bill of fare was
a lovely roast of beef (presented by the boys) both white + brown bread,
made by Mollie + the first in our town, canned corn, mashed potatoes +
gravey, chow-chow, for desert dried apple pie the first ever made in the
town.[38] every thing was done so nicely + I think we enjoyed it as much
as we would a dinner at home. each one highly praises the others work.
Mollie has had more experiance in cooking and we have learned to cook

---

[37]"Buffalo chips" were bison droppings which, when dried, could be burned for fires.
[38]"Chowchow" consisted of chopped mixed pickles in a mustard sauce.

without milk + <u>very</u> <u>little</u> butter we find necessary. our potatoes have been severely frozen + thawed, but in spite of all we <u>ring</u> <u>the</u> <u>water</u> out of them, slip off the skins and put them on to boil. We sewed this after noon after work was done I helped B. paint a hat band for Xmas. as the twilight came on, we put down our work + all 4 streached our weary bones upon the bed to talk it over. We can not realize the day at all. we took a little <u>snack</u> for supper, then Laura got out a bag of fresh pecans. we then made some most delicious caramels useing water instead of milk or cream + were surprised to find how very nice they were after we had played and fooled around untill we were tired, we again took up our work, while Mollie whoe is a very interesting reader, read aloud. we have begun Ruskin's "Crown of Wilde Olive."[39] The day has been perfect, the weather uncomfortably warm. we let our fire go out + open the door. ware our sun-bonnets with no wraps. We rather look for our men home to night + have tried to persuade Myers to hang out the "Beacon," which consists of a lantern hung high on a pole + can be seen from a long distance + many a time has it saved people from being lost on the plains.[40]

It is now 8.30 the wind has changed + it is getting <u>so</u> <u>cold</u>. we have just all decided to go to bed to <u>keep</u> <u>warm</u>. So ends our 1st Xmas day in Greely Co.

<u>Saturday</u> <u>Dec. 26, 85</u>

The weather is warm and pleasant again this morning we are expecting the teams + the mail to day. B + I ran over to the neighboring dug-out to see what time it was as our watch had stopped. got the work done early I began painting a pannel About noon B discovered the teams. we can see them several miles away + have nearly a half hour to prepare. we ran out to the wagons and got the mail. I got a lovely book and letter from Adam, and most surpriseing of all, I got an elegant satchet Xmas card from W. Larkins of Syracuse.[41] The boys came in + spent the eve Mollie + Mr Van took turns reading aloud from "Sweet Cicely," my new book.[42] then Mr. Van led the hyms + we all sang.

---

[39]English author John Ruskin published *The Crown of Wild Olive* in 1866.

[40]Beacon lights, like lighthouses along the shore, were used to guide travelers. The plains in Greeley County stretched for miles and were very, very flat.

[41]A "satchet Xmas card" would be a Christmas card with a scented sachet inside.

[42]*Sweet Cicely; or Josiah Allen as a Politician* (1885) was written by best-selling humor writer and women's rights author Marietta Holley.

Sunday 27 Dec—85

It is warm to day but cloudy + misty. had breakfast 8.30 of codfish, potatoes + bread. at 1/2 after 10 we were all dressed for church and everything was in order for the service. Mr Van came down stairs (ladder) +
while he searched a scripture lesson, whisteled hymn tunes softly to himself. Ham came in from the barn looking very nice. Myers also straggeled
in. then a knock at the door + the 3 other boys, [Hamilton J.] Proffitt. . .,
[Wilbert L.] Wright + [Robert W.] Hufford were admited all were ready
for service, with long coats, standing collars. first all sang several hymns,
then Scripture reading by Rev Van. Songs, a prayer, songs, then Our minister read some stories + good extracts from the Christian Advocate.[43]
then after a few remarks the conversation became general. after an hour
or so the boys went home for dinner + we got some hot corn mush, coffee, fried bacon.[44]

Myers goes to see the mules. (joke) 5.30 we have all just come from a
walk over the plains, started about 2.30—9 of us. the married men went
by themselves comming home but we 6 young ones ran and played
around like children.

Ham is such a tease but we all like him so much. Mr P. and Mollie
seemed to have taken a mutual likeing.

Monday
~~Tuesday~~ 29. 85

This morning + all night + yesterday it has rained a warm gentle rain, but
this afternoon the wind is from the north. it is snowing + dreadfully cold
the boys were in last eve. + we read aloud "Sweet Cecily" then played
pedro.[45]

Tuesday
~~Wednesday~~ 30. 85

Snowed + blowed dreadfully all day. Mr Prophet came over toward eve.
Laura baked bread to day, her first in the dug-out. this is a great occasion

---

[43]The *Christian Advocate* was a popular magazine with a Christian theme.

[44]"Corn mush" was cornmeal boiled in water.

[45]"Pedro" is the collective term for several types of Auction Pitch card games, all
based on the addition of the five of trump (pedro) as a counting card.

which we all look foreward to. with Mr Van, Ham + the rest of us all sat
along time in the twilight, sang hymns, told stories, &. &. while we were
prepairing supper about 6.30 we heard a wrap at the door + who should
come in but Several of the <u>Harper</u> <u>boys</u>. it was storming dreadfully, + a
great wonder that they ever found their way. their team had <u>stuck</u> down
in the river bed + they had walked up carrying their blankets + were
nearly frozen. there were 5 with the driver, Mr. [Charles C.] Share,
[Thomas] Kennedy, Newman + [Carter] Hutchison. We prepaired a very
nice supper, so we thought. we played a few game of cards and managed
to stow them away for the night up stairs. I wrote to Adam + sent some
work to Boston Art Company.

~~Wednesday~~
<u>Thursday</u> <u>Dec</u>. 30, 85

This day is lovely so braceing + clear the storm is over but the snow still
lingers. we got the boys their breakfast and charged a 1.00 apiece for their
entertainment. This is begenning our Hotel + we are proud of our 5.00.
    We were all up at 4.30 + the teams started early, taeking Mr Van, Ham
+ Prophet. So to-day we are alone with Myers who has been out hunting
nearly all day in hopes of shooting a beef but contented himself by bringing home a Jack-rabbit. I began painting primroses on a letter holder.

<u>Thursday</u> <u>31 85</u>

The wind has blown hard all day but the sun is bright + warm. we breakfasted at 7.30. Myers took his gun + lunch + went to work on the school
section.[46] we are left alone all day. when the dishes were done some
worked while we took turns in reading "Aulnay Tower" by Blanche W.
Howard we find it very good + interesting.[47] Just before dinner I read an
Essay from Bacon to help our appetites. after dinner which consisted of
bean soup, corn gems + molasses, we sat around the stove, told stories +
read each others <u>old</u> <u>love</u> <u>letters</u>.[48] we had a great deal of fun + laughed
much at each others expence. the days seem a little long some times,

[46]"The school section" referred to section sixteen. The income from the sale of section
sixteen of every township (which had thirty-six sections) was reserved for public education.

[47]Blanche Willis Howard published the novel *Aulnay Tower* in 1885.

[48]"Corn gems" were muffins, sometimes unleavened, made of coarse corn meal.

especially when Ham + Mr Van are away so much but we have not been lonely or discontented and frequently ask each other "Why is this thus?" I painted on a letter holder + finished it up with primroses. "Very pretty" so they all say. We read several chapters, then retired early.

Volume 5

January 1, 1886–August 3, 1886

This is N. Y. day. it is quite snowy + cold. we were awakened about 8 o-clock by Rob comming after the gun. antelope were in sight + great was the excitement. Myers was soon also on their track, so we ate our breakfast of corn-cakes + molasses with out his exhilerating presence. Mr Campbell + Jessie had sent us by the Harper boys 2 chickens, appels, cranberries + a can of fruit. the chickens we have had in the satchel on the signal stick on top of the dug-out. the wind had blown them down several times but we persevered. today brought them in + the great event was offeciated in by Laura who with a lavish hand prepaired an abundance of sage dressing. B and I rung out the frozen potatoes. Mollie prepaired the cranberry sauce, with white + brown bread + the indispensible gravy (which is a substitute for butter) formed our N. Y. dinner. At 1 o-clock as we were about to sit down to our meal, we heard voices + saw the welcome faces of Ham + the mules. the boys were true to their promise + were here to take dinner with us. Mr [the Rev. Lewis J.] Van Landingham + [W. C.] Gerard also came the last two had gotten behind the teams + had walked 12 miles.

We were anxious about the mail + soon had it distributed. I got 2 letters from Adam + papers we sat long in the twilight this eve + all sang hymns + told stories. our long twilight talks save oil, + are very pleasant. Rob shot an antelope + brot us over nearly half + said when wanted more the other quarter was at our disposal, also a Jack-rabbit the boys <u>are</u> <u>very</u> <u>kind</u>. Mr Myers brought me a pair of Jack-rabbit ears which I am going to keep for a relic.

Last night and to day we are having the benefit of one of the most <u>dreadful</u> <u>blizzards</u> that old Kansas men say they ever saw. it is snowing +

blowing. it is impossible to breath a moment with the wind directly in ones face. Laura and I attempted to go to the <u>improvement</u> but could only get a few feet away from the door.[1] how thankful we all feel to think our dug-out is so warm + comfortable. our water has given out. there is no more within six miles, but we are melting snow for ourselves + the four mules. the snow has drifted into the outerstairway so that Ham worked along time before he succeeded in getting out at all. All morning Ham, Myers + the rest have been diligently melting snow in the boiler to water the mules and <u>for</u> <u>our</u> <u>own</u> <u>use</u>.[2] our water has given out and the lake is 6 miles distant where they get the usual supply. nobody seems to care or worry at all, but use snow water to drink + cook with. the blizzard is dreadful B + I started for the improvement but snow + wind were so blinding + strong that we only could get a few feet away from the door. the men come in with their faces covered with ice + snow but we are so comfortable in our <u>dugout</u> to be sure there are 8 of us in this one room all day, but reading aloud by turns in "Sweet Cicely" and Tennyson is quite the thing. we sew, crochet + have good times while underground as we are we defy the worst weather.

Sunday January 3. 86

The storm is not yet over but the sun shines brightly. at 10.30 the boys came over to Service. they stayed untill after 1 o'clock then Laura put in the roast of venison, while I sit me down to write. The services this morning were very pathetic as our minister prayed for "the dear ones at home" for their safety + health, his feelings entirely over came him. it was a long pause before he could continue. all sang a long time then drifted into pleasant conversation. we loaded the boys with reading matter + they took their departure.

Monday 4. '86

Cold and stormy again but the sun shines brightly. breakfast is over, we 4 girls + ham are sitting around the table wreiting. Myers is melting snow for the mules. Mr Gerard is stopping up the cracks in the house where the snow has drifted in. all are busy + contented. Mr Gerard

---

[1]"Improvement" meaning outhouse.

[2]"Boiler" being a large metal vessel, usually copper, for heating water, usually for doing laundry.

brought 2 chickens so to day all assisted in getting the dinner which consisted of baked potatoes, chicken, gravy + dumplings.

Eve—we have just been over to see the boys. the prairie is perfectily beautiful. the irregular drifts of snow on the great level plain resembel a white capped sea. the sun has just set + the delicate pink of the horizon blends in, makeing a beautiful picture.

Tuesday 5. 86

Our team with Myers, Mr. Van + Gerard started for Syracuse. the day is very pleasant. We have been out nearly all day. Mollie and Mr. Prophet have tried slideing down the drifts on a board. We have to melt all of the snow that we want for water and are melting enough to wash to morrow. this afternoon the boys took the team + went to kill an a beef. of course we wanted to go for the ride and we went too, for 1 1/2 miles all standing up in the wagon such fun as we had, but the roads were dreadful. when we came to the drifts and the mules broke through so that they lay down discouraged, we got out and walked along with the boys. we were all very hilarious + had a lovely time. we left the boys and walked back breaking through the crust at nearly every step, but how we did laugh. we have just as much fun as we can and act jolly, [whether] we feel it or not. comming by the boys dug-out we went in put their table on top of the bed, dressed up a pillow with muffler, hat + coat, improvised a wagon + horse out of a stool put the lines in his hand. at every addition to the toilet he grew funnier and funnier. we gave him a gun + satchel + he looked very rakeish + life like. we pinned a placard on his coat, "Had enough of Greely. good-bye. & &" (joke) When the boys came we heard a great uproar they appreciated it as much as we I am sure. they all came over in the eve. we read aloud a chapter in "Sweet Cicely." I started my first bread. Wrote to Lee and Adam + sent it to day.

Wednesday 6—86

This has been a hard day we all agree. we washed + each had a three weeks wash to contend with. we had to stop & melt snow between times, but we got through at last. oh so tired we were I baked my bread 6 loaves and we all agree that it is lovely and I am satisfied that it is. we had to stop and rest once in a while none of us have been used to work of late. it seems we are always melting snow + our floor is always wet from the stove to the door. the mules have to be watered + we have tried to fill a barrel with the melted snow for the teams when it comes from town. The wind is comming from the north + is bitter cold. this is evening the boys have just gone. I gave them a loaf of my bread to sampel. our coal is nearly gone. the blizzard has begun afresh. the boys have been out of coal for some days + have begun on the lumber for fuel. we expect to do the same soon if our team can not get through.

The boys started for water to day 6 miles, but were obliged to return without it the drifts were to deep, so we went to melting snow again. This eve it has grown very stormy. Proffitt + Hufford were over spent a part of the eve. we all retired early to save oil + fuel.

<u>Thursday</u> 7 <u>January</u> 86

The wind blew dreadfully all night. the windows were nearly an inch deep with frost. we arose at 8 o.c. the floor was drifted full of snow, shelves, table, our clothes, were drifted nearly under + it is <u>so</u> <u>cold</u>. Ham made the fire but when he started to feed the mules, our stairway was full of fine, packed snow. he had nothing but the spade to work his way out with—no light was seen when the door was opened, nothing but a wall of snow with the impression of the door on it. Ham had a great time to find the barn. nothing can be seen of <u>our</u> dug-out but the stove pipe comming up through the snow. it has stormed all day the same. it is so cold, so wet + snowy in the house that for a time my heart failed me. Belle also was forced to shed an occasional tear but kept up bravely. we thought of our comfortable homes, + we five little orphans, as we call ourselves away out here in the wilderness, coal almost gone + very little oil. we began to burn the short boards upstairs that we thought we could do with out. this is indeed a blizzard + no prospect of our teams for more than a week if this continues. Yesterday we began to read aloud "<u>Barnaby</u> <u>Rudge</u>" + read quite a good deal to day.[3] we regaled ourselves with a dinner of rice soup. we have all tried to be gay and when we felt the bluest have sung the loud- est. At 3 o'clock it is getting dark. the snow doth sift in dreadfully. Ham has gone to water the mules and was obliged to force away through the window, where he handed in the coal for the eve + we handed out the water for the mules. I never before saw such a cold time. it would be death in half an hour out side, the wind is so piercing + the snow so blinding. I cannot describe how dreadful it all is + how many times to day some of our party has said "I wished I was home and I wouldent be in Greely." The

---

[3]*Barnaby Rudge* (1844) was originally a drama in two acts by Charles Dickens.

snow began melting caused by the heat of the stove. our bed is covered with pans to catch the water that persists in running down in streams.

Friday January 8. 86

The sun is shineing but it is very cold. Ham has been digging the mules out of the stable. We girls got out this afternoon for a little run and went up to the boys. we read, Ironed, sewed the boys were in several times— came in for the eve and we played poker.

Saturday 9. 86

Cold, but the sun shines. We are looking for the team to day. have been burning lumber to keep warm. I ironed + read an Essay in Bacon, sewed, & &. boys came in often to keep warm. had a dinner of corn-bread + steak. I tried cooking dried appels. I began with a 1/2 pail full when I got through we had enough to last us for nearly a week. they do swell so. its quite a joke. The boys came over and spent the first part of the eve. we have only enough oil to hang a Beacon for the teams so we opened the front of the stove, burned pine and by the firelight all as close to the stove as we could get we sang songs (the boys all sing well), told stories and talked of home. we had quite a little excitement thought we heard signal guns. Ham hung up the beacon and fired off the revolver, while B. shot off the gun. It is snowing again and all indications are in favor of another blizzard.

Sunday Jan. 10

The sun is shineing brightly and [thoroughly?] enough to keep the water running through the roof, but we've enough pans to nearly cover the floor. This does'ent seem like Sunday without Mr Van. we read + wrote letters, the boys came down after dinner and spent part of the eve. we are looking for the teams every minute. I wrote "A little old ~~log~~ sod shanty on the claim" for all of the boys. Laura baked a dried apple cake—first cake we have had since we left Harper. The coyotes have been running over the roof last night, and leaving their tracks around the door. All are dreadfully worried about the teams for fear they started back before the blizzard as they intended to do, and were lost or frozen.

Monday 11. 86 January

The boys were in all morning, playing cards + reading. after dinner they hitched the mules to the lumber wagon and 8 of us stood up in the box + rode to the river. They intended to break the road for the team from Syracuse. we had such a time to get there the mules stuck half way + it was impossible to draw the wagon further so they unhitched + all walked. the crust was so strong in some places that it bore the team up. As we neared the house comming back, we saw what we first thought was a wilde horse but a closer inspection proved it to be a solitary horseman. We all reached the barn at the same time and who should this gentleman proove to be but Larkins the strawberry blonde from Syracuse. Three men from Syracuse were lost on the plains in the last blizzard + frozen to death. one of them succeeded in walking 40 hrs through that dreadful storm but was badly frozen when he reached Syracuse + told of the dreadful suffering of the party. Young Chapman died first + the others unable to carry him further wrapped him in blankets + left him on the prairie. his body has not yet been found. Mr Larkins was on the committee to hunt him up and so rode over here to see how we were getting along. he saw the team + said they will be here to night. In Syracuse the suffering has been extreme. trains have been blocked for over a week + people are out of coal, but Mr Van by dint of manuevering succeeded in getting us 1/2 ton. he and Myers came in this eve brought the mail. I got a letter from Adam + papers. We are so glad to have father Van back. he is just like a father to all the boys. he is hardly warmed before we begin to tell him all the little things of interest that have happened while he smiles indulgently or laughs out heartily while we all talk at once. the boys are all over again to night. We played a few games of cards for Mr L's entertainment, had prayers and retired.

Tuesday 12. 86

Pleasant but cold. Larkins started soon after breakfast. Mr Hufford has heard bad news + starts for home to day.

Mr [William] Blakeman and Mr Beals distant neighbors of ours (6 miles) made us quite a visit. Mr B is young + very nice one of the nicest fellows I have seen in Kansas. he has been a professional skater. Mr Van went with Rob to Waukeena, all started togeather.[4] The boys were in sev-

---

[4]"Waukeena" being Wakeeney, Kansas, county seat of Trego county, in the northwest central part of the state.

eral times this afternoon. Mollie + Mr P., Ham and B went hunting coyotes. the boys Lute + Proffitt came in for the eve. I was so surprised and
pleased when during the eve Mr P. took from his pocket a (22 short)
<u>revolver</u> and a box of <u>catrages</u> + presented it to me with "the compli-
ments of the bachelors club."[5] I cant imagine why they did it but it was
awfully nice + kind + something that I have wanted so much, but if I do
say it they have admired my shooting very much. They have thrown up
the cans while I have shot them on the fly, & & & + seem to think it something unusual for a girl to shoot. I wrote home + sent it by Mr Van. he
wont be home untill Saturday.

<u>Wednesday 13. 86</u>

Pleasant + sunny but cold. While we were at breakfast Mr Proffitt came
over in a neighborly way to borrow our wash-board. The two gentlemen
are going to wash to day. we are invited over to see them at work. <u>We
girls</u> have divided the work systemmatically, we think. Mollie and Laura
begin this morn to do the cooking + sweeping and dish-washing, while B
+ I tend to the beds. we will change around every week.

<u>Thursday 14. 86</u>

Pleasant. the morning has been very short. Laura and I filled an engagement over to the boys dug-out about 11 o'clock. Laura made them some
bisquet [biscuits], as they had the meat already cooked she also made
them some <u>noodels</u>, while I ammused them with the cards + practised
shooting with my little revolver at the knot-holes in the room. We g[o]
over often + bake up things for the boys as neither know any thing about
cooking + are to timid to try, notwithstanding the no. of receipts we have
written off for them. of course it's fun for us and not prudent for them to
live on hot cakes + meat.

After dinner we girls went hunting jack-rabbits with Ham but the
rabbits were none the worse for it. we read aloud in "Barnaby Rudge." I
finished up my mending.

Last night the boys came over and we began reading aloud "Altiora
Peto" a novel by Laurence Oliphant, and this eve they are in again.[6] they
are quite as interested in the book as we. it is <u>beautifully written</u>, so fresh,
bright and original.

[5]"22 short revolver" is a .22 caliber handgun.

[6]*Altiora Peto* by Laurence Oliphant was published in 1883.

January 15. Friday '86

Another <u>Blizzard</u> this morning, snowing + storming so that it is impossible to see a few feet ahead of one we breakfasted at 8.30 but before that time the boys, Wright + Proffitt, were over. Their watch had stopped, so they had been up several hours, had their dishes done + thought it must be nearly noon. we invited them to spend the day + partake of bean-soup + corn-bread ~~for dinner~~ which they did. I sewed nearly all morning got my skirt nearly done, then we read aloud, &. &. &. such dreadful cold + stormy days we find it more social for all to get togeather, so we congregate in the Palace. we think we are very select, just <u>our town</u>, but we keep each other from getting lonesome.

Saturday <u>16</u> '86

It has been cold and stormy all day. B. is suffering with an ulcerated tooth. we read aloud most of the time to day in "Barnaby Rudge." The boys came over early in the eve. Mr W. has made a cribbage board + I am instructing the boys in said game. we read aloud in "Altiora Peto."

<u>Sunday</u> 17 January '86

Very cold and stormy again to day. The frost has been nearly <u>an inch</u> thick on our windows all day. we find it hard to keep warm away from the stove, so form a semicircle around the stove + read + &. &. we had breakfast this morning at 9.30 and dinner at 3.30. it consisted of a hash-pie + corn bread. we use gravy instead of butter as we are just about out of that article. the boys spent the evening with us.

<u>Monday</u> January 18 '86

The sun is shineing today. B. has been in bed nearly all morning with her tooth-ache but is better now. I have been sewing + writeing letters. I wrote to Adam. 12 pages to Harry. ~~also to Aunt Frank~~. we had our breakfast 9.30. The boys came over soon after + made a pleasant morning call. I have been reading aloud to Belle in "Barriers Burned Away" <u>E. P. Roe</u>.[7] it is now 4.30 Laura is prepairing our dinner of <u>noodels</u> + <u>boiled meat</u>. The boys have just been after an antelope (beef).

[7]*Barriers Burned Away* by the Reverend Edward Payson Roe was a novel about the Great Chicago Fire of 1871, published in 1872.

Myers brought in a grey wolf that he had poisoned with strychnine.[8] the boys were in this evening. Mr Prophett is very comical + pre-
tends to be dreadfully affraid of said wolf. he is now on the floor in
front of it, at a safe distance as it stands up alone frozen stiff, trying to
keep it at bay by the power of the human eye. after profound meditation, he said solemnly that he new how to skin it + preserve it whole, by
simply making a hole in the top of its head + pulling its body through.
he is nearly 6 foot + not being extremely boney is quite good-looking,
but he is the most rediculous fellow. he keeps us lively with his
nonsence. we hear a gentle tapping at the door. on looking out find him
sitting on the bottom stair-step. he jumps up with alacrity on seeing us
+ is <u>so</u> <u>glad</u> <u>to</u> <u>see</u> <u>us</u> he invariably loses his cap or his gloves when it is
time for him to go home, so is obliged to stay half an hour longer to
hunt them up. then he is "<u>so</u> <u>glad</u>."

Tuesday January 19, '86

Very blizzardy + so cold to day. this is one of the <u>coldest</u> days we have
had, almost equal to the <u>January 7</u> when so many were frozen. The boys
were in this morning + called. I have been sewing + reading aloud.

Friday 22 '86.

It has been quite cold to day this evening it is extremely so. I made bread
to day all alone + light bisquet for dinner. it was very nice.
Wednesday afternoon late we were all unprepared for company of
course. Mollie and Mr Proffett were playing cards B. had just washed her
hair in kerosene, Laura was snoozing + I had just set down to crochet
when without any warning, our door opened and <u>Minnie</u> <u>came</u> <u>in</u>.[9] We
were <u>so glad</u> to see her but had that day given her up. Mr Girard + a driver were also along. they went to Syracuse again next morning. Just as we
were prepairing supper Mr Van came in from Wallace where he has been
for nearly a week.[10] we got a quantity of mail. I had 4 letters from Adam,
besides papers, &. &. I sent a letter to Mother. <u>Thursday</u> was quite warm
the snow melted very much. Mr Van tied the mules out to graze where
the grass was visible. we are out of hay + also salt, B. Powder, cornmeal,
&. &. but are getting along without.

---

[8]"Strychnine," developed in 1819, was a poison commonly used to kill rodents.

[9]"B" may have been trying to rid her hair of lice by washing with kerosene.

[10]The town of Wallace lies about 25 miles north of Tribune.

Wednesday 27 January

For several days the weather has been quite warm. it has rained some and the ~~weather has~~ snow is going off slowly. Yesterday we washed, or rather B + Minnie did while I did all of the housework and the girls visited us. We are reading "7 Oaks" by Holland aloud in the evenings for the boys as well as our own benefit.[11] I heard the coyotes howling last night for the first time + its the most gloomy sound that one can imagine in the dead of the night. Ham was on top of the house looking for wolves this morning when he discovered a speck in the distance. both the feald glass and opera glass were brought to beare up the distant object, which we found to be the returning team from Syracuse Mr Van and Myers. Mr Girard soon came in a carriage with the mail. I got a very interesting letter from Lee and one from Adam. I wrote to Adam, also Ella Walton, to send back to morrow.

Minnie is so nice, I like her very much. Mr Girard is with us this eve. he + Minnie are playing Patience.[12] B + I are visiting the girls this week. it is their turn to do the housework.

January 30—86

For several days it has been warm and pleasant the snow is going off rapidly. Yesterday afternoon our dugout was thrown into a flutter of excitement. on scouring the plains with the field-glass Laura discovered the team comming. it was an hour off, so we were all dressed and ready to receive Mr Campbell and his brother Boss + Ham. we had been expecting them + were so glad to see them. Mr C had been quite anxious about us during the cold weather + several times expressed the relief he felt at finding us so happy + comfortable. we also got the mail. I got two letters from Adam. my Amature and papers.[13] Yesterday (29) we all felt to good for any thing + made chocolate caromels. Had batter cakes for dinner because the stove smoked. Yesterday I was sick with fever + lay down all day. To day the boys all went to work on the school-section. Mr C took his team + our party + went that way (5 miles) for a drive. I dident feel well enough so stayed home + practised the guytar + kept up the fire. they were back at 2 o.c. we had a lovely roast of beef + bean soup. Mr C

---

[11]*The Story of Sevenoaks* by Josiah Gilbert Holland was published in 1875.

[12]"Patience" is also known as solitaire.

[13]"Amature" may mean armature, a form used by artists for sculpting.

brought us a turkey, fruit, &. &. which we were very thankful for. Nig, Mr Proffett's dog died this morning. <u>poisoned</u> with <u>wolf</u> <u>bait</u>.

This eve the 30<u>th</u> the boys came over early. we had baked mush + molasses for supper. after the dishes were put away Mr C read several selections from W. Carlton's "City Ballads" then we, 11 of us, old + young, married + single, entered with <u>great</u> <u>zest</u> into playing games.[14] When we were through Mr C. sold the <u>forfeits</u> over Minnie's head and we had real old fashioned times in drawing-stone, measuring tape, + building a bridge.[15] We laughed untill we were nearly sick. Everyone entered into it with great spirit even Myers and the rafters of our little dugout rang + rang again with peals of genuine laughter. then we started a romance. Each one added to it as it went around it was a strange weird tale. Mr C. made it very funny and at last finished it up by the heroin's escape from a six-story window, &. &. Twas 10.30 when the boys went home and nearly 12. when we retired. I practised a long time on the guytar to day + like it so much.

January 31. 86

This morning is like spring day. the birds are singing, the snow is going fast but it is quite mudy. the thermometer in the shade + on the cold side of the house is 41° above. we sit writeing with the door open + the gentle breeze rusteling my pompadore.[16] Mr C + brother have gone for a walk. we are to have <u>turkey</u> for dinner that Jessie sent us.

February 1. –86

A lovely day very warm. Mr C's our neighbors, Ham + we five girls started in the wagon with the mules for Greely Center, 3 1/2 miles distant. when we came to the river bed, all were obliged to get out and walk, the snow drifts were melting fast. we had gone only two miles when we passed through a blizzard. it grew intensely cold. the boys gave us the

---

[14]Michigan poet Will Carleton published *City Ballads* in 1885.

[15]This passage is a reference to some sort of game; "forfeits" are markers deposited or made when one makes a mistake in a game, and are then redeemed on payment of a "fine" such as a kiss.

[16]"Pompadore" being a pompadour, a style of dressing the hair high over the forehead either by drawing long hair over a roll or by brushing short hair back so that it stands erect.

robes + walked to keep warm. we lost our way. the clouds had obscured the [sun?] but when it was over + we saw the blizzard going north, the sun came out + turning our mules very cold we returned to the warmth of our dug-out. The evening was passed pleasantly by Mr C's reading to us. the boys were over All sang hymns untill bedtime.

February 2. '86

I wrote to Jessie + put it in Mr C's letter to her, also to Adam + Harry. Mr. C's with Ham to drive started for Wallace 35 miles distant + thinking to make the trip in one day. it was storming when they started, but it did not clear up as they intended, so Ham told us all about it when he came back on Thursday. they struggled against the storm which had grown so bad that the mules ahead were not visable. they lost the road + walked all the way to keep warm. it was intensely cold Mr C tried to keep his brother awake by arguments + by occasionally tripping him up untill he himself was obliged to succumb to the stupor that was stealing over him and say "boys I can stand this no longer if it wasn't for home and the Greely Co. girls I would just as soon die as not" and wanted to stop + rest but they kept him walking knowing the fatal sleep that was creeping over him. At this critical moment Ham tripped + fell over the section line.[17] hope sprung anew, and spurred them to renewed efforts. soon they found an old trail + were soon at the cow-boys ranch + found to their disgust that after traveling all day against the wind that they had only accomplished nine miles.

On one day of this week Dave Hutchison came + stayed over night. brought us the mail. on Saturday afternoon Mr Jackson + "Peg" cam from Wallace made themselves very agreeable during the eve. I wrote a long letter to Lee they brought us some crackers + oysters for a treat. Everyone is very kind to the "Greely Girls."

Sunday Morning

Mr Jackson + driver started this morning for Syracuse. the boys came over to invite us to drive out on our land where they had been putting up our houses. the mules + wagon were soon ready. the day was lovely but just as were about to start, Mr Rogers and son drove up and made a little call. were out of coal so we sold them a bushel, though we could ill spare

---

[17]"Sections" of 640 acres each were staked out by surveyors and homesteaders with various kinds of markers and occasionally fencing or rope.

it. I have wondered in my mind whether this was right or not, but togeather we considered the circumstances and concluded it was. this gent had two sons frozen to death in the last blizzard.

we had a lovely ride. the boys stayed to lunch and we read "John Halifax" in the afternoon.[18] about 4.30 with the glass we saw the team from Syracuse comming about 6 miles away. all was excitement. we could not wait for the mail but taking our hats we started to meet them. we walked for 2 miles + distinctly heard them talking before we could see them. at last they came over the hill. joyfully we greeted them. we waved our shawls while the boys their hats. Ham, Mr Beals + Biney were there. the contents of the mail bag was soon emptied upon the plains, while each sought for what most interested them. I got a nice letter from Adam + mother. Mr Campbell sent a letter all in rhyme to "The Greely Girls." B. and Ham went along with the team Mr Wright and Laura went next, then Mr B. + I. Last of the proscession came Minnie and Biniey. while Mr Proffett + Mollie waited for us in the river-bed.

Wednesday 10 '86

The boys Biney + Ham started to town for horse feed and we are left alone.

Tuesday they got ready to start but there came up a dreadful blizzard. the boys came over about 10.30 but it stormed so that they were unable to find their way home, so they spent the eve with us.

Thursday 11, '86

Another lovely day. B has a cold. I practised Gaskells Compendium + on the guitar till my fingers were sore. boys came over. we read aloud and looked for the team but it came not. The girls slept upstairs last night. I decorated the house to day for "The comming of Sallie."

February 19. '86

Windy and Pleasant. Mr Jackson left this morning for Syracuse. he came last eve. + brought Mollie with him Saturday 13 late in the evening Mr Van + wife, Mr Myers and wife, the Harper boys, Peg + Mr Morgan came.

---

[18]*Gentleman John Halifax* (1856) was a moralistic novel about an orphan who rose in society to wed the heroine.

it was about 11.30 before we got them settled, fed and warmed. I got a nice letter from Harry and Ad.

Sunday <u>14</u> at noon Ham came with the team. soon came Erwin and [John C.V.] Kelly. the last two are very nice gentelmen.

Monday <u>15</u> Mr Van with Myers + wives moved over to their house on the school-section. The teams + ~~our company have all gone and~~ Mr Girard came with a load. Tuesday <u>16</u> The teams and company all left us, also taking Mollie to prove up school-land, Garden City. our neighbors also have gone, leaving we four girls in possession of the town. we straightway began to clean house. changed everything around, put up curtains to our cupboard, to our windows, &. &. Everything shines. the walls are covered with pictures. Everything is so pretty and home-like that we are more in love with the place than ever. About 5.30 when everything was looking its best Mr Bishop + young Dr More came in bringing our mail and will be with us untill tomorrow. I got a letter from Adam and a pretty valentine from Syracuse but I have no idea who sent it. The boys were very nice and agreeable. Dr sings lovely + plays the guytar. Mr B. laughs. both are fond of "<u>mince</u> <u>pie</u>." it was nearly 12 o.c. before we retired and enjoyed the evening so much. Dr. sang & played for us a long time in the morning about 10.30 they reluctently after starting many times, they succeeded in getting off.

The eve Wednesday 17 we spent all alone. B. loaded up Ham's <u>self cocker</u> + I my little revolver after drawing our curtains we felt safe.[19] Thursday 18—we baked up pies, cookies, &. &. prepairing again for company then it was that Mr J. came bringing Mollie. She was so glad to get home again and hardly knew our rooms. about 9.30 Mr. Wright + Proffitt came in the teams had stopped for the night about 14 miles from here + the two boys <u>walked</u> all the way in. They were dreadfully tired. we made them stay for supper + warm. during the eve Mr [Benjamin F.] Webb + friend, new neighbors, came in to get their mail. Feb. 19. Mr Jackson has gone. our work was nicely done up when Mr Workman from Greeley Center called, then in again came Mr Webb. we are looking hourly for the teams. Ham came in at 12.30 his team with the four mules had stuck in the river-bed in the snow. he had had no breakfast + while he partook of the necessaries of life, he vowed he could do nothing with out the assistance of we five, so all went + stood in statuelike sublimity on the bank while the boys toiled with pick + spade. Got a letter from Adam and the papers.

[19]"Self-cocker" was a self-cocking firearm.

February 20. '86 Saturday

This is a very warm lovely day. Our neighbors from all around have taken turns to day in comming in to see us. a teamster arriveing with Mr Erwin's lumber was here for breakfast. Mr Proffitt put a window in our upstairs. I gave Laura and Mollie both their first lessons in painting. I sent a long letter home to day.

Sunday 21. '86

A lovely day. Laura B. M + Ham + P also Mr W. walked over to our land. M & I were to tired so bathed + dressed about 2.30 Mr Beals + Blakeman called. after dinner they called again, also some of our other neighbors. we talked Drama and decided on the part for the "Octoroon."[20] Then Ham thought of a scheme to break the monotony of our lives, so when Mr B + Blakeman were ready to go, he took the giddy mules to the wagon and we girls with Mr Wright + Proffitt took them home, six miles. then waited there untill the moon came up at 9.25 we had a nice visit. it seemed so good to see some one else besides our own family. we found our neighbors to be <u>very</u> <u>nice</u> intelligent people. we got home 11.30 awfully hungry, but nothing to eat but cold rice-cakes and a ginger-snap apiece. rations were low. our mules walked all the way over and back. we had a lovely time. the first place we have been since we came here.

Monday 22. '86 February

Washingtons birthday. I gave Mollie + Laura painting lessons. Then we walked up to Mr Kellie's house that the boys were working on + visited them for some time. Mrs Van came this morning from her school-section to stay with us untill Mr Van comes from Syracuse the teams all went this morning.

This eve as we sat around the table at our different occupations, our five neighbors from <u>over</u> <u>the</u> <u>draw</u>, Mr Proctor, two Mr Webbs, [John] Sc[h]uyler + Carpenter came near our window + sang.[21] Oh! <u>so</u> <u>lovely</u> several pretty selections. then one played the flute, it was <u>so</u> <u>beautiful</u> and they sing so well togeather Mr W. has one of the prettiest tenor voices I

[20]*Octoroon* was an 1859 play by Dion Boucicault, based on an English novel about slavery. The play features the character Zoë, a mixed-blood slave whose lover must sell her to a man they both hate.

[21]A "draw" is a gully, made by fast-running water, usually by floods.

ever heard. we applauded greatly + called them in and we all spent a pleasant evening togeather. B. and I cleaned our yard to day. I went down to the lake behind the barn for a pail of water, the day was so lovely. I found one little spear of grass that was new + green, the first herald of spring. I brought it in and pinned it to the wall before the admireing gaze of the girls, then I counted the months before May and again we thought how short would be our exile, for time so far has tripped the light fantastic toe right merily for us.[22]

Tuesday 23 '86

We washed this morning. in the afternoon I ironed + gave Mollie a painting lesson. Mr Proctor was here to tea. B. made a real cake and put jellie between the layers. The boys were in a couple of times and spent the eve with us. we read John Halifax. the girls went up to Mr. Kellie's house and hung up the hammock.

Wednesday 24. 86

Very pleasant. Mr Beals came over to day. we girls with Proffitt + Wright Ham + Mr B. walked up to Mr. Kellie' house + swung in the hammock. There came up an april shower but it was of short duration. the wind is very strong. we saw the teams comming from S. all went to the river to meet them. straightway we emptied the contents of the mailbag upon the grass. I got a letter from Adam, Aunt Ella + a box of gum. it was impossible to walk against the wind so B + I rode up on the wagon. I stood up and the wind blew me down, its strength is great. We had a pleasant time in the eve with music + games.

Thursday 25. 86

Mr + Mrs Van mooved into Mr Kellies house 1/2 mile north. Mr B. did not start for home untill after dinner. We were out doors all morning. we went after the mules, Minnie, B. Mr. B, Ham + I, that were larrioted out on the prairie + in the gaiety of our humor tried to induce the aged animals to play circus around their stakes.[23] Dave H. came over from Hector,

[22]"Trip the light fantastic" usually referred to dancing at a party; here meaning time has flown quickly.

[23]"Larrioted out" animals referred to using a long rope to tether grazing animals so they would not get lost on the plains.

4 miles distant.[24] when he went in the house to see the other girls, Mr B + I snipped his gun, a self loader + shot out all of the loads at a tin-can. B + Ham went down behind the barn to try the plow.[25]

Our neighbors from over the draw who will here after be known as The 5 were in most of the morning signing papers with Mr Van and The 2 also In the eve we had a lovely time. the supper dishes were hardly done when a rap at the door + The 5 made their appearance in a body. they are so jolly + nice. they proposed a serenade on Mr + Mrs Van so after chatting a while all went quietly the 1/2 mile, notwithstanding the badger hole. the boys have formed a quartet + sing perfectly togeather Frank Web has one of the sweetest tenors that I ever heard. after singing we called awhile. they seemed very much pleased at the music. the boys came in + stayed till 10.30. Gum was passed by way of refreshment.[26] thus ended a very happy day.

Friday 26 '86

A very strong wind to day. Mr Proctor came over after the team to moove into B's + my dugout so they will be near their work. Minnie + B. went with him. Laura went with Ham to look at his claim. Mollie + I stayed home to write letters. I took a lesson on the guytar yesterday. this makes three in all. I am practising on it quite hard + am so in hopes to learn it before I go home. The 5 were all in to day to call. old Mr Beals was here. No 2 were over in the eve + we finished "John Halifax."

Saturday 27. 86

We had four new arrivals this morning, gentelmen from Newton. they with the rest of our neighbors came in this eve. we had more than enough for progressive euchere, so that game was introduced + we had a very exciteing time.

---

[24]Hector, now a ghost town, was four miles north of present-day Horace, Kansas, and founded by the Greeley County Land and Town Company in December 1885. It survived for less than a year and was transplanted lock, stock and businesses to Tribune by November 1886.

[25]A "self-loader" refers most likely to a repeating rifle, such as the 1873 Winchester, which had a magazine to hold a quantity of bullets.

[26]Modern chewing gum was invented about 1850.

Sunday—28. February.

Cold + cloudy. Mr + Mrs Van came down at 11. o'c. and we had service the boys were all over. Mr Van talked to us all very nicely, had scripture read + singing We spent most of the day around the stove.

Monday March 1 86.

Snowing + cloudy but not very cold. We were up at 4. o'c to give Ham an early start for Syracuse. Mr Proctor + Mr Van also went. B. + I rode as far as the river on the coupeling pole.[27] Minnie went to stay all night with Mrs. Van. the boys were all in.

March 2. Tuesday, 1886

snowing, blowing + cloudy we could not get out at all to day. The boys were all in during the day. I had a very bad headache + accomplished nothing. B. put a plaster on the back of my neck which blistered it severly, hence I carry my head very straight.[28]

March 3. Wednesday

Very cold snowy misty + generally disagreeable. It is B.s + my time to do the work I arose + made the fire it was Oh so cold! had oatmeal corncakes + bacon for breakfast. B + I have sworn off this month from coffee + tea, so we all strengthened ourselves with hot-water. for dinner corn muffins + ham, apple sauce made from dried appels. we have no eggs butter, or milk for our muffins but they were very nice without. we also had Hominy cakes, these are made by mixing a little water salt + flour with the Hominy + frying it in lard.[29] (Evening) the teams came at 3.30. Minnie came home from Mrs Vs we were so glad to see her again. I got letters

[27]"Coupeling pole" meaning coupling pole, a pole that joins the pair of front wheels to the pair of rear wheels of a wagon, like the drive shaft on a car. When there is no wagon box on the wagon, it is a convenient place to sit.

[28]A "plaster" was a medicinal substance, such as mustard, spread on a cloth and applied to the body to heal, soothe, or heat an area. It was thought to draw out the pain or infection, or to serve as a counterirritant, meaning the pain it caused would distract the patient from any other pain and, presumably, confuse pain nerves as well.

[29]"Hominy" are hulled kernels of corn, usually ground into grits and cooked with water to make a mush; it was also sold canned in water. Drained of water, it is then usually sautéed in bacon drippings, oil, lard, or butter.

from Adam Mother + Harry. I wrote a letter ~~to~~ home to send in tomorrows mail. Mr Chapman remembered we "Greeley Girls" with a nice package of confectionary.[30] The boys were all in this afternoon and got their mail.

March 7 Sunday '86.

To day was lovely + warm. during the morning Mr Web came in. Mr Chapman + Dave came over from Horace, Mr C. on his way to S—he had a good team + we dashed up to Mr V and all over section 9—first buggy ride I have had since I came.[31] We had Sunday school at 11.30. This afternoon we all went walking. I had Dave, Laura, the young Surveyor, Mr Jenkins B + H Mollie + Mr P. in the afternoon the boys called. Mr Webb + brother + their two friends who came on Friday, Mr [Homer R.] McPherson and Mr Boak. We went to our Lake after Frank + I, then all played catch awhile. in the eve we wrote letters.

Thursday 4 Mr Beals came down to see about the play. We all walked up to Mr. Van's new house the boys had'ent it quite finished but we had a little dance of our own and a good time. This evening Mr. Webb's friends came, also two loads from Wallace, men, whom we accomidated, there were 9 that slept upstairs.

The boys all came over this eve our room was full, but we had a very pleasant time.

Wednesday 5.

Mr Beals went home this afternoon. Mr Chapman + Dave called + stayed to dinner. The boys were over this eve. the teams came home bringing the mail. got a letter from Adam. The Surveyor began to mark out our town on Saturday men are seen in all directions on the prairie.[32] Great excitement

---

[30]"Confectionary" meaning candy.

[31]Horace would become the railroad center for this area in August of 1887. The railroad meant that Horace survived, while other towns in the area, such as Hector, collapsed. Horace remained important enough for a post office until 1965, when the office was closed and the mail sent to Tribune.

[32]A "surveyor" laid out and mapped the streets and lots for a new town. To "mark out" a town meant to draw the property lines.

Monday 8 86 March

The boys were all in during the day. The weather was vareable it snowed + rained + shone alternately. the surveying went on part of the day. in the eveg the Dramatic troup met here + we read over + discussed the play.

Tuesday. 9.

This morning when we arose there was several inches of snow on the ground + still snowing but by noon it was gone + the sun shineing. the boys happened in several times. at noon just before they went to survey, some one of the boys put a board over our stove pipe. We couldent imagine what ailed the stove, it smoaked so. soon Ham discovered the cause + we laughed heartily.[33] I coppied my II Act. helped Mollie paint thistels. Minnie and I are working togeather + it keeps us busy most of the time for we have so much company. Yesterday I painted snow-birds for Laura + she made the pies for me.

Wednesday 10. 86

Mollie + B. began working togeather this morning. Minnie + I will visit. Laura expects to leave us soon + go home for a few weeks and work in the office. The wind is blowing dreadfully. B. + I started for the barn but I was blown back, landing in my own stair way. I gladly took shelter. The boys were in with letters for us to have mailed. our whole town bring their letters here for us to send out, so we keep a sort of a P. O. Mrs Van is mooving + stopped here for the afternoon. Mr Girard came this afternoon from Wallace. I practised quite hard on the guytar and studied on my part for the play. tis so stormy that the surveyor (Mr Jenkins) could not work so we are all assembeled. We girls got a lovely box of Gunthers Candy from Charley Smith, but it lasted only a short time. it just went to the spot. Oh how we enjoyed it.

Thursday 11 '86

Slight snow on the ground this morning but cloudy. Laura + Ham started for S—+ we girls all rode to the hill, then came by Mrs Van's + called. Laura has gone to stay for a month or more. we feel very sorry to have our party so broken up.

---

[33]Placing a board over the stove pipe at the chimney end meant the smoke from the stove would flow into the house instead of outside—a practical joke.

Friday. 12. March '86

We had two arrivals last night, Mr [Robert] Pringle + [Wallace] Rankin.

To day Mr Chapman called + Mr G—went to S—Tis very windy but pleasant. the Surveyers are all at work. The work has begun on the addition that will be made to the Palace for a sleeping apartment. the boys were all in this afternoon. I sent a letter home to day.

Saturday. 13. 86

A lovely day, windy B. + Mollie did their Saturday baking. Mr Larkins came in the afternoon + brought our mail. I got two letters from home. one from Lee also Harry, also from Sam Hall our claim friend. indeed it was a good one. the boys were over. Minnie + I took the mail out to the boys who are surveying. In the eve some of the boys came in again and ten of us went over + serenaded Mr Van + wife. we had such fun + the moon was lovely. I went with F. Webb. comming home we all got scattered. when we began to think at all about our direction, there wasent a soul in sight. we found we had wandered a mile to far east. we soon found Belle + Larkins they were also "looking at claims." we concluded we would just as soon walk the rest of the night. well, by 11- o-c we got home found the rest of our party in the hammock, which is swung in the new building, (gents sleeping apartments) without a roof which lets in the moon light. we then geathered in the "Palace" after singing for some time we retired + blew out our light at 12. sharp when we thought it time for the gentlemen to go we gently hint by singing "Good night Ladies" it took effect + laughing, there was a stampede for the door.

Sunday 14. March

A lovely day very warm. breakfast at 7.30. Minnie + I took a walk to the lake behind the barn for water. After breakfast we discovered two people approaching from Hector. we were all on the roof with the glass. It prooved to be Mr. Cunningham +

after calling, they went to look for land, then Mr Weaver came over + stayed for sunday-school. our lesson was from the book of Est[h]er. much interest was displayed, our singing was good. before the service was over Mr Beals came in to spend the day + talk Drama. we have such jolly times, + such nice young people. About 4- o-c we saw Ham coming from S—about 12 of us went to the river to meet him. got a letter from Adam. I devoted my evening to Mr Larkins. B + H went over to Mr Vans.

prairie fires are beautiful at night.[34] It was 12- o-c before Mollie + B finished their letters. Ham goes to S. in the morning + must rise @ 4 Minnie + I shook hands over it that we would not go to bed for only 4 hrs sleep so wrote untill 2- o-c, then took a lunch. as it was monday 15 we played Calafornia Jack, then sat by the stove + talked untill 4- o-c when we called Ham.[35] we felt very frisky + went with him to feed the mules we three then swung in the hammock + sang untill breakfast. the day-break was beautiful. Minnie + I wondered how we could possibly sleep every morn + miss it all. they make a great deal of fun of us. We numbered 13 for tea. Mrs Van is with us to night. boys all came over. Moon lovely all sat on the roof of our dug-out + serenaded it. Frank W. + I went to the river after water + slid down the snow drifts. Larkins and Chapman are here.

All retired promptly 12.15

<u>Tuesday 16</u>. <u>March</u> 86

Breakfast at 6.30. a lovely day. we began a large wash at 8 o-clock. by 11 it was all done, dried + sprinkeled for ironing.[36] thats the way we do things in Greeley. boys were in several times during the day. Mollie + Minnie went this afternoon to Hector with Larkins + Chapman. B + I pre-paired the meal + in eve wrote letters. She went to Mrs. Van's to spend night + keep her company. I wrote to Adam. the prairie fire is beautiful, but it is circeling us very near 'tis almost to the barn boys are doing what they can with back-fires and wet bags. [37] Mr. K's house barely escaped the flames. we have Mr Reed from Newton and Mr Frazer from Chicago both very nice. Mr Jenkins is here yet surveying.

Minnie + I are the investigating committee, tis our business to find out the affairs of all new comers + post ourselves accordingly. this we do with great alacrity. Mr [A. C.] Van Aken is our head man + drops in occa-sionally with information that he has gleaned. this is when new arrivals

---

[34]Lightning strikes, which set prairie grass alight every spring, burned the grass enough to keep it healthy and under control.

[35]"Calafornia Jack" was California Jack, a form of "All Fours" card game.

[36]Dried clothes were sprinkled with water, rolled up and put aside until they could be ironed. This prevented wrinkles from setting in.

[37]"Back fires" were lit to burn over an area so the prairie fire would not have enough fuel to burn it again; "wet bags," usually of burlap, were used to beat out sparks and cinders.

come in or teams stop. Mr Pringle and Rankin have a nice dog which is an addition to our live stock, this with <u>our</u> <u>chickens</u> we feed scraps daily, with all ceremony.

Wednesday 17 '86

Minnie and I began work. Lovely and warm. Mr Beals came down in the afternoon. We swung in the hammock untill we saw the teams comming then went to meet them. The well diggers came, also the two teams + Mr Girard. We met Mrs Van + B. across the river + had a pleasant chat. Mr B. + I walked up behind the wagon + talked of "the weather + things." in the eve the boys came over but the girls were all out for a stroll. Mr B. + I went to the river, finding a good smooth board, in the hilarity of our spirits proceeded to slide down hill. twas great fun and the moon was lovely.

Thursday 18 '86

Mr B. was here all day and the girls left him for me to entertain. he is awfully jolly, so nice + polite. we held the hammock down our usual time. in evening strolled by the light of the moon. the girls were all out again. there is a great rush for the hammock every evening + lots of fun over it. The boys came in this eve. and B. formed them into a quartet. they sang beautifully. We had a hard sand storm to day. our cupboard was sifted full, sand was in all of our vituals, but such is Greeley Co.[38]

Friday 19, '86

Rather cool to day. Mr B. went home. Our housework occupies most of our time. we are boarding the "well-men" + surveyor. The boys happened in during the day. we girls have had real comfortable jolly times togeather to day. It snowed to day + the wind has been blowing a gale The weather has been very fickel of late. I made cookies to day. 'tis indeed the <u>somethingless</u> out of the <u>nothingless</u>.

Minnie and I have had an [experience] with the prairie fire. it has burned all around us + as far over the plain as we can see it looks as

---

[38]Sand storms were common if enough prairie grass was burned away and a strong wind blew the dirt or "sand" into every nook and cranny of a home. "Vituals" meaning victuals or food.

though our dug outs had been taken up and set down on a piece of black bristle board. Mr Van Aken was working near when it came to the back of the house. we were in side + the first we knew of it we heard a <u>mighty roar</u> like an approaching storm. on looking out saw a sheet of flames hurried on by the wind approaching our new building. Mr. Van A. started a back fire + we three fought bravely—but Minnie + I were alone an hour afterward when the flames again broke out. the wind changed + brought them furiously toward the barn + loose lumber. I started my first backfire + we worked hard with the broom + wet sacks, but we saved our barn + all our belongings. B. was at Mrs Van's.

March 20 '86

Very windy + cold. we baked + did our Saturdays work. the men could not work on account of weather so all set around the stove in the way. I took a snooze in the hammock. We got mail to day. In the eve. F. Webb came in, also Pringle + Rankin + we had a sing, practised for a serenade. there has been a continual skuffle for the hammock to day 'tis never allowed to cool. F. + I got it for an hour or more by pure stratagy, + enjoyed it much while the full moon beamed. Dave H. came over from H. + spent the eve. I entertained him while the rest sang + we talked over old times.

March 21 '86

This is a lovely day and Sunday at that. This morning there were five gentelmen came over from Hector + Horace to attend Sunday school. it was a very pleasant gathering, about 20 in number, discussions were animated + singing good. Minnie, Jenks, B, + Ham walked to their claims this afternoon + took their lunch. Dave promised to take me to my tree claim tomorrow or soon.[39] Mr Chapman came + brought some confectionary.

---

[39]A "tree claim" was an additional 160 acres of land homesteaders could have if they planted a certain acreage of trees on the original homestead. This meant an extra half-section of land for the price of a few trees, but with no guarantee the parcels of land would be next to each other.

March 23. Wednesday '86

Cloudy + sultry. Minnie + I are through with our week of work and feel as happy as a school boy on Saturday. We went to the river with Ham to get a bbl. of water.[40] had a good time all day. Dave called, also Mr Blakeman + friends. The Webb boys all got home to day. Mr Proctor came with provisions. I helped Mollie hammer brass, + began my doylies, also made some chocolate candy, with walnuts.[41] Minnie + I took Mr Wright his mail, then went toward our claims to meet Ham, for he has been plowing for us, + got a ride in the wagon. wrote a letter to Mother this eve. Got our mail at 12 o-clock last night. The well-diggers brought it. We had retired but hastily dressed + got supper for them. then taking our letters to bed and putting the lamp on the shelf we enjoyed ourselves very much with our home news.

Saturday 27 '86

Snowed hard last night. this morning it is very cold still snowing + blowing dreadfully. This is as bad as any of our blizzards in the winter and is so cold in the house that we cant keep warm. The gents sit around the room with their overcoats + hats on. Mr Kellies teams got in this morning, + the men (5 of them) are busy putting up something up to protect their horses. our "Palace" is full of men + we can hardly moove.

Mollie's two brothers came on Friday. Washie + Boss. I got a letter from Adam saying she would start Monday. B + I are nearly wilde.

Sunday 28. 86

Awfully cold, still blowing the snow in a blizzardy fashion the snow blew in all over the beds last night and the shelves are drifted over. we have been all morning digging our belongings out of the snow + wiping up the water as it melts. the doorway was drifted full + Ham had to go in + out from the upstairs window. I am writeing this on my lap. its so cold we can't sit in the back part of the room.

---

[40]"Bbl." meaning barrel.

[41]"Doylies" were doilies, circles or rectangles of lace and fabric used to protect and decorate tabletops and furniture.

March 31. '86

Belle + I started for Syracuse this morning with Ham + Mr. Kellie to meet Adam, who will be here Thursday morning. the day was lovely, but not warm enough to discard our winter cloaks + hats. All of our town nearly have gone in to day to vote for the County Seat.[42] we got there early in the afternoon, did our marketing for the next few months. had calls in the afternoon + eve + a goodtime generally.

April 1st '86 Thursday

Very pleasant. we were up at 4 o-c with 5 of the gentelmen B + I went to meet Adam. At 6. o.c she came the train being due any time between 4 + 8. Oh the joy of such a meeting and triumphantly we escorted her to the Hotel for breakfast and about 8.45 we with Mr Campbell as an addition to our load minus Mr K—started for Tribune.[43] Just before we reached there up came a blizzard it grew intensely cold but we had plenty of wraps + were soon home. This eve we girls wrote up items for the first paper the "Greeley Tribune" which will be printed at Harper next week.

April 4 86 Sunday

We had Sunday School this morning, the first lesson—leaves. It has been snowing all day. B. and Ham drove out to Mr Beals.

Mollie, Minnie + Proctor have gone to see Mr Scott who has been quite sick. our apothecary shop came in use for they had no medacine + no way of getting it.[44] Minnie went over yesterday + doctored him up. his life was dispaired of but I think with the aid of the medacine she will bring him through.

April 5th 1886

Cloudy but warm Mrs Van. came over + spent the afternoon. B. A. + I went after buffalo chips to the river-bed. B & I cleaned up stairs today.

[42]Voting for the county seat was an election to determine in which town the county seat of government would be located, usually a hotly-contested election, since county business meant an economic windfall.

[43]After "Chappaqua" was surveyed, the name became Tribune, its current name.

[44]An "apothecary shop" was a pharmacy, but in this case referred to the girls' stock of medical supplies.

This eve I wrote to Ella and Laura R. Adam has a bad cold + coff so does'ent enter yet into the spirit of things. Dr Moore called on his way to Mr Scott's several calls from strange gents from the other town.

April 11. Sunday '86

This has been our week to work. A., B. + I so we have been pretty busy + hardly done any thing else. we have 17 + 18 every meal.

Mr Girard and family came yesterday, also Mrs Taylors son Edd. We had 35 for Sunday School to day in our "Palace." after the dinner was over, B. A. Ham + Mr Taylor + I called on the Rankins. the sky looked dark + threatening. it rained quite hard for a while. the roof was like a sieve, the rain fell in upon us. we held the boys hats to catch it. then all went to Mr Wrights house a mile away. Wrote a letter to Mother this eve. we had lunch at 7.30 of bread + butter, prunes, pickels, chocolate cake. gave a lap supper for 17 or more.[45] We are having April Showers.

April 14 '86

Wednesday morning. this is the day that we have set apart to moove from the "Palace" and give up our hotel life + live with Minnie in her 10 x 12 on her claim. She has furnished the house + every thing needful and we three board her for the rent. Our mooving has unsetteled nearly every family in town. Campbell brothers + Mollie have mooved on their Claim 1/2 mile from us. Mr and Mrs Girard have taken our place in the "Palace." Mrs Taylor + two sons, Will and Edd also moove to their land in a few days. they are such a nice family. Mrs T—is a lovely old lady + reminds me so much of Grandma Garrow. We girls did a very large wash this morning besides cooking for nearly twenty. our family is very large. Dr Moore called this afternoon + helped us put our defects [effects] in to the wagon. B + I wrode out first with Ham, then soon came Minnie + Adam on the top of a large load of goods. we got supper in our new home, several of the gents called before it was dark and Frank Webb spent the eve.

April 15 '86

We finished setteling our house had 8 gent. callers. B and I did the bakeing. Just at noon Dave came upon his poney and invited us to a dance this

---

[45]A "lap supper" would be a buffet, where diners balanced their plates in their laps.

eve. at Hector. it had just been thought of this morning. We were delighted and wore our second bests.[46] Dave came after a load and Ham + Belle. Frank W. + I went in Mr K livery carriage the night was lovely + moonlight. dance was in a new store building 16 x 24. there are only two ladies in the town, rather aged, married + keep the Hotel. we five were the only ladies that danced so we had it all our own way, but of course we danced evry set. At 12- o-c a lovely supper was served, then we danced untill 2 a.m. met ever so many nice gents. there was nothing rough at all + we had a <u>lovely</u> time. Mr Beals was there but has been quite sick and looks wretchedly. we got home at 3 a.m. Will Taylor, Frank W. + Ham came in to warm and for an hour + 1/2 we talked it all over. the went home a little before 5 a.m. we girls then changed our dresses, washed the supper dishes + swept out. About 6- o-c Mollie and Dr Moore came over from Campbells + made us quite a lengthy call. they had both like ourselves concluded that it was not worth while to go to bed. We girls when our breakfast was over all streached our weary bones out accross the bed + slept untill noon.

April 17. 86 <u>Saturday</u>

This morning Adam and I went over to Mollie's 3/4 of a mile, did baking. Minnie G. called. Ham was here during the morning. after dinner we three, B. being too tired walked into town 1 1/2 miles the first time we had started to walk both ways. in all I have walked more than <u>five miles</u> to day. had a good time in town. stayed long at Mrs Girards, "(the Palace)" there were a number of new arrivals. called at Rankins. stopped where the boys were at work + had real old fashioned visits with all of them. rode a while with Ham on the coupeling pole. went on the Wallace road to meet Mr Proctor. he had taffy for us. our provisions came to day. we waited untill the boys were through with their work. Frank W. + Ham came out with us + put a hammock on each end of our house fastening an end of each to the house + the other to a 4 x 6. they then banked up our house with sod, for the wind has been blowing very hard the wind blows in through the cracks, + up through the cracks in the floor + comes with such force that it keeps our carpet flapping furiously. it even lifts the tax [tacks] out of it. the boys stayed to supper & went home 11.55 p.m. the moon was lovely + we enjoyed the ~~moon~~ + hammocks.

---

[46]"Second bests" were outfits not good enough for church, but better than the clothes worn to do chores.

Sunday April 18. 86

We arose at 7.30 breakfast about 8.30. it is dreadfully windy. we have given up all hopes of walking in to church. the wind is so strong that it is impossible to stand up against it. we are in terror for fear the little 10 x 12 will go over. The front of the house weaves in and out, tis almost impossible to write. a bottle of liquid on the shelf has been slop[p]ing over though only about 2/3 full. the girls are out in the hammocks. F. W. came over and spent the morning. In the afternoon and evening we had calls, Mr's Proctor, Taylor, Webb, Ham, and the Campbells called at the door in the buggy. Mr Beals also called.

Monday Morning Apr– 19. 86

This morning Adam + Belle began to do the work this week. pleasant but windy. had breakfast at 9.30. Wrote letters to Harry, Mother and Lee.
    Minnie and Adam went to town after tea. came home with Frank W. + Ham.

Tuesday April 20. 86

We all got up this morning in excellent humor.
    Minnie + Adam are deeply interested in a game of Patience Belle is making dough-nuts. I have just been out in the back yard sketching ~~our~~ the position of our two hammocks + house it began to rain, quite a hard shower and it evry crack + knot-hole it dripped in upon us. we covered the bed with goassemeres set our empty pans + cups around, then had great fun dogging the drops.[47]
    Minnie + A. have gone over to Mollies after lard + the doughnuts + B. are taking a rest. I begin this day to keep the books for the firm of Graham and Smith.

April 21. 86 Wednesday

Mollie came over last eve and stayed all night.
    The storm that Foster predicted has been with us all day in the shape of hard rain storms, wind and hail. we four girls have not been able to get out of the house in consequence of the same but we have had a very cosey time by ourselves. we made candy + had an exciteing time trying to

[47]"Goassameres" meaning gossamer, a gauzelike fabric.

dodge the drops as they came through the roof but they are to quick for us and we are getting rather damp. it is keeping us busy to get our 4 stiff clean sunbonnets in a dry place. I look from the window when the wind was very strong + what a harrowing sight met my eyes. there there was our <u>oil</u> <u>can</u> bounding over the prairie our large jug in full persuit. there is nothing to stop them so we are waiting for the wind to change + bring them back.[48] the wind has been very strong at times we have had our doubts at times of the stability of our structure, so while the side toward the wind is weaving in + out, each arm them selves with a flat-iron to be as heavy as they can + form along the shakey side + act as a prop.[49]

April Saturday. 24, 86

Morning in Greeley Co. 5.30 a.m. we girls have just gotten home from the <u>Horrice</u> [Horace] <u>dance</u>. Mr Taylor has just got the fire started + Ham is lunching from the cubbord. About 8 o-clock last eve the team came for us. Mr Larkins, Webb, Ham and W. Taylor were the gents in our load. there were two teams. the night was cloudy, threatening rain. Ham walked ahead a great part of the way to keep us on the road but nevertheless in an unforseen moment we missed it + went wandering over the prairie with not even a star to give us the points of the compass. the boys were scattered around trying to find some land-marks when they came to the river bank it was very steep so we girls got out with Billie Taylor + crossed on foot while the team went farther down. we walked about 1 1/2 miles before they found a way through + caught up with us. we all kept whis-teling + calling to keep togeather, but still we were wandering at random while the clouds grew darker + more threatening. soon we saw a dim light which we thought must be in the direction of H. we took heart + followed it. after going several miles it grew no brighter + began to elude us like a will-o-wisp.[50] we all climbed into the wagon, the boys giving up their search for the road and then + there we held a consultation. The other team was lost sight of from the start. the consultation ended as it began and a feeling of sadness came on us. Soon in answer to our calls came pis-tol shots. Soon Dave + several gents appeared upon the scene. we were

[48]The "oil can" was probably an empty can of kerosene, used for refilling kerosene lamps.

[49]A "flat-iron" was a heavy iron used for pressing clothes.

[50]A "will-o-wisp" meaning will-of-the-wisp, an old English term meaning an elusive or delusive goal.

very near the Hotel. the boys were going home from the dance it was nearly 11. there had been no ladies there untill <u>our six</u> came. at the Hotel they had all retired but they lighted up + let us come in not any to soon for the storm raged fearfully. we could do nothing but make the best of it. we had a very pleasant time. danced untill 4 o-clock we were obliged to stay for it was to dark to venture out so as the morn was breaking we said good-bye and started. it was after 5 o-c when we passed through Tribune people were stirring in the village, but we passed through quietly feeling rather numerous. Mr Taylor + Ham stayed for breakfast. it is, we concluded the first time we had to bring our company home for breakfast.

We girls slept at intervals and were <u>so</u> <u>tired</u>. Minnie and Mr Taylor walked to the stone quarry Billie stayed all day. Late in the afternoon there came up a dreadful storm + rained so it was impossible for him to go home. it rained down through the cracks dreadfully, dry places were very scarce. Billie dozed upright in a corner. A + Minnie lay across the bed under the gossamers with several tin pans and cups on top of them. Belle found that the rain could not come through the table so curled up under it. getting up on the trunks with a pan resting on the side of my head to catch the drop that persisted in falling in my face I slept comfortably. about 9.30 the rain stopped. we girls took our shawls + lay accross the bed + Billie had a couch on the floor. it seemed as though we had only gone to sleep when we were wakened by the rain in our faces. it was then 12.30. we arose + resumed our former positions untill morning.

<u>Easter</u> <u>Sunday</u>
<u>April</u> <u>25 1886</u>

Been raining hard all morning Everything is flooded out as well as in. we did not undress last night so were ready for breakfast at 7.30. it was a tired though jolly party. by 10.30 the sun was shineing though the wind was so strong that our little 10 x 12 quaked with fear.

In the afternoon Ham came up and in the eve Mr Proctor + C. Hutchison.

<u>Monday</u> <u>26. 86. April</u>

First monday after easter sunday shall hereafter in our own private calenders be known as blue monday. our feelings ebbed low. we felt so disgusted with our selves + everything else that we <u>swore</u> <u>off</u> dancing while in Greeley Co. except the private parties in our own town. Adam +

Minnie had a lunch + walked to town after the mail. Belle + I went over to our land + set out 35 trees apiece, or rather sprouted buckeyes, which is one + the same.[51] The girls came home feeling much better + we had a jollification. began to think we werent such <u>tough</u> characters. another resolution we made that day was to send the boys home at 10- o-clock sharp. F. Webb came over + we tried the new rule with good effect.

April 27. 86 <u>Tuesday</u>

This is a lovely still day. We did our work + lounged around on the bed. three slats in the same have refused longer to support our tired frames, but sink to the floor in spite of all we can do leaving a great hollow. Mr Van and Kelley called for us to sign papers for advertising.[52] it has been delayed by the interference of one Sparks, the U.S. Land Commissioner hence it will be untill the 11 of June before we can prove up. A. and M. walked to town for mail. B wrote letters and I painted. we began to read aloud "Portia" by the Duchess, all feeling the want of something light + bright.[53]

April 28. 86 <u>Wednesday</u>

This is a lovely day but cool and awfully windy. our bbl. of water is nearly gone. This morning it was so low that Minnie called upon us to decide whether we would use the remaining water for our coffee, or would we prefur to wash. the former suited us best and a damp wash-rag went 'round the crowd. after breakfast Minnie + A. took the pails + searched for a lake. At 1/2 m distant they found one with muddy thoug[h] very good water. Frank Webb came over early this evening and with we girls all spent the eve at his brothers 1/2 m. away. had a good time.

April 29. <u>Thursday</u> '86

B. and I were home all afternoon alone. A and M. went into town after the mail. In the morning B + I took the picture + pails + hunted for water. We

---

[51]"Sprouted buckeyes" were horse chestnuts that had sprouted.

[52]"Papers for advertising" refers to the advertisement that all homesteaders placed in a newspaper that described the land they claimed so that if anyone else had claim to it, the information would be part of the public record and, presumably, would inform other claimants, thus preserving their rights to the land.

[53]*Porta; or By Passions Rocked*, by Duchess (a pseudonym) was Number 72 of publisher F. M. Lupton's 1880s' *Chimney Corner* series, which included short stories by Sir Arthur Conan Doyle.

found a small lake (a buffalow wallow where the late rain had collected.)[54] it resembled circus lemonade in color but we were grateful though dreadfully affraid of snakes + mountain lion so carried a revolver + knife. we were 3/4 of a mile from home.

The girls came home about 9.30 with Mr Proctor and Ham.

April 30. Friday. 86

about 8.30 as we were eating breakfast, Ham with two of the boys dashed up to our door, well mounted + armed. they had just started out in search for a couple of mountain lion that had been frequently seen in our neighborhood. they made the scene hideous by assumeing the air of cow-boys + uttering unearthly yells. We are all invited to spend the day at Mrs Vans but I have taken cold in my eye which is quite enflamed so stay at home + keep it polticed. our dog Piso keeps me company we both expect the lion to walk in at any moment.

May 14. Friday

We woke up at 9- o-c this morn + had breakfast 10.30 it is raining occasionally in showers all night the wind blew so that we thought our house would be wafted away. Yesterday morn. Mr Schneyder came at 5.30 a.m. to put tar paper on our roof. stayed to breakfast + was here untill nearly noon visiting, playing pedro with Adam + telling our fortunes. he is a very obliging little dutch boy. he + his dog Rex are good characters.

I had my trees set out on Wednesday. we four girls caught a ride down this W— afternoon with the Taylor boys. came home by moonlight with Frank Web. we thought we would have a sing so geathered up the people as we went along when we reached a partly finished store building where the organ was, we had over 40. we sang awhile then someone brought in a violin one string was partly gone but they peaced it out with a tar rope by the light of a lantern we danced merrily untill 10.30, then we walked home

Saturday 15 '86. May

we went to the stone quarry with Ham + Mr Proctor on the wagons. got large quantities of wilde flowers. comming home all were walking. Adam

[54]A "buffalo wallow" resulted from bison wallowing around, or rolling about in soft mud. Water collected in the depression that the animals created.

+ I stepped over a rattle snake 9 rattels Ham put his foot on it in the badger hole + cut its head off with his knife. In the eve the boys sent a wagon for us + we danced until 15 of 12— in Rankins building. I went with Frank. All had the best time we have had yet. Our <u>advertisement</u> came out <u>this week</u> for first time.

<u>Sunday</u> 16. <u>86</u>. <u>May</u>

A. M. + I walked in to Sunday School this morning. had a little shower on the way. over 70 were present + the school was organized. we are in Mr Proctors class. it rained hard + our teacher brought us home in the wagon. in afternoon He took Ham + us over to Mr Campbells where Laura opened the long looked for box of candy from Mr Fisher. went to town pump came home in the wagon by moon light.[55]

<u>Sunday</u> <u>May 23</u>. <u>86</u>

This morning was warm + pleasant. Ham + T. White came out after us in the spring wagon. we dident know where the S. School was to be held but we saw them mooving the organ + followed it. it was in an unfinished building seats were arranged impromtu. betwen 60 + 70 were present. we that sat behind the organ had just opened our mouths to sing the first hymn when the props gave way + the seat came down. the music of the organ was lost mid the exclamations of surprise that followed, but the superintendent + our teacher brought in a couple of bundels of shingels + peace was restored. Then when we had just finished reading the lesson Lo! a long seat at our right came down suddenly + many found themselves on the floor more shingles, + the lesson went on without interruption. we voted the services at 2.30 a.m. after this. had a little sing after it was over.

Minnie + I had engagements with Frank + Billy Taylor but they failed to make their appearance so we felt very wrathy + stayed home all after noon + missed going to Horrice [Horace] with T. White, Ham B. + Adam. but we had calls all afternoon 12 people in all. F + Ham took us all down town in the Hack + we had a sing at Mrs King's in the eve we came home with the boys. they stayed untill 11- o-c + we retired at 12- o-c.

---

[55]"Town pump": Many towns had a hand-operated water pump at a convenient location where residents could collect water for their household use.

Last Wednesday 19—we had a social given by all the ladies of Tribune. they contributed cake, we bought Lemons + had lemonade for refreshments. between 60 + 70 were present; had a very successful time, played bean-bags and games. <u>Thursday</u> eve was prayer meeting not very good attendance only 25. we walked down + back came home with the boys by moonlight.

<u>Monday</u> <u>May</u> <u>24</u> <u>86</u>

Minnie and I begin to work

<u>June</u> 1st <u>1886</u>. Tuesday

I began to day to write up the past week as near as I can remember. have been so busy of late doing nothing in particular but going to town + entertaining callers. Yesterday morning B + I mooved into our own house. cleaned it all up on Saturday. had 15 callers in all. Minnie + I went to town in afternoon to get mail. 4 Harper boys said they were comming up to play whist + we had a very pleasant time they went at 11.30 after which we four had quite a fright with a centipede. we had intended to sleep at <u>our</u> home to night so had sent our beds down. B. did not feel like walking over so the girls took pity on us and let us stay with them three slept in the bed + I slept on top of the trunks. Thursday 4 gents from Harper + Tribune spent the eve with us.

Saturday we had invited company. Mr Moffett, Proctor, Hutchinson + Hofmaster, and gave them refreshments of lemonade + cake. had a good time, played bean-bags. Sunday Ham + Proctor came up with the light wagon + took us to S. School we stayed in all afternoon, coupeled off + came home in the eve—I with Mr Hoffmaster, a widdower 32 yrs very soft. we took a ride &. &. &.

This morning June 1s[t] 86 we have had too calls it is sultry + warm. it has been threatening to storm. This afternoon M. + I rode into town on the spring wagon. Adam came in with Johnnie Rankin on a load of stones.[56] we played bean-bags in front of Moffitts loafed did our shopping + came home early. B and I then started home 1/2 mile. it was threatening rain + about dark it began to pour. I fastened a heavy blanket on one side of the house so that when the rain fell upon it, it would run off on the floor. it was streached tightly over the bed high up + formed a

[56]Limestone boulders littered Kansas; "a load of stones" was probably a reference to a wagon filled with stones removed from a field to prepare it for cultivation.

sort of canopy under which we were to sleep. B. was lying down and by the light of the lantern I was reading the latest news aloud, when above the flashing of the lightning + roar of thunder, we heard the voice of Ham out side. he and Mr Glenn had stopped at No 11 + the girls were so worried that they dispatched him immediatly. we insisted on sticking it out, but when told the mud on the floor would be 6 in deep by morning we hastily covered up what we had + got into the wagon the faithful mules fairly tore up the sod as they tore along over the Prairie. we arrived at No 11 drenched + were welcomed with open arms. We played cards untill 9.30 when Adam Ham + Mr Glenn went to the dance, in honor of the Harper boys. notwithstanding the scarcity of bedding the girls tried to accomidate us + I slept on the trunks as usual. Adam got home at 2- o-clock. she had walked home, being unable to get a team at that time in the morning. most of the ladies stayed in all night. A. was drenched but very hilarious had a lovely time. we left the beacon out. we saw a centipede in the house last night and all rose up in arms.

June 2. Wednesday '86

it rained very hard + is cloudy all day. we did not wake up this morning untill 15 of 11. Mr Beals + Mr Proffitt called on horse back before we were quite dressed but we were soon out + entertained them. Adam made a malaga cake this afternoon.[57] we had our breakfast + dinner togeather. we have laughed + talked all day while we tried to compose ourselves to write letters. decided to have candy, so made butter-scotch. I rote to Mother + Ella Walton. the bed all broke down + the girls are carpentering. our house + bedding is so wet that we did not go home but slept on the trunk.

June 3. 86 Thursday

A lovely morning but cool got up early. B + I went home + to work dried out our house. I made garden, planted parsnips + peas. in afternoon Mr Kennedy, Misses Andrews McClure & C Gallier drove out on their way to stone quarry. All played bean bags. M. A. + I walked to town got a ride home with Kennedy + McClure. they stayed to tea. B + I went home to spend the night. Ham called in the eve. I took his horse & loaped over the

---

[57]"Malagas" (here probably dried before using) are white, firm-fleshed grapes from southern California.

plains to No 11 our dugout was very damp. The mold was over the ground floor + up the sides of our natural plaster, a little lake of water in on side that had not dried up the bedding was almost wet in spite of being out in the sun, but we kept our lantern burning + with our firearms under our heads slept as soundly as could be.

Friday
June 4. 86 ~~Saturday~~

B and I came over 7.30 to breakfast + found the girls ready to receive us. Minnie went in town with W. Rankin + spent the day. Ham and Walter Proffitt came out and spent the eve. we sat in the hammocks untill 9.30 then we four started for our dug-out we took a lantern + felt positive that we could find the house. we walked + walked. we had lost sight of Ham untill he fired his revolver to give us his direction. we did the same. Kept calling + whisteling to each other but still no house. we walked for another long time. W. + I found our selves in Laura's door yard 2 m E- of town we afterward found the others. spread out the slickers + sat down to rest + consult. we had so much fun, then continued our search. we saw a small object ahead + when we got to it found it to be the place we started from No 11 twas between 12 + 1 o.clock so we gave up the idea of "holding down our claims" + the girls took us in I rested peacefully on the cover of M's trunk the others took a third of the one bed without a murmer.

Saturday 5. 86. June

We ordered the surrey wagon for this morning.[58] Ham brought it out. we four went to hunt a man to do our plowing. we were south several miles called at Mrs Taylors. had a lovely time rode untill noon. did our shopping drove home for our dinner + were back to town by 1.10 where we spent the afternoon organized a "Ladies Society" + made arrangements for a moonlight festival on the 16th B + I slept on our land without inturruption.

Sunday 6—86 June

In afternoon at 2.30 Mr Proctor + Hoffmaster came for us in the lumber-wagon. Adam stayed home to meditate + write letters. Had a lovely time.

[58]A "surrey" was a four-wheeled, two-seater carriage used mainly for pleasure riding.

some Horrice boys were over. They voted our sunday school at 9. O-clock Mr Hutchinson + Moffitt came back with us in the wagon. Mr M. + I spent the eve in the hammock during an animated conversation. about 9.30 we with Ham + B. started for our home. we sat on the roof + talked long in the moonlight then went in side while the moon shone in at the windows we all four sat on the edge of the bed for a few minutes as our chairs are minus, when to our surprise the whole affair gave away without warning + fell into pieces like the "One hoss Shay."[59] we arose and went back to the girls at No 11 who took pity on us and let me sleep on the trunk we had so much fun.

Monday 7. 86 June

B. and I slept at our dug-out. I papered in the afternoon.[60] Dave called. A drove of 9 wilde horses passed here persued by cow-boys.
   Dicky Wilson + Ham spent the eve with us at our home.

Tuesday 8. 86. June

Our men are plowing and B. and I stopped to advise them before going to breakfast. In the afternoon Adam and I walked to town in 30 minutes This is the fastest time on reckord came back before dark. had a good visit with the boys + made a few calls. Snyder and his dog came up + spent the eve with us. did not go to our home. had a light shower to day. Made great preperations to wash tomorrow

Wednesday 9. 86. June

Began washing, our last in Greeley Co we hope and the first for three weeks. I wrote to Mother. Ike put the tar paper on our house.[61] Robinson and [Andrew J.] Crane, our workmen are boarding with us for dinners.

---

[59]"The Wonderful One-Horse Shay" from a poem by Oliver Wendell Holmes entitled "The Deacon's Masterpiece," was often found in early schoolbooks. It told of a church deacon who vowed to build a shay, or carriage, so it would not wear out because every part of it was as good as every other part. It ran a hundred years "to a day" and all of a sudden went to pieces. Schoolchildren memorized and recited such poetry as part of their education.

[60]"Papering" presumably referred to putting newspapers or wallpaper on the walls to stop the drafts and decorate.

[61]"Tar paper" placed on the outside of the house walls was water-resistant.

Thursday 10 June

I was at home in dug-out this morning, papering + making it look cosy. About 4.15 all started for town twas awfully hot we got there to late for the Ladies meeting, so it was postponed. we took supper at the "Smith's Sisters." thought there would be prayer meeting but after, were disappointed so had private meetings. Mr Moffitt + I occupied Mr Proctors unfinished building. I wone a bet off of the moon. we started home about 11- found Ham + B. already home. one couple occupied the corner of the roof, other the top of the trunk in side of dug-out. our hoose did us credit + looked very pretty. had a lovely time. Saw the light extinguished at No 11 + heard the boys say "good night." our company departed at 1.30. Moon was lovely. B + I got a letter from W. Glenn, Harper, correcting a might be error in our advertisment. twas very kind for it might have hindered our prooving up.

Friday. June 11. 86

We were delayed in getting our coal. Adam + I came over after breakfast + carried away all the wood we could find. we have an immence ironing to do + nothing to work with. we accomplished as much as we could untill wood was gone. made mock-mince-pies for dinner. very warm, wind is blowing hard. C. Hutchison spent the afternoon eve + took tea with us.

I am writeing this in my own home. tis getting late 9.10. B. went to Mrs Campbells + Ham will stop for her a dreadful storm is threatening us but I have doors + windows open as I write by the light of a lantern. Ham's self-cocking six-shooter + catridge belt is buckeled arround my waist, the ring revolver is at my left hand. Thus equipped I await further development. Ham + Belle came soon. got papers + letters. Adam + C. Hutchison came over to see if there was any mail, thinking they saw the signal.

Saturday 12, 86.

A very uneventful day. Minnie + I baked chocolate cake, Lemon + dried currant pies. wind blew dreadfully all day had several light showers. girls went to town after supper. I came to my dug-out to write a letter. The watch stopped so that we had no time at all and could only judge meal time by our appetites. F. Webb and Mrs Brecount called in the dog cart.[62] Later Ham B. + Adam came with the two mules to the light wagon. all went over to Lauras + called. got a letter from Lee.

[62]A "dog-cart" was a two-wheeled carriage with transverse seats, set back to back.

Sunday June 13. 86.

Very warm. B + I went to breakfast at No 11 at 6.30. S. School at 9. Mr Proctor came for us in the light wagon. had a good time. after it was over Mr Moffitt + I went into the unfinished hotel climbed upon a saw-horse + talked about "the crops" &. &. &. he rode home with us. Ham came in afternoon. Thermometer at noon 93° in the shade We told our teacher we would walk in, in the afternoon and stay to prayer meeting and he would bring us home in the wagon, but we were lazy and thought they would come out anyway if we did not go in, so about 8.30 we walked down the road about a mile + waited but lo! no one came. we came back still looking + we three involuntary sat down in the hammock. it suddenly gave way, so we arrose disconsilate. thus passed the eve. it blew dreadfully. I went home. found Ham asleep on the bed while Belle was sound asleep on the roof. such sochibility. the beacon burned brightly, and I got there safely.

Monday 14. 86 June

Belle and I hastened over this morning quite early 7.30. all were excited over the great ironing that we had planned to do. B + I went to Mrs Campbells + borrowed irons. The meat man drove up to our door + we had fresh meat first we had seen since last winter.[63] I am affraid we dident enjoy it as much as we might had we not forgotten how it ought to taste. Robison plowed for us + was here to dinner. Adam + Minnie went to town for the mail. Belle + I ironed faithfully all afternoon. I wrote a letter to Mr Glenn in reply to his advise about our advertising. Everyone seems so interested in our prooving up. thermometer 105° in the shade. we brought it in where we were ironing + it ran up to 128. this we think is decidedly hot.

Tuesday 15. 86

Belle + I ironed in the afternoon. Adam + Minnie went with Hoffmaster to sow cane on his farm.[64] the horses started suddenly + Adam fell on the wheel spraining her shoulder. B. + I went home early walked around

---

[63]Fresh meat was sometimes delivered door-to-door in towns, so the arrival of a meat-man at the dugout would have constituted a sign of civilization in Greeley County

[64]"Cane" meaning possibly sorghum: a syrup from it is a substitute for cane sugar..

very disconsilate not knowing what to do with ourselves, when Hutchison and Moffit came over. spent the eve. Mr M. + I walked to shenkels unfinished house untill 11.30. boys went home 12.30.

<u>Wednesday 16. 86</u>

B + I arrose early. went over to Lauras. caught a ride with Hoffmaster. Just got home when Mr Moffitt drove up with a little <u>wilde</u> <u>horse</u> first time it had been hitched single we had a lovely ride.

Adam had baked the cake for the social. we went down town in the afternoon. took tea at Mrs Millers where we had been invited. helped arrange the room for the social. had a love time, ~~in the~~ came home with Mr M. sat on the roof + talked. retired at 2. o-cl

~~Thursday 17 86~~
<u>Monday, June 21 86</u>

This is the day that we are advertised to proove up, so Ham got the surrey with Laura as witness we four went to Syracuse Mr Van + Proffitt also went. went to bank + got cheque cashed for $400.00 got through with business without trouble. deputy was young and bashful. Mr. McPherson was very nice + in eve—took Laura + I to the sand-hills it was so lovely. we crossed the Arkansas river which was very pretty and reminded me of our river at home. Shopped next morning, started at 8 o'clock, at 12 m. home A man had a young badger, so I brought him home.[65] got here at 7. found Minnie some better. we ordered the Dr + he will be here this eve.

<u>Wednesday June 24</u>

Adam + I came from the dug-out to breakfast. We had a hard time getting here the eve. before + were lost on the prairie. A + I went to town in the morning. C Hutchison walked home with us. he + Adam went to stone quarry. I went down to dug-out to write letters. I sat writing + hearing a noise looked up + found myself confronted by a young rattle snake 3/4 of a yd long he had crawled out of the earth above the table + was watching me as he plied his little black tongue. I retreated he also. Adam came soon + we hunted but he was nowhere to be found we have the satisfaction of knowing that he is somewhere in the house and liable to crawl out

[65]The *Greeley County Tribune* reported that Julia had christened the badger "Flaxy."

on the table at any moment. there are a few couples invited to Mrs Finches this eve. Carter + Mr Moffitt found the rigs were all taken so came up + spent the eve. we had as usual rather a hard time to find our way. Adam took the inside + Mr M. + I sat on the roof + talked untill Carter was ready to go at after 2. o-clock. we forgot our lantern so retired in the dark in great fear of the snake.

July 12 1886

This morning Adam started for Michigan with Mr Hoffmaster for a traveling [companion] as far as Chicago. its awfully lonely without her. Minnie was down town all afternoon. Ham was here all morning. Miss Moffitt spent the afternoon with B. + I. we went to P. O. loafed awhile got a letter from Mother and Lee. Hutchie wanted me to go on top of the hotel so I went + for nearly an hour we stayed, enjoying the beauties of Tribune + surrounding country. we had a nice visit. he has promised to tell me something to night about somebody (name unknown) that is <u>very</u> <u>very</u> nice.[66]

Minnie + I put the clothes to soak, + rolled our bbl. down to the well + filled it retired early.

July 15th 86

Went to well at noon with Minnie. shopped. got home for dinner.

Mr Bloom came up in the afternoon with his pet mule. wanted me to ride it but no saddle was to be found. In eve. went horse back riding on Prince with Mr Moffitt. went to his farm, then over my land to see how the crops were. went over 12 miles got home 11.30. had a <u>lovely</u> time. evening cool + very bright. Ham + B. spent the eve at Mr Fletchers, so they say, but they had the gray mules + took a lovely ride. Minnie + Mr Brown were on a tare. while we waited for B., M + I decided to take Smiths boiler home. was then about 1- o-clock. found great fun in beating a march on its sides as we went through the deserted streets. saw Mr M. comming from landing [?] his horse. all played a game of croquet. I wrote to Adam untill after 2. o-c I sat up last eve untill 4.30 to copy my part in the drama. was out on Section 4 first part of eve. Thermometer 105° in shade.

---

[66]Carter Hutchinson's secret may have involved the engagement of Laura Rodman and P. A. Scroggins, who married September 21, 1886, in Greeley County's first wedding.

Friday 16. 1886

Very pleasant ironed some + baked. M. went off with Mr Brown. B. did the shopping.

July 28. 86. Wednesday

The elements are raging again to night. great clowds obscure the horizon while the frisky lightening not content to roam the sky alone must needs waken the thunder from its sleep and set it to grumbeling and roaring angerly after each vivid flash.

Even the buffalo grass forgets to curl as it holds up its head to drink in the moisture while it plants its feet deeper, + firmer into the fertile soil of Greely Co.[67]

August 3rd 1886

Went to the dance given in our honor last eve. with Mr Moffitt. had a good. went about 9.30. sat on the lumber pile + talked before going in. at 11.30 it was raining hard + when it slacked went to supper Mrs Morgan. Belle + I helped to wait on the tabels + wash dishes for they were both so tired. we got our feet very wet.

Philadelphia girls were all over. after the supper, we did not go back B. went home + Mr Bloom + I washed up the dishes + helped Mrs M. untill after 3 a.m. The Phil—Ladies + escorts with a host of others turned it all into a social + entertained each other all night, the rain + floods being to dangerous to venture we had a comfortable seat made of the tent on the floor + had a lovely time untill breakfast was ready at 6.30. then came up + changed my dress + Mr M. + I went to the river which is indeed a river this morning. it was so deep + rapid that teams could not pass. Walter + I strayed a long ways along its banks. we rescued a keg from the deep. went to Mrs Weavers + called, then to my land + investigated the crops. house was full of water 4 ft. + everything was floating. then to Minnies + got home 11.30 in time to make toilets for dinner, for we are boarding at Mrs Morgans.[68] we walked 5 miles + were rather tired

[67]"Buffalo grass" is the common name for *Buchloë dactyloides*, a low-growing grass common on the Great Plains and the western United States. It is rich grass for livestock grazing.

[68]"Make toilets for dinner" meaning to make a toilette, a French term for primping and readying oneself for a social occasion.

after sitting up all night. W. + Ham have bet the cigar that I go to sleep this afternoon + I am determined not to. called up on Carter + had a nice chat. am hunting a piece to read at the temperance meeting to night, though dont intend to go for Walter insists on my staying away + I ~~promised~~ he promised anything I could ask if I would comply + I accepted upon a certain condition he agreed to do it + we shook hands and then I told the condition, that he was to go in my place. He had said before decidedly that nothing would induce him to go. so he was quite taken back but valued his word as highly as I do mine + wont back out. so he goes + I stay home alone.

Julia's diary ends here. The *Greeley County Tribune* later reported that the five original "Greeley Girls" went to Wakeeney, Kansas, on August 6 to make their final proofs on their claims and the same were accepted by August 12, 1886. The five girls soon separated: Laura Rodman married in the following September; Julia the following May; Minnie Smith left and later married. Belle Graham left Kansas after an accident with a runaway horse. She returned to Michigan and married a hardware dealer from Chicago, Henry H. Daw, in Buchanan, Michigan, on September 14, 1887, and moved to Chicago. Mary Campbell stayed, married H. J. Proffitt, and was appointed the first postmistress of Tribune.

The "Palace Hotel" is now remembered only by the members of the historical society and the town: the sod grown over, the songs grown faint, the Kansas prairie wind blowing it all away.

Appendix 1

Who Addie Knew

Census records and genealogical histories abound with information regarding the people Addie mentions in passing in her diaries. For the reader's convenience, such information is listed below, and the name is marked in the text with an asterisk (*). Ages given are from the 1880 census. Names are in alphabetical order by the name as it first appears in the text (in quotation marks below). If only a surname was in the text, it is used to determine the order in which the name appears.

"Allie Bradley" (also "Al"), at age seventeen was Fanny's older sister, Alice.

"Eddie Aymar" was the nine-year-old son of restaurant proprietor Albert Aymar.

"Clifford Benson" was the eighteen-year-old son of Jack and Kathie Benson and a student in Berrien Springs.

"Bert" was Bertha Tudor, age ten.

"Jen Boon," Eugenia E. Boon, was a twenty-three-year-old schoolteacher from Berrien Springs.

"Jim Boon" was son of the town blacksmith, Jacob.

"Page Boon" refers to H. Page Boon, a twenty-six-year-old Berrien Springs farmer.

"Jule Brown" was Julius C. Brown (1863–1902), son of Abigail and Ethan Allen Brown, a former state representative. Jule moved to Benton Harbor and worked as a fruit buyer in the thriving fruit market of lower Michigan.

"Victoria Vibla Brown" of Buchanan, Michigan, was fifteen years old in 1882.

"Bunny" was probably Blanche Tudor, six-year-old sister of Bertha and May.

"Nal Colvin" was eighteen-year-old Rinaldo I. Colvin, son of Austin and Ellen Colvin, a Berrien Springs student.

"Tom Dispennet" was the fourteen-year-old son of Andrew Dispennet and a student in Berrien Springs.

"Mr. Roscoe Dix" was the partner of Thomas Lee Wilkinson, Jr. in his abstract and title firm; his son Roscoe was ten; his son "Win"(for Winifred) was eight.

"Mrs. Dixe" was Virginia Dix, wife of Thomas Lee Wilkinson's partner, Roscoe D. Dix, and a seamstress in Berrien Springs.

"Fred Dougherty" was Frederick A. of Louisville, Kentucky, formerly of Berrien Springs, and twenty-six years old in 1882.

"Gus Dudly" was Augustus M. Dudley of Berrien Springs, a twenty-one-year-old printer.

"Mate Dunn" referred to Mary E. Dunn, eighteen-year-old daughter of Edward and Mary Dunn, who would marry Addie's brother Harry in 1890.

"Clara Elliot" was the fourteen-year-old daughter of Thomas and Mary Elliot.

"Carrie Eply" was a twenty-five-year-old schoolteacher boarding with the Platt family.

"Mr. Essick" was probably fifty-six-year-old David Essick, a Berrien Springs butcher.

"Mrs. Euson" was probably Martha W. Euson, a forty-year-old housewife.

"Howard Ewalt" was a nineteen-year-old printer from Berrien Springs.

"Mrs. Ewalt" was probably Elvira Ewalt, a Berrien Springs widow and mother of Kit.

"Fanny" Bradley, age fifteen, was daughter of divorcée Emogene Bradley and sister of Allie.

"Fletcher Farley" was a twenty-seven-year-old Oronoko Township resident.

"Mr. Ford" was Thomas Ford who died at age thirty-eight on August 12, 1880.

"Fox'es" presumably referred to George W. and Louise M. Fox of Buchanan.

"Herm. Gaugler," born in 1867, was a son of Daniel G. W. and Elizabeth Gaugler.

"Rena Gaugler," born in 1877, was a daughter of Daniel G. W. and Elizabeth Gaugler.

"Elmer Gorham" was the fifteen-year-old son of Ira and Clara Gorham of Berrien Springs and a student.

"Mary Gould" was probably Mary S. Gould of Niles.

"Abby Gray" was fifteen-year-old Abbie, daughter of Amos and Sarah Gray of Berrien Springs.

"Mrs. Hall" was forty-eight-year-old widow Elizabeth.

"Nellie Hall" was the eleven-year-old daughter of Mrs. Hall, above.

"Mary Himes" was a thirteen-year-old daughter of Walter and Emmeline Himes of Buchanan.

"Gene Howe" was fourteen-year-old Eugene, son of Hezekiah and Lucretia Howe of Berrien Springs.

"Lillie B. Howe" was a twenty-one-year-old schoolteacher in Oronoko Township.

"Lora Howe" was the twelve-year-old daughter of Charles E. Howe of Buchanan.

"Mrs. Howe," the Sunday school teacher (February 28, 1881 entry), was Gene's mother.

"John Jacobs" was a forty-three-year-old laborer from Oronoko Township.

"Frank Kephart" was the seventeen-year-old son of Philip and Susan Kephart of Berrien Springs.

"Fannie Kessler" was the eighteen-year-old daughter of widower L. John Kessler of Berrien Township.

"Kit" was seventeen-year-old Kitty Elvira Ewalt, daughter of Elvira, a widowed housekeeper.

"Rome Knight" was probably Nathan Jerome Knight, twenty-one years old in 1882, and a farmer in Oronoko Township.

"Mrs. M.Mc.C.D.W." was Martha McClellan Wilson, a Washington, D.C. native and a very wealthy woman.

"Mr. Marquissee" was forty-two-year-old Lewis.

"Carrie Mars" was the eighteen-year-old daughter of Andrew and Susan Mars.

"Hugh Mars" was a twenty-year-old farmer in Berrien Springs.

"Mr. Mars" was probably Andrew Mars of Berrien Springs.

"Mrs. Martin" was possibly thirty-four-year-old Margaret L. Martin of Berrien Springs.

"Walter Martin" was eleven years old and lived in Berrien Springs.

"May and Susie" were the fourteen- and twelve-year-old daughters of fifty-five-year-old Darius Brown of Berrien Springs.

"May" Tudor was the eight-year-old daughter of thirty-year-old widow Sarah, and sister of Bertha and Blanche.

"Mrs. Miley" was Laura M. Miley, a fifty-three-year-old Niles housewife.

"Howard Miller," twenty-nine-year-old son of John and Mary Miller, lived in Berrien Springs.

"Minnie" was probably twenty-seven-year-old Minnie M. McOmber, wife of Frederick, publisher of the *Berrien Springs Era* newspaper.

"Annie O'dell" was Anna A. O'Dell, fifteen-year-old daughter of Greenlief and Mary O'Dell of Berrien Springs.

"Lutie Pardee" was sixteen-year-old Lucy Pardee.

"Mrs. Perkins" was probably Jennie A. Perkins, thirty-seven-year-old housewife.

"Ella Platt" was the twenty-five-year-old daughter of widowed housekeeper Aurelia Platt.

"Jim Platt," age twenty, was the son of Aurelia Platt and brother of Ella and Laura.

"Laura Platt" was the twenty-eight-year-old daughter of James and Aurelia Platt of Berrien Springs and Addie's future sister-in-law.

"John Reiber" was an eighteen-year-old printer in Berrien Springs.

"Mrs. Reiber" was Amelia, forty-three-year-old wife of Dr. William Reiber.

"Sade Reiber" was Sarah A. Reiber, a twenty-year-old Berrien Springs school-teacher.

"Jennie Senseny" was the daughter of George's paternal aunt, Rosalie M. Senseny of Chambersburg, Pennsylvania, and second cousin to Addie.

"Charlie Shearer" was a fourteen-year-old son of Malinda and Alpheus Shearer of Berrien Springs.

"Sherrill" refers to fourteen-year-old Winifred Sherrill and her father, Mark L. Sherrill of Galien Township in Berrien County.

"Charlie Smith" was nineteen-year-old Charles Smith, a Berrien Springs farm laborer.

"Hattie Smith," age eighteen, worked as a clerk in the Berrien Springs post office.

"Mr. Sparks" was probably Wilson Sparks, a fifty-year-old farmer in Oronoko Township.

"Ot Statler" was possibly thirteen-year-old Herbert O. Statler of Berrien Springs.

"Jim Steffy" was probably James S. Steffy of Berrien Springs.

"Will Stem" was William Stemm, the fourteen-year-old son of Samuel and Catherine Stemm of Oronoko Township. He and his family were Pennsylvania Germans.

"Gertie Stevens" was the sixteen-year-old daughter of Thomas L. and Hester B. Stevens of Niles and sister of Wirt.

"Sallie Tudor" was most likely Sarah J. Tudor, a thirty-three-year-old Berrien Springs widow.

"Charlie Turner" was fourteen-year-old Charles F. Turner of Berrien Springs.

"Cash and Kit Van Riper" refers to fifteen-year-old Cassius and presumably either Lulu E. (eighteen years old) or Ada B. (fourteen years old) Van Riper of Buchanan.

"Charlie Watson" was Charles B. Watson, age thirty-three.

"Willie Weaver" was fourteen-year-old William Weaver of Berrien Springs.

"Jack Wilk." refers to John Franklin Wilkinson, a younger brother of Thomas Lee Wilkinson, Jr.

"Chick Wilkinson" refers to Charles Albert Wilkinson, the youngest brother of Thomas Lee Wilkinson, Jr.

"Will D." probably refers to William Dougherty of Chicago.

"Wirt" was William Wirt Stevens, thirteen-year-old son of Thomas and Hester B. Stevens of Niles. His father was president of the First National Bank of Niles, his sister was Gertie.

Appendix 2

What Addie Read

One notable characteristic of Adeline Graham's life is the time she spent with books. Much of what Addie wrote reflected her literary interests and the reading common to educated people of the time. The classical works could be found in many classrooms, but Addie also loved fiction and read voluminously of some of the popular authors of the era.

Louisa May Alcott's novel *Little Women* (two volumes, 1868 and 1869) made a strong impression on Addie, as it has on generations of American girls. Addie, a tomboy herself, found a kindred, if fictional, spirit in the tomboyish and literary Josephine "Jo" March. In her diary entry of June 13, 1880, Addie noted that she had finished reading *Little Women* for the second time and wanted to emulate Jo: "I think I am naturally something like her," she wrote, "for everybody says I'm a 'perfect Jo March.'" Jo March is fifteen years old as *Little Women* opens, the same age Addie was when she began her diary.

Identifying strongly with Jo, Addie filled her diary with references to her role model. In one of her first entries, Addie writes that she had "found a splendid seet up in a little cherry tree" where she could sit and read, probably imitating Jo March, who read books while sitting in an apple tree. In her diary entry on May 19, 1880, Addie wrote of a "P.C." that probably referred to the March girls' secret literary society, the Pickwick Club, labeled "P.C." in Alcott's chapter title. Addie's identification with Jo lasted for years; while away at college, she recorded that she had written a letter to "Marmie," the pet name the March sisters also used for their mother.

Other references to *Little Women* abound in Addie's diary. Both Jo and Addie are "the man of the family" when their fathers are away, and each girl describes an elderly relative, Jo's Aunt March and Addie's grandmother, as a "fussy old lady" when she visits and cares for the woman. Addie also worked rather obscure words from *Little Women* into her "scribblings." When she sprains her ankle, it "aches like Sancho"; in the first chapter of *Little Women*, Jo has "been considered a 'Sancho' ever since she was born." Later, Addie refers to her infant nephew George as "nevvy," a term Jo uses for one of her sister Meg's twins—her own "nevvy" or nephew.

As did Jo March, Addie had a great fondness for both literature and writing, and she submitted several stories for publication. When she sat down to write, Addie noted in her diary that "genius burns." When Jo March worked at writing stories, she would seclude herself in her room, don her "scribbling suit," or a black pinafore and cap, and set to work. Family members would pop in to ask, "Does genius burn, Jo?"

Addie enjoyed several other Alcott novels, which are listed below. And like her fictional role model, Addie gave up ideas of a career for marriage and family life.

References to other popular works are sprinkled throughout Addie's diary. Such information about these works as was available, for the reader's convenience, is listed below in alphabetical order by the title Addie used when she first referred to the work. The diary text is marked with an asterisk (*) next to the titles for which the editors found information.

Among the Poets may have referred to a yearly "best poets" collection gathered by Augustine Austin Smith.

"Andersen" referred to the now-classic Hans Christian Andersen, author of *Andersen's Fairy Tales*.

"Anne" was *Anne: A Novel*, by Constance Fenimore Woolson, appearing in *Harper's Bazaar* in 1882.

Arthur Bonnicastle (1873) was a semi-autobiographical novel by Josiah Gilbert Holland (1819–1881) of a New England boy's life at Yale and in New York.

"Atlantics" refer to *Atlantic Monthly*, a popular magazine.

Aunt Serena: A Novel (1881) was by Blanche Willis Howard.

"Century" was a reference to *Scribner's Monthly Magazine*.

The Changed Brides (1869) was by best-selling author Emma Dorothy Eliza Nevitte Southworth, better known as E. D. E. N. Southworth.

Eight Cousins was by Louisa May Alcott.

Fair Barbarian (1881) was written by Frances Hodgson Burnett.

Frederick the Great is probably Thomas Carlyle's version, a six-volume work (1858–1865) entitled *The History of Frederick II of Prussia called Frederick the Great.*

Figs and Thistles (1879), written by Albion Winegar Tourgee, was set in Ohio and the South during the Civil War.

Glimpses Through (1873) was by Ellen L. Hollis.

Gulliver's Travels by Jonathan Swift was published in 1726.

"Harpers" magazine refers to *Harper's Monthly Magazine.*

The Head of the Family, by Dinah Maria Mulock Craik (1883), was one of a very inexpensive two-shilling novel series published by Macmillan Publishing Company. Craik specialized in children's books, fairy tales, poems and novels.

"Home and Fireside" was *Our Home and Fireside Magazine,* published by George Stinson between 1873–1889.

Hypatia (1853), by Charles Kingsley, was set in fifth-century Alexandria. The character Hypatia is a lecturer on Greek philosophy and a woman of unusual spiritual charm.

Idylls of the King is by the English author Alfred, Lord Tennyson.

"John Burns of Gettysburg" was a poem by Bret Harte (1836–1902).

"Katherina" was probably *Kathrina: Her Life and Mine, in a Poem* (1867) by Josiah Gilbert Holland.

A Knight of the Nineteenth Century (1877) was by the Reverend Edward Payson Roe.

"Letters of H. H." may refer to *[Letters] to H.H. Cumming, Esq., John D. Twiggs and George W. L. Twiggs,* published 1870–79.

"Life and Letters of Lord Macaulay" and "Macaulays Life and Letters" refers to *The Life and Letters of Lord Macaulay* that Sir George Otto Trevelyan published in 1876.

Life of Josephine existed in multiple editions. Most likely this was the one either by Cecil B. Hartley (1880) or P. C. Headley (1857). Both wrote of the life of Napoleon's wife, Josephine de Beauharnais.

"The Lightning Rod Dispenser" by Michigan poet Will Carleton was published in *Farm Festivals* in 1881.

Little Men (1871) was Louisa May Alcott's sequel to *Little Women*.

Little Women was by Louisa May Alcott.

Love's Labor Lost is a play by William Shakespeare.

Lucile was a novel in verse by Owen Meredith, the pen name of Edward Robert Bulwer Lytton, First Earl of Lytton (1831–1891).

Minna von Barnhelm (1767) was a comedy by Gotthold Ephraim Lessing.

A Modern Instance was a novel by William Dean Howells, published in 1881.

The Monastery (1820) by Sir Walter Scott was set in the reign of Queen Elizabeth I.

"Mrs. Lirriper's Lodging" was one of Charles Dickens' *Christmas Stories*, published in 1863.

"New Church Magazine" probably refers to *The Children's New-Church Magazine*, a monthly publication by William Carter and Brother that ran from 1862–1891.

An Old Fashioned Girl (1877) was by Louisa May Alcott.

Oldtown Folks (1869), written by Harriet Beecher Stowe (writer of the bestseller, *Uncle Tom's Cabin*), was a novel about life in Oldtown, New England, shortly after the American Revolution.

"One-Hoss Shay" is a reference to Oliver Wendell Holmes' poem, "The Deacon's Masterpiece: or The Wonderful One Horse Shay," that appeared in his *The Autocrat of the Breakfast Table* (1858).

One Summer (1875) was by Blanche Willis Howard.

"Prince Charlie" may be *Prince Charlie, the Young Chevalier*, by Johnes Meredith (1860). Bonnie Prince Charlie was pretender to the throne of England after the Civil War in the seventeenth century.

"A Psalm of Life" was a poem by Henry Wadsworth Longfellow.

Queechy (1852), a novel by Susan Warner, was a very popular, sentimental children's book about the life of orphan Fleda Ringgan in Queechy, Vermont.

Rose in Bloom was by Louisa May Alcott.

"The Schonberg Cotta Family" is Addie's reference to *The Chronicles of the Schonberg Cotta Family* (1867) by Elizabeth Charles Rundle.

"Scribner's" was *Scribner's Monthly Magazine*, also known as *The Century*. It published from 1870–1881.

Shirley (1849), a novel by Charlotte Brontë, was set in Yorkshire, England, at the end of the Napoleonic Wars. Its plot focuses on the depressed wool industry and the struggle between the hero, mill-owner Robert Gerand Moore, and the mill-workers.

"St. Nicholas" or "St. Nick" was *St. Nicholas' Magazine*, a popular magazine for young adults and children.

Talbury Girls was the novel by Mary Andrews Denison.

"Tangle Tales" was probably *Tanglewood Tales* (1853), Nathaniel Hawthorne's adaptation of six Greek myths.

Thaddeus of Warsaw (1803) was an historical novel by Jane Porter.

Thanatopsis (1817) was a poem by William Cullen Bryant.

Three People was a novel by the prolific "Pansy," pseudonym for a youth writer who published 353 titles during his/her career.

"Titcumb's Letters" was *Titcom's Letters to Young People, Single and Married* (1858) by Josiah Gilbert Holland.

Through One Administration (1881) was by Frances Hodgson Burnett.

Tom Brown's School Days was by Thomas Hughes.

The Two Glasses was a poem by Ella Wheeler Wilcox.

Uncle Tom's Cabin by Harriet Beecher Stowe (1850) was a best-selling anti-slavery novel.

"Undine and Sintram" most likely referred to one of the many editions of *Undine and Sintram*, published from 1830 on, by Friedrich Heinrich Karl, Freiherr de La Motte-Fouqué.

"Vicar of Wakefield" is *The Vicar of Wakefield* (1766), a novel about a British vicar and teacher written by Oliver Goldsmith.

Without a Home (1881) was by the Reverend Edward Payson Roe.

Index of Names and Places